ATS-68   ADMISSION TEST SERIES

This is your
PASSBOOK for...

Certified Protection Professional Examination (CPP)

Test Preparation Study Guide
Questions & Answers

COPYRIGHT NOTICE

This book is SOLELY intended for, is sold ONLY to, and its use is RESTRICTED to individual, bona fide applicants or candidates who qualify by virtue of having seriously filed applications for appropriate license, certificate, professional and/or promotional advancement, higher school matriculation, scholarship, or other legitimate requirements of education and/or governmental authorities.

This book is NOT intended for use, class instruction, tutoring, training, duplication, copying, reprinting, excerption, or adaptation, etc., by:

1) Other publishers
2) Proprietors and/or Instructors of "Coaching" and/or Preparatory Courses
3) Personnel and/or Training Divisions of commercial, industrial, and governmental organizations
4) Schools, colleges, or universities and/or their departments and staffs, including teachers and other personnel
5) Testing Agencies or Bureaus
6) Study groups which seek by the purchase of a single volume to copy and/or duplicate and/or adapt this material for use by the group as a whole without having purchased individual volumes for each of the members of the group
7) Et al.

Such persons would be in violation of appropriate Federal and State statutes.

PROVISION OF LICENSING AGREEMENTS – Recognized educational, commercial, industrial, and governmental institutions and organizations, and others legitimately engaged in educational pursuits, including training, testing, and measurement activities, may address request for a licensing agreement to the copyright owners, who will determine whether, and under what conditions, including fees and charges, the materials in this book may be used them. In other words, a licensing facility exists for the legitimate use of the material in this book on other than an individual basis. However, it is asseverated and affirmed here that the material in this book CANNOT be used without the receipt of the express permission of such a licensing agreement from the Publishers. Inquiries re licensing should be addressed to the company, attention rights and permissions department.

All rights reserved, including the right of reproduction in whole or in part, in any form or by any means, electronic or mechanical, including photocopying, recording, or by any information storage and retrieval system, without permission in writing from the Publisher.

Copyright © 2024 by
National Learning Corporation

212 Michael Drive, Syosset, NY 11791
(516) 921-8888 • www.passbooks.com
E-mail: info@passbooks.com

PASSBOOK® SERIES

THE *PASSBOOK® SERIES* has been created to prepare applicants and candidates for the ultimate academic battlefield – the examination room.

At some time in our lives, each and every one of us may be required to take an examination – for validation, matriculation, admission, qualification, registration, certification, or licensure.

Based on the assumption that every applicant or candidate has met the basic formal educational standards, has taken the required number of courses, and read the necessary texts, the *PASSBOOK® SERIES* furnishes the one special preparation which may assure passing with confidence, instead of failing with insecurity. Examination questions – together with answers – are furnished as the basic vehicle for study so that the mysteries of the examination and its compounding difficulties may be eliminated or diminished by a sure method.

This book is meant to help you pass your examination provided that you qualify and are serious in your objective.

The entire field is reviewed through the huge store of content information which is succinctly presented through a provocative and challenging approach – the question-and-answer method.

A climate of success is established by furnishing the correct answers at the end of each test.

You soon learn to recognize types of questions, forms of questions, and patterns of questioning. You may even begin to anticipate expected outcomes.

You perceive that many questions are repeated or adapted so that you can gain acute insights, which may enable you to score many sure points.

You learn how to confront new questions, or types of questions, and to attack them confidently and work out the correct answers.

You note objectives and emphases, and recognize pitfalls and dangers, so that you may make positive educational adjustments.

Moreover, you are kept fully informed in relation to new concepts, methods, practices, and directions in the field.

You discover that you are actually taking the examination all the time: you are preparing for the examination by "taking" an examination, not by reading extraneous and/or supererogatory textbooks.

In short, this PASSBOOK®, used directedly, should be an important factor in helping you to pass your test.

CERTIFIED PROTECTION PROFESSIONAL

BOARD CERTIFICATION IN SECURITY MANAGEMENT

The Certified Protection Professional designation is awarded to experienced security practitioners who have demonstrated in-depth knowledge and management skills in eight key areas of security. Those who have earned the CPP are ASIS board certified in security management.

Established in 1977, the CPP is widely acknowledged as the highest recognition of security professionals. The credential is given to individuals who have demonstrated expertise in security management principles, concepts, technology, and best practices. The CPP provides independent confirmation of a practitioner's ability to assume leadership responsibilities and address broad security concerns.

ELIGIBILITY REQUIREMENTS

Applicants must meet one of the following requirements to be accepted as a CPP candidate:

Work Experience:
Nine (9) years of security experience, including at least three (3) years in responsible charge of a security function

OR

Work Experience:
Seven (7) years of security experience, including at least three (3) years in responsible charge of a security function

And

Education:
An earned bachelor's degree or higher from an accredited institution of higher education

---

Eligibility requirements also include no prior conviction of any criminal offense that would reflect negatively on the security profession or on ASIS International and its certification programs.

EXAM STRUCTURE AND CONTENT

Candidates must pass a comprehensive examination consisting of approximately 200 multiple-choice questions testing their knowledge of eight major areas (domains) of security management before being awarded the CPP designation. The importance of each domain, and the tasks, knowledge, and skills within it, determines the specifications of the CPP examination. The relative order of importance of the domains determines the percentage of total exam questions.

Physical Security

- Survey facilities to manage/evaluate status of physical security, fire detection, and emergency/restoration capabilities.
- Select design, implements, and manage security measures to reduce risk of loss.
- Assess effectiveness of security measure by testing and monitoring.

Security Principles and Practices

- Plan, organize, direct, and manage the organization's security program to avoid/ control losses and apply the processes to provide secure work environment.

- Develop, manage, or conduct threat/ vulnerability analyses to determine the probable frequency and severity of natural and an-made disasters and criminal activity in the organization's profitability and/ r ability to deliver products/services.
- Evaluate methods to improve security and loss prevention systems on a continuous basis through auditing, review, and assessment.
- Develop and manage external relations programs with public sector law enforcement or other external organizations to assist in achievement of loss prevention objectives.
- Develop and present employee security awareness programs to achieve organizational goals and objectives.

Investigations

- Develop and manage investigative programs.
- Manage or conduct the collection and preservation of evidence to support post investigation actions (employee discipline, criminal or civil proceedings, arbitrate n).
- Manage or conduct surveillance processes.
- Manage or conduct investigative interviews.

Business Principles and Practices

- Develop and manage budgets and financial controls to achieve fiscal responsibility
- Develop, implement, and manage policies, procedures, plans, and directives to achieve organizational objectives.
- Develop procedures/techniques to measure and improve organizational productivity.
- Develop, implement, and manage staffing, leadership, training, and management programs in order to achieve organizational objectives.

Personnel Security

- Develop, implement, and manage background investigations in coordination with other departments and agencies to identify individuals for hiring and/or promotion.
- Develop, implement, manage, and evaluate policies, procedures, programs, and methods for personnel protection (excluding executive protection) to provide a secure work environment.
- Develop, implement, and manage executive protection programs to reduce security risks to executives and to ensure continued viability of the organization.
- Support the organization's efforts to reduce substance abuse in the workplace.

Emergency Practices

- Mitigate potential consequences of emergency situations by identifying and prioritizing potential hazards and risks and developing plans to manage exposure to loss.
- Prepare and plan how the organization will respond in an emergency.
- Manage activation of the emergency response plan to reduce loss.
- Recover from emergency situations through management of the restoration of vital services and facilities to minimum standards of operations and safety.

Information Security

- Survey information facilities, processes, and systems to evaluate current status of: physical security, procedural security, information systems security, employee awareness, and information destruction and recovery capabilities.
- Develop and implement policies and standards to ensure information is evaluated and protected against all forms of unauthorized/inadvertent access, use, disclosure, modification, destruction, or denial.
- Develop and manage a program of integrated security controls and safeguards to ensure confidentiality, integrity, availability, authentication, non-repudiation, accountability, recoverability, and audit ability of sensitive information and associated information technology resources and assets.
- Evaluate the effectiveness of the information security program's integrated security controls, to include related policies, procedures, and plans to ensure consistency with organization strategy, goals, and objectives.

Legal Aspects

- Develop and maintain security policies, procedures, and practices that comply with relevant elements of criminal, civil, administrative, and regulatory law to minimize adverse legal consequences.
- Provide coordination, assistance, and evidence such as documentation and testimony to support legal counsel in actual or potential criminal and/or civil proceedings
- Provide advice and assistance to management and others in developing performance requirements and contractual terms for security vendors/ suppliers and establish effective monitoring processes to ensure that organizational needs and contractual requirements are being met.
- Develop and maintain security
- Policies, procedures, and practices that comply with relevant laws regarding investigations, personnel security, and information security.

PREPARING FOR THE EXAM

The CPP exam is a self-study exam and candidates choose their own method of preparation. This Passbook® has been successfully used by many candidates and is highly recommended as a major contributing factor in passing the examination. Preparation is a major factor in exam success. Candidates are advised to prepare a study plan and make the necessary commitment of time to prepare adequately. Recent data suggest that a preparation time of at least 16 weeks appears to be a critical factor in CPP exam success.

Approved candidates have a two-year period of eligibility to schedule and pass the exam. Candidates should take advantage of several preparation resources and not rely on one preparation method. Because the CPP exam is comprehensive, it is strongly advised that candidates not rely solely on previous work experience.

RECERTIFICATION REQUIREMENTS

Practicing CPPs are required to participate in professional development activities and submit reports every three (3) years to maintain active certification. It is the CPP's responsibility to ensure that recertification credits claimed conform to the guidelines established by the Professional Certification Board. More information on CPP recertification is available at.

www.asisonline.org/certification/
recertification.htm.

HOW TO TAKE A TEST

You have studied long, hard and conscientiously.

With your official admission card in hand, and your heart pounding, you have been admitted to the examination room.

You note that there are several hundred other applicants in the examination room waiting to take the same test.

They all appear to be equally well prepared.

You know that nothing but your best effort will suffice. The "moment of truth" is at hand: you now have to demonstrate objectively, in writing, your knowledge of content and your understanding of subject matter.

You are fighting the most important battle of your life—to pass and/or score high on an examination which will determine your career and provide the economic basis for your livelihood.

What extra, special things should you know and should you do in taking the examination?

I. YOU MUST PASS AN EXAMINATION

A. WHAT EVERY CANDIDATE SHOULD KNOW
Examination applicants often ask us for help in preparing for the written test. What can I study in advance? What kinds of questions will be asked? How will the test be given? How will the papers be graded?

B. HOW ARE EXAMS DEVELOPED?
Examinations are carefully written by trained technicians who are specialists in the field known as "psychological measurement," in consultation with recognized authorities in the field of work that the test will cover. These experts recommend the subject matter areas or skills to be tested; only those knowledges or skills important to your success on the job are included. The most reliable books and source materials available are used as references. Together, the experts and technicians judge the difficulty level of the questions.
Test technicians know how to phrase questions so that the problem is clearly stated. Their ethics do not permit "trick" or "catch" questions. Questions may have been tried out on sample groups, or subjected to statistical analysis, to determine their usefulness.
Written tests are often used in combination with performance tests, ratings of training and experience, and oral interviews. All of these measures combine to form the best-known means of finding the right person for the right job.

II. HOW TO PASS THE WRITTEN TEST

A. BASIC STEPS

1) Study the announcement

How, then, can you know what subjects to study? Our best answer is: "Learn as much as possible about the class of positions for which you've applied." The exam will test the knowledge, skills and abilities needed to do the work.

Your most valuable source of information about the position you want is the official exam announcement. This announcement lists the training and experience qualifications. Check these standards and apply only if you come reasonably close to meeting them. Many jurisdictions preview the written test in the exam announcement by including a section called "Knowledge and Abilities Required," "Scope of the Examination," or some similar heading. Here you will find out specifically what fields will be tested.

2) Choose appropriate study materials

If the position for which you are applying is technical or advanced, you will read more advanced, specialized material. If you are already familiar with the basic principles of your field, elementary textbooks would waste your time. Concentrate on advanced textbooks and technical periodicals. Think through the concepts and review difficult problems in your field.

These are all general sources. You can get more ideas on your own initiative, following these leads. For example, training manuals and publications of the government agency which employs workers in your field can be useful, particularly for technical and professional positions. A letter or visit to the government department involved may result in more specific study suggestions, and certainly will provide you with a more definite idea of the exact nature of the position you are seeking.

3) Study this book!

III. KINDS OF TESTS

Tests are used for purposes other than measuring knowledge and ability to perform specified duties. For some positions, it is equally important to test ability to make adjustments to new situations or to profit from training. In others, basic mental abilities not dependent on information are essential. Questions which test these things may not appear as pertinent to the duties of the position as those which test for knowledge and information. Yet they are often highly important parts of a fair examination. For very general questions, it is almost impossible to help you direct your study efforts. What we can do is to point out some of the more common of these general abilities needed in public service positions and describe some typical questions.

1) General information

Broad, general information has been found useful for predicting job success in some kinds of work. This is tested in a variety of ways, from vocabulary lists to questions about current events. Basic background in some field of work, such as sociology or economics, may be sampled in a group of questions. Often these are principles which have become familiar to most persons through exposure rather than through formal training. It is difficult to advise you how to study for these questions; being alert to the world around you is our best suggestion.

2) Verbal ability

An example of an ability needed in many positions is verbal or language ability. Verbal ability is, in brief, the ability to use and understand words. Vocabulary and grammar tests are typical measures of this ability. Reading comprehension or paragraph interpretation questions are common in many kinds of civil service tests. You are given a paragraph of written material and asked to find its central meaning.

IV. KINDS OF QUESTIONS

1. Multiple-choice Questions

Most popular of the short-answer questions is the "multiple choice" or "best answer" question. It can be used, for example, to test for factual knowledge, ability to solve problems or judgment in meeting situations found at work.

A multiple-choice question is normally one of three types:
- It can begin with an incomplete statement followed by several possible endings. You are to find the one ending which best completes the statement, although some of the others may not be entirely wrong.
- It can also be a complete statement in the form of a question which is answered by choosing one of the statements listed.
- It can be in the form of a problem – again you select the best answer.

Here is an example of a multiple-choice question with a discussion which should give you some clues as to the method for choosing the right answer:

When an employee has a complaint about his assignment, the action which will best help him overcome his difficulty is to
    A. discuss his difficulty with his coworkers
    B. take the problem to the head of the organization
    C. take the problem to the person who gave him the assignment
    D. say nothing to anyone about his complaint

In answering this question, you should study each of the choices to find which is best. Consider choice "A" – Certainly an employee may discuss his complaint with fellow employees, but no change or improvement can result, and the complaint remains unresolved. Choice "B" is a poor choice since the head of the organization probably does not know what assignment you have been given, and taking your problem to him is known as "going over the head" of the supervisor. The supervisor, or person who made the assignment, is the person who can clarify it or correct any injustice. Choice "C" is, therefore, correct. To say nothing, as in choice "D," is unwise. Supervisors have and interest in knowing the problems employees are facing, and the employee is seeking a solution to his problem.

2. True/False

3. Matching Questions

Matching an answer from a column of choices within another column.

V. RECORDING YOUR ANSWERS

Computer terminals are used more and more today for many different kinds of exams.

For an examination with very few applicants, you may be told to record your answers in the test booklet itself. Separate answer sheets are much more common. If this separate answer sheet is to be scored by machine – and this is often the case – it is highly important that you mark your answers correctly in order to get credit.

VI. BEFORE THE TEST

YOUR PHYSICAL CONDITION IS IMPORTANT

If you are not well, you can't do your best work on tests. If you are half asleep, you can't do your best either. Here are some tips:

1) Get about the same amount of sleep you usually get. Don't stay up all night before the test, either partying or worrying—DON'T DO IT!
2) If you wear glasses, be sure to wear them when you go to take the test. This goes for hearing aids, too.
3) If you have any physical problems that may keep you from doing your best, be sure to tell the person giving the test. If you are sick or in poor health, you relay cannot do your best on any test. You can always come back and take the test some other time.

Common sense will help you find procedures to follow to get ready for an examination. Too many of us, however, overlook these sensible measures. Indeed, nervousness and fatigue have been found to be the most serious reasons why applicants fail to do their best on civil service tests. Here is a list of reminders:

- Begin your preparation early – Don't wait until the last minute to go scurrying around for books and materials or to find out what the position is all about.
- Prepare continuously – An hour a night for a week is better than an all-night cram session. This has been definitely established. What is more, a night a week for a month will return better dividends than crowding your study into a shorter period of time.
- Locate the place of the exam – You have been sent a notice telling you when and where to report for the examination. If the location is in a different town or otherwise unfamiliar to you, it would be well to inquire the best route and learn something about the building.
- Relax the night before the test – Allow your mind to rest. Do not study at all that night. Plan some mild recreation or diversion; then go to bed early and get a good night's sleep.
- Get up early enough to make a leisurely trip to the place for the test – This way unforeseen events, traffic snarls, unfamiliar buildings, etc. will not upset you.
- Dress comfortably – A written test is not a fashion show. You will be known by number and not by name, so wear something comfortable.
- Leave excess paraphernalia at home – Shopping bags and odd bundles will get in your way. You need bring only the items mentioned in the official notice you received; usually everything you need is provided. Do not bring reference books to the exam. They will only confuse those last minutes and be taken away from you when in the test room.

- Arrive somewhat ahead of time – If because of transportation schedules you must get there very early, bring a newspaper or magazine to take your mind off yourself while waiting.
- Locate the examination room – When you have found the proper room, you will be directed to the seat or part of the room where you will sit. Sometimes you are given a sheet of instructions to read while you are waiting. Do not fill out any forms until you are told to do so; just read them and be prepared.
- Relax and prepare to listen to the instructions
- If you have any physical problem that may keep you from doing your best, be sure to tell the test administrator. If you are sick or in poor health, you really cannot do your best on the exam. You can come back and take the test some other time.

VII. AT THE TEST

The day of the test is here and you have the test booklet in your hand. The temptation to get going is very strong. Caution! There is more to success than knowing the right answers. You must know how to identify your papers and understand variations in the type of short-answer question used in this particular examination. Follow these suggestions for maximum results from your efforts:

1) Cooperate with the monitor

The test administrator has a duty to create a situation in which you can be as much at ease as possible. He will give instructions, tell you when to begin, check to see that you are marking your answer sheet correctly, and so on. He is not there to guard you, although he will see that your competitors do not take unfair advantage. He wants to help you do your best.

2) Listen to all instructions

Don't jump the gun! Wait until you understand all directions. In most civil service tests you get more time than you need to answer the questions. So don't be in a hurry. Read each word of instructions until you clearly understand the meaning. Study the examples, listen to all announcements and follow directions. Ask questions if you do not understand what to do.

3) Identify your papers

Civil service exams are usually identified by number only. You will be assigned a number; you must not put your name on your test papers. Be sure to copy your number correctly. Since more than one exam may be given, copy your exact examination title.

4) Plan your time

Unless you are told that a test is a "speed" or "rate of work" test, speed itself is usually not important. Time enough to answer all the questions will be provided, but this does not mean that you have all day. An overall time limit has been set. Divide the total time (in minutes) by the number of questions to determine the approximate time you have for each question.

5) Do not linger over difficult questions

If you come across a difficult question, mark it with a paper clip (useful to have along) and come back to it when you have been through the booklet. One caution if you do this – be sure to skip a number on your answer sheet as well. Check often to be sure that you have not lost your place and that you are marking in the row numbered the same as the question you are answering.

6) Read the questions
Be sure you know what the question asks! Many capable people are unsuccessful because they failed to read the questions correctly.

7) Answer all questions
Unless you have been instructed that a penalty will be deducted for incorrect answers, it is better to guess than to omit a question.

8) Speed tests
It is often better NOT to guess on speed tests. It has been found that on timed tests people are tempted to spend the last few seconds before time is called in marking answers at random – without even reading them – in the hope of picking up a few extra points. To discourage this practice, the instructions may warn you that your score will be "corrected" for guessing. That is, a penalty will be applied. The incorrect answers will be deducted from the correct ones, or some other penalty formula will be used.

9) Review your answers
If you finish before time is called, go back to the questions you guessed or omitted to give them further thought. Review other answers if you have time.

10) Return your test materials
If you are ready to leave before others have finished or time is called, take ALL your materials to the monitor and leave quietly. Never take any test material with you. The monitor can discover whose papers are not complete, and taking a test booklet may be grounds for disqualification.

VIII. EXAMINATION TECHNIQUES

1) Read the general instructions carefully. These are usually printed on the first page of the exam booklet. As a rule, these instructions refer to the timing of the examination; the fact that you should not start work until the signal and must stop work at a signal, etc. If there are any special instructions, such as a choice of questions to be answered, make sure that you note this instruction carefully.

2) When you are ready to start work on the examination, that is as soon as the signal has been given, read the instructions to each question booklet, underline any key words or phrases, such as least, best, outline, describe and the like. In this way you will tend to answer as requested rather than discover on reviewing your paper that you listed without describing, that you selected the worst choice rather than the best choice, etc.

3) If the examination is of the objective or multiple-choice type – that is, each question will also give a series of possible answers: A, B, C or D, and you are called upon to select the best answer and write the letter next to that answer on your answer paper – it is advisable to start answering each question in turn. There may be anywhere from 50 to 100 such questions in the three or four hours allotted and you can see how much time would be taken if you read through all the questions before beginning to answer any. Furthermore, if you

come across a question or group of questions which you know would be difficult to answer, it would undoubtedly affect your handling of all the other questions.

4) If the examination is of the essay type and contains but a few questions, it is a moot point as to whether you should read all the questions before starting to answer any one. Of course, if you are given a choice – say five out of seven and the like – then it is essential to read all the questions so you can eliminate the two that are most difficult. If, however, you are asked to answer all the questions, there may be danger in trying to answer the easiest one first because you may find that you will spend too much time on it. The best technique is to answer the first question, then proceed to the second, etc.

5) Time your answers. Before the exam begins, write down the time it started, then add the time allowed for the examination and write down the time it must be completed, then divide the time available somewhat as follows:
   - If 3-1/2 hours are allowed, that would be 210 minutes. If you have 80 objective-type questions, that would be an average of 2-1/2 minutes per question. Allow yourself no more than 2 minutes per question, or a total of 160 minutes, which will permit about 50 minutes to review.
   - If for the time allotment of 210 minutes there are 7 essay questions to answer, that would average about 30 minutes a question. Give yourself only 25 minutes per question so that you have about 35 minutes to review.

6) The most important instruction is to read each question and make sure you know what is wanted. The second most important instruction is to time yourself properly so that you answer every question. The third most important instruction is to answer every question. Guess if you have to but include something for each question. Remember that you will receive no credit for a blank and will probably receive some credit if you write something in answer to an essay question. If you guess a letter – say "B" for a multiple-choice question – you may have guessed right. If you leave a blank as an answer to a multiple-choice question, the examiners may respect your feelings but it will not add a point to your score. Some exams may penalize you for wrong answers, so in such cases only, you may not want to guess unless you have some basis for your answer.

7) Suggestions
   a. Objective-type questions
      1. Examine the question booklet for proper sequence of pages and questions
      2. Read all instructions carefully
      3. Skip any question which seems too difficult; return to it after all other questions have been answered
      4. Apportion your time properly; do not spend too much time on any single question or group of questions
      5. Note and underline key words – all, most, fewest, least, best, worst, same, opposite, etc.
      6. Pay particular attention to negatives
      7. Note unusual option, e.g., unduly long, short, complex, different or similar in content to the body of the question
      8. Observe the use of "hedging" words – probably, may, most likely, etc.

9. Make sure that your answer is put next to the same number as the question
10. Do not second-guess unless you have good reason to believe the second answer is definitely more correct
11. Cross out original answer if you decide another answer is more accurate; do not erase until you are ready to hand your paper in
12. Answer all questions; guess unless instructed otherwise
13. Leave time for review

b. Essay questions
1. Read each question carefully
2. Determine exactly what is wanted. Underline key words or phrases.
3. Decide on outline or paragraph answer
4. Include many different points and elements unless asked to develop any one or two points or elements
5. Show impartiality by giving pros and cons unless directed to select one side only
6. Make and write down any assumptions you find necessary to answer the questions
7. Watch your English, grammar, punctuation and choice of words
8. Time your answers; don't crowd material

8) Answering the essay question

Most essay questions can be answered by framing the specific response around several key words or ideas. Here are a few such key words or ideas:

M's: manpower, materials, methods, money, management
P's: purpose, program, policy, plan, procedure, practice, problems, pitfalls, personnel, public relations

a. Six basic steps in handling problems:
1. Preliminary plan and background development
2. Collect information, data and facts
3. Analyze and interpret information, data and facts
4. Analyze and develop solutions as well as make recommendations
5. Prepare report and sell recommendations
6. Install recommendations and follow up effectiveness

b. Pitfalls to avoid
1. Taking things for granted – A statement of the situation does not necessarily imply that each of the elements is necessarily true; for example, a complaint may be invalid and biased so that all that can be taken for granted is that a complaint has been registered
2. Considering only one side of a situation – Wherever possible, indicate several alternatives and then point out the reasons you selected the best one
3. Failing to indicate follow up – Whenever your answer indicates action on your part, make certain that you will take proper follow-up action to see how successful your recommendations, procedures or actions turn out to be
4. Taking too long in answering any single question – Remember to time your answers properly

EXAMINATION SECTION

EXAMINATION SECTION
TEST 1

DIRECTIONS: Each question or incomplete statement is followed by several suggested answers or completions. Select the one that BEST answers the question or completes the statement. *PRINT THE LETTER OF THE CORRECT ANSWER IN THE SPACE AT THE RIGHT.*

1. In cases when a security officer has been commissioned or deputized with special police or peace officer powers, it is usually true that this type of power

    A. is unlikely to hold up in court
    B. applies statewide, but only for a limited amount of time
    C. is limited to the region or municipality of jurisdiction covered by the law enforcement agency that has granted it
    D. is limited to the grounds and buildings of the officer's employer

    1.____

2. MacGregor's Theory X of management assumes that an average worker

    A. will be self-directed if he or she is committed to objectives
    B. welcomes change
    C. will seek responsibility if rewards address higher needs
    D. would rather follow than lead

    2.____

3. In developing an emergency response plan, an organization needs to take into account the threats to computerized data. Typically, fires resulting in temperatures above 125-150 degrees F will melt the base media composition of any photographic or machine-readable media.

    A. 98-110
    B. 125-150
    C. 200-212
    D. 300-500

    3.____

4. What is the term for a condition that may create or increase the probability of a loss?

    A. Endangerment
    B. Risk
    C. Peril
    D. Hazard

    4.____

5. As part of the process for creating a loss prevention program, a business evaluates its existing resources. Typically, the FIRST step in this evaluation is to

    A. assess existing management capabilities
    B. compensate for inadequacies
    C. review the historical development of existing protection practices
    D. assess the company's physical capability to protect property and personnel

    5.____

6. In an employment screening interview,

    A. the interviewer is mostly focused on finding the single best person for the position
    B. a candidate's personality is generally of little importance
    C. the interviewer usually knows every detail of about the position being discussed
    D. the interviewer is usually not trained in interview methodology

    6.____

7. As a rule, a padlock shackle should be case-hardened and measure a minimum of _____ of an inch thick.

    A. 1/8
    B. 5/16
    C. 7/16
    D. 3/8

8. As a rule of thumb, if more than _____ percent of an organization's records are described as "vital," the process by which these records are evaluated should be examined.

    A. 5
    B. 10
    C. 20
    D. 30

9. A security manager at a large retail chain is building a department from the ground up, and is considering the way in which jobs should be grouped.
   Most often, the rationale for this process is based on the

    A. necessity for coordinating different tasks
    B. established lines of communication
    C. existing industry standards
    D. established formal hierarchy

10. The role of an ombudsperson at a large security firm would be to

    A. coordinate financial policy
    B. handle employee grievances and ethical problems
    C. facilitate communications
    D. initiate action plans

11. Employees at a workplace should be trained in "de-escalation" skills that might help to defuse an aggressive coworker. Which of the following is NOT one of these skills.

    A. Avoiding any eye contact
    B. Using open-ended questions
    C. Encouraging the aggressor to articulate their feelings
    D. Using crisis-related code words that will alert select staff members of the incident without tipping off the aggressor

12. A security officer at a federal building is asked to deliver a document marked *ORCON*. This means that

    A. the information has been provided by a commercial firm or private source under an express or implied understanding that the information will be protected as a trade secret or proprietary data with actual value.
    B. any additional distribution or inclusion in another document must be approved by the originator of the document.
    C. the information is subject to a formal access control system established by the Director of Central Intelligence
    D. the document must be handled through special cryptographic channels

13. Cost-of-loss formulas typically include a single figure for the cost of a permanent replacement of a lost asset. Which of the following costs are NOT components of the "permanent replacement cost" as it is used in these formulas? 13.____

    A. Cost of temporary substitute
    B. Make-ready or preparation costs
    C. Purchase price or manufacturing cost
    D. Freight or shipping charges

14. The three types of evidence are 14.____

    A. photographic, taped, and spoken
    B. sworn, eyewitness, and hearsay
    C. narrative, testimonial, and circumstantial
    D. testimonial, documentary, and real

15. To ensure proper perimeter security at a large installation, parking spaces should, if possible, be set back at least _____ feet from the building. 15.____

    A. 100
    B. 300
    C. 500
    D. 750

16. If a security scheme is to include warning signs, the signs should be installed along the area's physical barriers and at entry points. The signs should be posted at intervals of no more than _____ feet 16.____

    A. 25
    B. 50
    C. 100
    D. 200

17. The business improvement district (BID) method for dividing public safety responsibilities between public law enforcement and private security is an example of a(n) _____ relationship. 17.____

    A. umbrella
    B. contractual
    C. topic-specific
    D. informal

18. Which of the following is NOT typically a goal of an investigative report? 18.____

    A. Providing the reader with a clear picture of an incident
    B. Inspiring the reader to further action
    C. Influencing the reader's attitude
    D. Suggesting how to proceed from the facts of the report

19. A security manager wants to increase job satisfaction among his employees through job rotation. A potential disadvantage associated with this approach is that it

    A. involves a temporary decrease in productivity
    B. can require extensive retraining
    C. can make work burdensome and repetitive
    D. doesn't provide substantive changes in job content

20. The employees at a large security organization are attempting to unionize. In order for the National Labor Relations Board to be appropriately petitioned to hold a representation election to determine whether employees in a bargaining unit can be represented by a union, at least _____ % of the bargaining unit's employees must sign an authorization card.

    A. 10
    B. 30
    C. 51
    D. 75

21. A security officer is writing a report describing stolen property. The items that would appear FIRST on the list would have

    A. initials or personal marks
    B. numerical characteristics
    C. identifying characteristics
    D. a definite market value

22. A liaison officer at a large private security firm is attempting to maintain a working relationship between the corresponding functional departments at the firm and local law enforcement. Usually, a good time to meet with officers in functional departments is
    I. when a criminal offense has been committed
    II. 15-20 minutes before the start of their shifts
    III. over a meal
    IV. at the end of the day

    A. I only
    B. I, II and IV
    C. II and III
    D. I, II, III and IV

23. If a master key is coded 52345 and an individual key X in the system is coded 52123, what other key code in the system could open the same door as key X?

    A. 52135
    B. 52145
    C. 52344
    D. 52543

24. What is the most widely used illegal drug?

    A. Ecstasy (MDMA)
    B. Marijuana
    C. Methamphetamine
    D. Cocaine

25. The ideal motion detection device for a large warehouse with multiple aisles is a(n) _____ detector.   25._____

    A. microwave
    B. ultrasonic
    C. proximity
    D. thermal

KEY (CORRECT ANSWERS)

1. D
2. D
3. B
4. D
5. A

6. B
7. C
8. B
9. A
10. B

11. A
12. B
13. A
14. D
15. B

16. C
17. B
18. D
19. D
20. B

21. B
22. C
23. B
24. B
25. B

TEST 2

DIRECTIONS: Each question or incomplete statement is followed by several suggested answers or completions. Select the one that BEST answers the question or completes the statement. *PRINT THE LETTER OF THE CORRECT ANSWER IN THE SPACE AT THE RIGHT.*

1. In a large security organization that employs at least some union members, union members are sometimes given preferences over nonunion members in areas such as hiring, promotion, and layoff. Preferences given in this situation are often likely to violate the provisions of the

    A. Taft-Hartley Act
    B. Wagner Act
    C. Landrum-Griffin Act
    D. Fair Labor Standards Act

    1.____

2. The first step in ensuring that an organization will be able to function following a disaster is most often a

    A. designation of an alternative headquarters
    B. responsive alert system
    C. well structured vital records program
    D. detailed public relations strategy

    2.____

3. If it is possible to isolate an area from a facility's HVAC system, first priority should be given to the

    A. data center
    B. security central command center
    C. mail room
    D. executive offices

    3.____

4. In high-security areas where personnel are constantly coming and going-and often forget to lock the door behind them, the _____ lock is recommended.

    A. interlocking deadbolt rimlock
    B. electromagnetic
    C. bar
    D. automatic deadlatch

    4.____

5. Regardless of whether a business of product- or service-oriented, the initial requirement in creating a loss prevention program is to

    A. identify the business purpose
    B. define protection activities
    C. identify specific vulnerabilities
    D. define protection objectives

    5.____

6. Which of the following 5-digit lock codes would be MOST desirable as a master key combination?

    A. 13526
    B. 21919
    C. 91519
    D. 88888

    6.____

7. For spot protection of a row of ten or so filing cabinets, the most appropriate motion detection device would be a(n) _____ detector.

   A. thermal
   B. ultrasonic
   C. microwave
   D. proximity

8. At most government agencies, if an Executive Director becomes suddenly absent for any reason, the _____ will automatically step into the role of Acting Executive Director.

   A. Program Director
   B. Deputy Director
   C. Ombudsperson
   D. Chief Financial Officer

9. In organizational management, "span of control" refers to the

   A. number of people reporting to one manager
   B. formalized rules and procedures
   C. separation of operating units
   D. centralization of decision-making

10. Which of the following types of fences is LEAST likely to be approved for protecting restricted areas?

    A. Chain link
    B. Wood
    C. Barbed wire
    D. Concertina

11. Historical research has revealed a number of characteristics that are generally-but not exclusively-associated with the perpetrators of workplace violence. Which of the following is NOT one of these characteristics?

    A. Chronic complainer
    B. Male between 25 and 40 years of age
    C. Job as core of one's identity
    D. Overly talkative with coworkers

12. A security team is assigning a criticality rating to a potential loss that would have a noticeable impact on earnings as reflected in the operating statement and would require attention from the senior executive management. Usually, this kind of loss would be rated

    A. fatal
    B. very serious
    C. moderately serious
    D. relatively unimportant

13. The report of an incident should include each of the following, EXCEPT the

    A. approximate time the incident occurred
    B. name and badge number of any police officers who attended
    C. officer's opinion about the cause of the incident
    D. names of those who were involved in the incident

14. In some areas of the country, private security organizations and public law enforcement agencies establish cooperative relationships that are formalized by such activities as shared training programs, legislative lobbying, and public/private information and resource networks. The primary motivation for this degree of formalization is to

    A. establish a structure that will increase the longevity of the relationship
    B. expand the powers of arrest for private security officers
    C. streamline the amount of time and money spent on the relationship
    D. establish legal protections for the work of private security organizations

15. Which of the following organizational characteristics reflects the concept of high complexity?

    A. Functional departments
    B. Low degree of specialization
    C. Narrow spans of control
    D. Centralized authority

16. A personality/attitude assessment that is appropriate for college-aged and older adults is the

    A. Edwards Personal Preference Schedule (EPPS)
    B. Ohio Vocational Interest Survey (OVIS, OVIS II)
    C. Otis-Lennon Mental Ability Test (OLMAT)
    D. Work Values Inventory (WVI)

17. In federal protocols, information that must be controlled to protect the national security is assigned one of three levels of classification. If the information's unauthorized disclosure could reasonably be expected to cause serious damage to the national security, it is classified

    A. confidential
    B. for official use only
    C. top secret
    D. restricted

18. In criminal investigation, physical specimens of known origin are known as

    A. artifacts
    B. testimonials
    C. documents
    D. exemplars

19. The _____ method of risk classification tends to function most effectively when there is only one unfavorable factor to consider.

    A. judgement
    B. sliding
    C. numerical
    D. expert

20. In addition to solid, ethical work, an officer's best defense against a lawsuit or complaint is

    A. a good lawyer
    B. testimony from trusted character witnesses
    C. clear, detailed records and reports
    D. an aggressive counterclaim

21. A liaison or partnership between private security and public law enforcement can create trust and understanding between the parties involved. Which of the following strategies is LEAST likely to help maintain a program?

    A. Limiting communications to individual cases or problem incidents
    B. Incorporating similar operational procedures
    C. Staying aware of each others' mission statements and standards
    D. Linking computer or information systems

22. In most burglary cases, the most likely suspects are

    A. employees
    B. family members
    C. friends
    D. one-time visitors

23. Pure risk
    I. can be deflected or transferred to another party through a contract or insurance policy
    II. is the inherent risk involved in conducting everyday business
    III. involve the chance of both profit and loss
    IV. presents only the prospect of loss

    A. I and II
    B. I and III
    C. I and IV
    D. II and III

24. For a private company, the main advantage of hiring contract security personnel, rather than using their own proprietary security personnel, is

    A. higher quality of personnel
    B. greater loyalty
    C. a substantial reduction in cost
    D. a higher degree of deterrence

25. In describing the organizational structure of a security department, the term _____ 25._____
refers to the number of different units at the same administrative level.

    A. horizontal differentiation
    B. vertical differentiation
    C. scatter
    D. spread

KEY (CORRECT ANSWERS)

1.	A	11.	D
2.	C	12.	C
3.	C	13.	C
4.	D	14.	A
5.	A	15.	C
6.	A	16.	A
7.	D	17.	A
8.	B	18.	D
9.	A	19.	A
10.	B	20.	C

21. A
22. A
23. B
24. C
25. A

TEST 3

DIRECTIONS: Each question or incomplete statement is followed by several suggested answers or completions. Select the one that BEST answers the question or completes the statement. *PRINT THE LETTER OF THE CORRECT ANSWER IN THE SPACE AT THE RIGHT.*

1. The notebook of a security officer may be used to
   I. illustrate the officer's skill and efficiency
   II. aid in the writing of reports
   III. aid in giving accurate testimony in court
   IV. provide documentary evidence of a proper search

   A. I and II
   B. I, II, and III
   C. II and IV
   D. I, II, III and IV

   1._____

2. The failure to _____ is NOT generally considered a major reason for security losses.

   A. recognize vulnerabilities
   B. accept a certain level of risk
   C. use the proper countermeasures
   D. consider change

   2._____

3. An owner wants to install ultrasonic detection devices throughout her building as security devices. To insure against false alarms, the receivers and transmitters should be

   A. aimed directly at each other
   B. of different makes
   C. both directed into the direction of air flow
   D. installed side by side, about three feet apart

   3._____

4. Which of the following is NOT a function that is performed during the risk mitigation process?

   A. Identifying particular risks to an organization, facility, or project
   B. Obtaining insurance
   C. Contingency planning
   D. Developing system policies, procedures, and standards

   4._____

5. Which of the following is NOT a Crime Prevention Through Environmental Design (CPTED) strategy?

   A. Obscuring the border definitions of controlled spaces in order to deceive or confuse potential intruders.
   B. Locating gathering areas in places with natural surveillance and access control
   C. Placing unsafe activities in safe spots to overcome vulnerability
   D. Providing clearly marked transition zones that indicate movement from public to private spaces.

   5._____

11

6. Under the Omnibus Crime Control and Safe Streets Act of 1968, as amended by the Electronic Communications Privacy Act of 1986, electronic communications generated at a company workstation are protected from interception by employers and/or law enforcement agencies during the time they are
    I. stored on a hard drive
    II. being typed
    III. in the sender's "sent" box
    IV. traveling along the network medium to an outside device that is not owned by the employer

    A. I and III
    B. II only
    C. IV only
    D. I, II, III and IV

7. For high-security areas, probably the least costly lock that would prove acceptable is the _____ lock.

    A. tubular deadbolt
    B. pin-tumbler
    C. interlocking deadbolt rimlock
    D. bar

8. Typically, the exposure to loss from pure risk falls into six categories. Which of the following is NOT one of these categories?

    A. Fraud and criminal violence
    B. Adverse legal judgements
    C. Technical obsolescence of assets
    D. Physical damage to assets

9. A security manager is working with associates on an operating plan for the entire security organization. Another term for this type of plan is _____ plan.

    A. tactical
    B. SBU
    C. functional
    D. daily

10. Directs costs of losses include each of the following, EXCEPT

    A. employees
    B. information
    C. negotiable instruments
    D. property

11. The truth verification technique known as "statement analysis" rests on the belief that

    A. hypnosis does not increase the likelihood that a person will tell the truth
    B. changes in physiological functions occur involuntarily as a response to a stressful activity
    C. most subjects do not attempt to lie directly, but simply edit or withhold information
    D. a deceptive person's autonomic or involuntary nervous system causes an audible increase in the micro-tremor frequency of his/her voice

12. The most foolproof way to secure an information system after it has been compromised is to   12.____

    A. close the network breach
    B. change all passwords and rotate workstations
    C. find and delete the virus or other intrusive program
    D. reinstall it from a known good source

13. During an interview, which of the following suspect behaviors is LEAST likely to be interpreted as deceptive?   13.____

    A. Dilation of the pupils when viewing evidence
    B. Crossing one's legs
    C. Yawning or stretching
    D. Blushing

14. Ideally, security kiosks that are installed at access points should   14.____
    I. have three-lane traffic capability
    II. be self-contained, with a restroom, refrigerator, etc.
    III. use card readers or other automated access in place of security personnel
    IV. built of concrete block and bulletproof glass

    A. I and II
    B. I, II and IV
    C. III and IV
    D. I, II, III and IV

15. Which of the following types of locks offers the highest security in most residential applications?   15.____

    A. Lever
    B. Disc tumbler
    C. Warded
    D. Pin tumbler

16. A security manager at a large private company views himself as both the leader of a team responsible for protecting and enlarging its own resources, and a member of the administrative staff charged with reducing operating costs. This situation is an example of   16.____

    A. the Hawthorne effect
    B. cognitive dissonance
    C. intrapersonal conflict
    D. role ambiguity

17. In arson cases, an accelerant would be indicated by each of the following, EXCEPT   17.____

    A. melted copper, aluminum, and other metals
    B. 22 minutes or fewer elapsed from ignition to flashpoint
    C. deep cracks and crevices in wood
    D. melted windows and/or mirrors

18. The _____ Act is the federal statute that identifies unfair labor union practices.

    A. Wagner
    B. Taft-Hartley
    C. Fair Labor Standards
    D. Landrum-Griffin

19. Of the following personnel selection procedures, the LEAST costly is usually

    A. the employment interview
    B. employment tests
    C. background and reference checks
    D. preliminary screening

20. A large security firm employs the top-down method of budgeting. This method does NOT work very well when

    A. unit managers have limited knowledge of the current situation
    B. there is a financial crisis
    C. business needs necessitate close coordination among units
    D. the budgeting process must be performed quickly

21. For sketching an outdoor crime scene, the _____ method is preferred.

    A. triangulation
    B. coordinate
    C. cross-projection
    D. single spiral

22. At a large industrial plant, Stan White, a police officer, moonlights as a private guard. A worker on the night shift is caught leaving the building with three shop tools in his coverall pockets. The worker is taken to the plant manager's office for an interview. It is probably in the owner's best interest for this interview to be conducted by

    A. officer White
    B. the owner
    C. the plant manager
    D. a lower level executive

23. Assertive behavior is a key element in a security manager's strategy for resolving conflict among employees. Which of the following stages in assertive behavior is generally performed LAST?

    A. Presenting problem-solving strategies
    B. Indicating consequences
    C. Describing the behavior that is the source of the conflict
    D. Empathizing

24. Among the private security activities that have caused administrative headaches and frustration for public law enforcement in the recent past, the issue that has done the most to strain relations between private security and police is

    A. the "turf" mentality
    B. an explosion in white-collar crime

C. false alarms
D. the overextension of private security officers' powers of arrest

25. Which of the following is an issue confronting private security today? 25.____

   A. A generalized lack of training and qualifications among private security guards
   B. The legal status of police officers working as private security guards
   C. Reluctance of many enterprises to hire private security guards on a contract basis
   D. The indefinite legal status and authority of private security guards

KEY (CORRECT ANSWERS)

1. B	11. C
2. B	12. D
3. D	13. B
4. A	14. B
5. A	15. D
6. C	16. C
7. C	17. D
8. C	18. B
9. A	19. D
10. A	20. D

21. A
22. D
23. B
24. C
25. B

EXAMINATION SECTION
TEST 1

DIRECTIONS: Each question or incomplete statement is followed by several suggested answers or completions. Select the one that BEST answers the question or completes the statement. *PRINT THE LETTER OF THE CORRECT ANSWER IN THE SPACE AT THE RIGHT.*

1. In devising countermeasures to a security threat, each countermeasure is evaluated in terms of the consistency with which the countermeasure achieves its functional objective over a large number of similar cases. This is known as countermeasure

   A. reliability
   B. surprisability
   C. validity
   D. repeatability

   1._____

2. If an ultrasonic detection system is used as a security device, the installer should be careful to set the frequency of the unit above a minimum of _____ cycles per second, which is well past the threshold of human hearing.

   A. 18,000
   B. 23,000
   C. 35,000
   D. 50,000

   2._____

3. Which of the following, as evidence, is most likely to have individual rather than class characteristics?

   A. Hair
   B. Partial fingerprint
   C. Handwriting
   D. Fibers

   3._____

4. _____ risk offers the opportunity for both gain and loss.

   A. Assumed
   B. Speculative
   C. Presumed
   D. Pure

   4._____

5. Which of the following is an example of risk deflection?

   A. Disaster planning and response
   B. Second-party contracting
   C. Forming specific organizational roles to handle risk events
   D. Developing production schedule alternatives

   5._____

6. The functions of risk management include each of the following, EXCEPT

   A. loss control
   B. loss indemnification
   C. loss detection
   D. loss prevention

   6._____

7. When marking off an outdoor crime scene, the standard perimeter is _____ square feet.

   A. 20
   B. 40
   C. 60
   D. 80

8. Which of the following is NOT an appropriate security measure for a high-priority area in a facility?

   A. Scheduled mobile security patrols
   B. Constantly monitored CCTV
   C. Motion detectors
   D. Access control

9. "Implied consent" for the monitoring of an employee's e-mail and online activity in the workplace is established by

   A. the employee's agreement to work on network equipment that is owned by the organization
   B. a verbal warning or a message posted at login that indicates there will be periodic monitoring
   C. the fact that there is no legal basis for denying the monitoring of employees' online activity
   D. signed permission by an employee granting the employer the right to monitor communications at his/her discretion

10. An ultimate goal of a liaison or partnership between private security and public law enforcement is to maintain the program indefinitely. Which of the following is LEAST likely to lead to a failure to maintain this relationship?

    A. Long-term tenure of founders or coordinators
    B. Personality conflict
    C. Single-source funding
    D. Off-topic meetings

11. In the presentation of physical evidence, continuity in the chain of custody is important because it

    A. substantiates that the evidence was not tampered with
    B. takes the place of reports, which are not admissible as evidence
    C. is required by law
    D. decreases the likelihood that an officer will have to take the stand

12. Of the following, the type of lock offering the LEAST amount of security is _____ the _____ lock.

    A. pin-tumbler
    B. lever-tumbler
    C. electromagnetic
    D. disc-tumbler

13. The most likely vector of attack for a computer virus is as a(n)

    A. HTML e-mail with embedded scripts
    B. Java application subscript on the World Wide Web
    C. e-mail with a malformed MIME header
    D. attachment to an e-mail

14. A security officer is interviewing a suspect in a theft at a public building. Which of the following suspect behaviors is MOST likely to be interpreted as deceptive?

    A. Keeping responses consistently short
    B. Referring the officer to witnesses
    C. Repeating questions immediately after they are asked
    D. Requesting legal counsel

15. A security administrative staff is adopting the "Boulwarism" approach to collective bargaining if it

    A. views the opposition as an adversary but recognizes that an agreement must be worked out along legal guidelines
    B. offers compromise, flexibility, and tolerance in order to bring negotiations to a speedy conclusion
    C. presents an initial offer as a final offer that will not be altered by negotiation
    D. responds to labor's offer by mirroring the negotiators' style

16. An employer advocates the use of the "hot stove" method of employee discipline-making the consequences so severe for small infractions that their repetition is unlikely. The main disadvantage associated with this approach is that it

    A. is likely to encourage the personal bias of the manager
    B. creates records that may later prove incriminating
    C. does not take individual and situational differences into account
    D. offers deferred, rather than short-term, benefits

17. A security manager wants to shape policies and practices through periodic departmental meetings during which the group will determine the organization's future. Each of the following is considered to be an effective way for managers to prevent the phenomenon known as "groupthink," EXCEPT

    A. implementing a time delay between preliminary and final decision-making
    B. pressuring dissenters
    C. regularly rotating in new group members
    D. inviting attendance by managers from other departments in the organization

18. During an investigation, an officer makes a mistake in his notebook. The proper way to correct the error is to

    A. neatly black out the entire mistaken section and start again
    B. erase the error completely with a clean eraser
    C. leave it and correct it later, when writing the report
    D. draw a single line through it and start again

19. A _____ key is made to fit only one lock.

    A. bit
    B. master
    C. change
    D. warded

20. In recent years, experts studying the relationship between private security and public law enforcement have noted a perception of differing motivating factors for each sector. In fact, these experts note, the common factor motivating each is

    A. profit
    B. loss prevention
    C. protection of the general citizenry
    D. justice

21. Which of the following applicant screening devices is specifically designed to identify applicants who are less prone to be involved in counterproductive incidents and have a higher degree of work ethic?

    A. Minnesota Multiphasic Personality Inventory (MMPI)
    B. Reid Report
    C. Polygraph
    D. Stanton Survey

22. The budgeting process at a large security firm is likely to have each of the following positive effects, EXCEPT

    A. keeping managers informed about organizational activities
    B. providing standards against which supervisor's performance can be evaluated
    C. encouraging innovative thinking to meet resource allocation
    D. enhancing coordination across units

23. When risk transfer is used as a method for loss prevention at an organization, it is important to remember that this strategy

    A. sometimes increases risk exposures in other areas of the organization
    B. tends to significantly alter the conduct of business
    C. should be used in support of, rather than instead of, protection practices
    D. retains generally higher risks than other strategies

24. Which of the following statements is/are true about an emergency operations plan (EOP)?

    I. It specifies how people and property will be protected in emergencies
    II. It assigns responsibility for mitigation concerns to local officials
    III. It identifies resources available for use during operations
    IV. It establishes lines of authority

    A. I and II
    B. I, III and IV
    C. II and III
    D. I, II, III and IV

25. A security manager wants to shape policies and practices through periodic departmental meetings during which the group will determine the organization's future. Which of the following statements about group decision-making is FALSE?

   A. Groups to be more conservative than individuals with an organization's resources.
   B. Group members often exaggerate their commitment to bad ideas, in order to fit in
   C. Group decisions tend to dilute responsibility.
   D. Group meetings are among the slowest and most costly ways of getting things done.

25._____

KEY (CORRECT ANSWERS)

1. A
2. C
3. C
4. B
5. B

6. C
7. B
8. A
9. B
10. A

11. A
12. B
13. D
14. C
15. C

16. C
17. B
18. D
19. C
20. B

21. D
22. C
23. C
24. B
25. A

TEST 2

DIRECTIONS: Each question or incomplete statement is followed by several suggested answers or completions. Select the one that BEST answers the question or completes the statement. *PRINT THE LETTER OF THE CORRECT ANSWER IN THE SPACE AT THE RIGHT.*

1. A security officer with typical training and authority
   I. is subject to the 4th Amendment protections against unreasonable searches and seizures
   II. must supply Miranda warnings to people or suspects before questioning
   III. must see a misdemeanor committed in its entirety in order to make an arrest
   IV. usually does not have the authority to detain suspects

   A. I and II
   B. I, III and IV
   C. IV only
   D. I, II, III and IV

   1._____

2. A security manager is formulating a protocol for behavior modification within his department. Which of the following should be avoided?

   A. Using positive reinforcement rarely, to avoid an inflated sense of achievement
   B. Identifying the exact behaviors that will be targeted for modification
   C. Generally ignoring minor undesirable behaviors
   D. Using punishment only in unusual circumstances

   2._____

3. Federal government information that is classified as SECRET may _____ within the United States and its territories.
   I. be sent by registered mail
   II. be sent by express mail
   III. be sent by first class mail
   IV. not be mailed under any circumstances

   A. I only
   B. I and II
   C. I, II and III
   D. IV only

   3._____

4. Which of the following areas at a facility is most likely to be classified as "medium-priority" for surveillance purposes?

   A. HVAC systems
   B. Individual offices
   C. Computer server room/data center
   D. Power supply

   4._____

5. While private security officers often suffer from police officers' inaccurate perception of their training, skills, and roles, they are sometimes likely to hold a few stereotypical ideas of their own about public law enforcement officers. Generally, a private security officer is LEAST likely to believe a public law enforcement agency

   5._____

A. does not sufficient train individual officers to perform well in most situations
B. shows disdain for private security officers
C. is structured to respond to crimes after they have occurred, rather than to prevent them in the first place
D. has little accountability for crimes committed within their jurisdictions

6. After a crime has been committed, a security officer's role is usually

   A. search and seizure
   B. apprehension and detention
   C. deterrence
   D. observing and reporting

7. Frequently, when a criminal act causes a loss for a business, judges require only the _____ of the tangible property to be associated with prosecution.

   A. full replacement value
   B. retail value
   C. cost value plus prosecution and recovery
   D. cost value

8. In the terminology of power bases, _____ power is delegated from higher established authorities to others?

   A. reward
   B. referent
   C. legitimate
   D. personal

9. Under the incident command system (ICS) framework, written plans are required when
   I. the resources of multiple agencies are used
   II. multiple jurisdictions are involved
   III. the incident requires changes in personnel shifts or equipment
   IV. the incident involves hazardous materials

   A. I only
   B. I, II, and III
   C. II and III
   D. I, II, III and IV

10. To initiate an effective cooperative program between private security and public law enforcement, a private security liaison officer should FIRST

    A. make the law enforcement agency aware of what the company is seeking from the relationship
    B. attempt to earn the respect of the law enforcement agency
    C. set up interviews with key law enforcement officials
    D. research the law enforcement agency and their work

11. Which of the following types of personality assessments is often avoided by managers because of its association with psychological problems?

    A. Behavioral measure
    B. Inkblot test

C. Minnesota Multiphasic Personality Inventory (MMPI)
D. Myers-Briggs Type Indicator (MBTI)

12. Most commercial break-ins are done through

   A. basements or other subterranean access points
   B. windows and doors
   C. adjacent buildings
   D. parking areas

13. In most statement reports, the final component is the

   A. affidavit
   B. attestation
   C. notary seal
   D. ID paragraph

14. Which of the following steps in the budgetary process is usually performed LAST?

   A. Planning activities in detail
   B. Combining unit budgets
   C. Outlining resource restraints
   D. Formulating performance targets

15. The typical maximum holding force of an electromagnetic lock is about _____ lbs.

   A. 750
   B. 1500
   C. 2500
   D. 4000

16. Which of the following is an example of dynamic risk?

   A. Profit loss
   B. Liability loss
   C. Personnel-related loss
   D. Direct property loss

17. A private security officer comes across a crime scene. The officer should

   A. begin canvassing for witnesses
   B. collect and bag physical evidence while handling it as little as possible
   C. notify the police
   D. mark the location of every moveable object on the scene

18. Of the following, which is LEAST useful as a security device?

   A. Motion sensor
   B. Photoelectric sensor
   C. Thermal detector
   D. Pulsed infrared detector

19. The conditions that will worsen or increase asset exposure to risk of loss can be divided into major categories. Which of the following is NOT one of these categories?

A. Age of assets
B. Political environment
C. Social environment
D. Historical experience

20. Which of the following is NOT a stimulant? 20._____

    A. Oxycodone
    B. Cocaine
    C. Nicotine
    D. Ritalin

21. The ID paragraph in an interview report typically does NOT include the subject's 21._____

    A. race or ethnicity
    B. dependents
    C. age
    D. place of employment

22. A security organization's plan for the acquisition or divestiture of a major fixed asset, 22._____
    such as an electronic security system, is included in the _____ budget.

    A. expense budget
    B. balance sheet
    C. capital expenditures budget
    D. profit budget

23. In threat analysis, one method of presenting overall risk is to use a scatter plot. This is a 23._____
    method of plotting each risk on a graph whose axes are

    A. cost and frequency
    B. cost and probability
    C. category and cost
    D. category and frequency

24. According to the portrait parle system for describing a suspect, which of the following 24._____
    features would be LEAST important to a description?

    A. hair
    B. chin
    C. lips
    D. eyes

25. Guidelines for protecting trade secrets do NOT include 25._____

    A. clearly document trade secrets and the policies for their disclosure in the employee handbook, as a basis for possible legal action
    B. having new and existing employees sign non-competition and proprietary information agreements that protect the company both during and after their employment
    C. document non-competition agreements separately from employee handbooks
    D. have non-competition agreements signed separately from employee handbooks

KEY (CORRECT ANSWERS)

1. C
2. A
3. B
4. B
5. A

6. D
7. D
8. C
9. B
10. D

11. C
12. B
13. B
14. B
15. B

16. A
17. C
18. B
19. A
20. A

21. A
22. C
23. A
24. A
25. A

TEST 3

DIRECTIONS: Each question or incomplete statement is followed by several suggested answers or completions. Select the one that BEST answers the question or completes the statement. *PRINT THE LETTER OF THE CORRECT ANSWER IN THE SPACE AT THE RIGHT.*

1. In an interview that conforms to the Reid technique, the questioner usually 1.____
    I. tries to actively persuade a confession through moral justification
    II. begins with a short non-accusatory interview by another person
    III. transitions immediately between the initial interview and the interrogation
    IV. opens the interrogation with a monologue that discourages the suspect from denials or explanations

    A. I only
    B. I, II and IV
    C. III only
    D. I, II, III and IV

2. Which of the following is NOT a common method of protecting vital records? 2.____

    A. Off-site secure storage
    B. Encryption
    C. Duplication and dispersal
    D. On-site secure storage

3. Which of the following areas at a facility is LEAST likely to be a high-priority area for surveillance? 3.____

    A. Common areas or workspaces
    B. Power supply
    C. Entrances and exits
    D. Mail room

4. Security consoles in a large installation should NOT be 4.____

    A. equipped with communications systems
    B. conveniently located
    C. staffed with professionally trained personnel to document access
    D. equipped with monitoring systems

5. The collective bargaining process involves each of the following commonly accepted functions, EXCEPT to 5.____

    A. establish a method for the settlement of disputes during the lifetime of a contract
    B. administer agreements
    C. determine the appropriate collective bargaining units among groups of workers
    D. establish and revise the rules of the workplace

6. In the case of a fire, a security officer's primary responsibility is to 6.____

    A. protect the building from theft
    B. "knock down" any hot spots

C. organize and conduct an orderly evacuation
D. ensure the proper function of the sprinkler system

7. Legal criteria for the definition of a "trade secret" include whether the information
    I. has commercial value to the owner by virtue of its not being widely known
    II. is the subject of efforts by the owner to maintain its confidentiality
    III. could reasonably be considered to be unique or novel
    IV. is known by anyone outside the company

    A. I only
    B. I and II
    C. I, II and IV
    D. II, III and IV

8. Usually, the most difficult part of an investigative report to write is the

    A. portrait parle
    B. summation
    C. narrative
    D. introduction

9. Which of the following federal laws established the National Labor Relations Board (NLRB)?

    A. Norris-LaGuardia Act
    B. Wagner Act
    C. Taft-Hartley Act
    D. Landrum-Griffin Act

10. Private security organizations and public law enforcement agencies still suffer, to a degree, from problems in communication. At the root of most of these problems is the

    A. infrequent contact between personnel
    B. working officer's perception of the private security guard
    C. informal nature of most cooperative programs
    D. overlapping powers of arrest

11. _____ physical evidence links a suspect to a crime.

    A. Direct
    B. Marginal
    C. Associative
    D. Inclusive

12. Which of the following statements about master key systems is FALSE?

    A. They generally reduce the security of locks.
    B. Master keys operate a different shear line from individual keys in the system.
    C. Cylinders that are master keyed use an additional set of pins.
    D. They are not possible with disc-tumbler locks.

13. Which of the following would NOT be an example of a security department's discretionary costs?

A. Utilities
B. Equipment
C. Accounting fees
D. Materials/supplies

14. In the incident command system (ICS) framework, the ideal number of subordinates under a single supervisor during an incident would be

   A. 3
   B. 5
   C. 7
   D. 9

15. The main problem associated with motion-sensor intruder alarms is that they

   A. are limited in application to areas in which there is already no motion
   B. have a pre-set sensitivity that is not adjustable to accommodate different situations
   C. are more costly than barrier fences
   D. cannot cover long, narrow areas such as hallways

16. Defining a security problem involves an accurate assessment of the kinds of threats or risks affecting the assets to be safeguarded. This assessment is known as

   A. event criticality
   B. loss event probability
   C. loss event frequency
   D. loss event profile

17. Which of the following types of computer viruses is frequently used for the purpose of embezzlement?

   A. Logic bomb
   B. Trojan horse
   C. Stealth
   D. Boot

18. An officer is collecting paint specimens at a crime scene. Generally, good practice is to
   I. lift the specimens with tape
   II. remove the samples with a wooden implement
   III. chip down to the substrate before removal
   IV. use a scraper

   A. I and III
   B. I, II and IV
   C. II and III
   D. I, II, III and IV

19. Which of the following is NOT an outward sign that a person has been using marijuana?

   A. Memory impairment
   B. Red eyes
   C. Constricted pupils
   D. Slowed reaction time

20. A security manager achieves a broad span of control through the use of confrontation as a means of resolving conflict. Which of the following is NOT a guideline for this approach?

    A. Establishing a common goal
    B. Withholding key information during the confrontation
    C. Clarifying each party's strengths and weaknesses
    D. Committing to a flexible position

21. Hertzberg's motivational model identifies _____ as a motivating factor for employees.

    A. job security
    B. punishment
    C. achievement
    D. working conditions

22. At a manufacturing plant that employs about 400, some vandalism has occurred. The security manager arranges interviews with several employees. As part of his interviewing strategy, the security manager tries to induce a certain amount of stress, in order to observe the subjects' reactions. Which of the following responses to these stress-inducing questions or comments is often interpreted as a sign of guilt?
    I. Making an attempt to bond with or seduce the questioner
    II. Admitting stress and saying something such as "I shouldn't be here."
    III. Engaging in "stalling tactics" such as hair-combing or rear ranging clothes
    IV. Accusing the questioner of unfair harassment

    A. I and II
    B. I, III and IV
    C. III and IV
    D. I, II, III and IV

23. Each of the following should be named in a risk management plan, EXCEPT

    A. specific individual risks
    B. the timing of risk management activities
    C. the managerial approach to risk
    D. organizational roles and responsibilities for handling risks

24. A liaison officer at a large private security firm is charged with establishing a solid working relationship with local law enforcement. In the past, police and private security have suffered from strained relations, and after attempting several times, and in several different ways, to contact the precinct captain about initiating such a relationship, the liaison officer has yet to receive a response. The most productive and prudent next step for the liaison officer would be to

    A. appeal to the chief of police and mention the captain's reluctance
    B. begin a public relations campaign in which local media are contacted and told of the private security organization's desire to form a relationship
    C. drop the matter and wait for the police to initiate an outreach
    D. invite the police crime prevention officer for a tour of the private facility

25. Generally, a security officer has the authority to search suspects for
    I. personal property and identification
    II. contraband (narcotics)
    III. physical evidence of a crime
    IV. weapons, when there is a reasonable suspicion that the suspect has a weapon

    A. I only
    B. I, II and III
    C. IV only
    D. I, II, III and IV

KEY (CORRECT ANSWERS)

1.	B	11.	C
2.	B	12.	D
3.	A	13.	A
4.	B	14.	B
5.	C	15.	A
6.	C	16.	D
7.	B	17.	B
8.	C	18.	C
9.	B	19.	C
10.	B	20.	B

21. C
22. D
23. A
24. D
25. C

EXAMINATION SECTION
TEST 1

DIRECTIONS: Each question or incomplete statement is followed by several suggested answers or completions. Select the one that BEST answers the question or completes the statement. *PRINT THE LETTER OF THE CORRECT ANSWER IN THE SPACE AT THE RIGHT.*

1. The control box of a hard-wired security alarm system
    I. must have a button-actuated switch
    II. should incorporate an inside noisemaker
    III. should have a test switch that will check components
    IV. give an instant alarm mode that bypasses the exit/entry delay

    A. I, II and IV
    B. II only
    C. II, III and IV
    D. I, II, III and IV

    1._____

2. Each of the following is considered to be a depressant, EXCEPT

    A. methaqualone
    B. methadone
    C. chloral hydrate
    D. alcohol

    2._____

3. In emergency planning, the term "vulnerability assessment" is most accurately defined as the

    A. systematic protocol for determining the cost of risk
    B. determination of the likelihood of an event's occurrence
    C. determination of possible hazards that may cause harm
    D. implementation of specific interventions to reduce risk

    3._____

4. Optimum security lighting at a facility is achieved by
    I. even light on bordering areas
    II. glaring lights in the eyes of an intruder
    III. little or no light on security patrol routes
    IV. combining lighting with other measures such as posts, fences, and alarm systems

    A. I and II
    B. I, III and IV
    C. II, III and IV
    D. I, II, III and IV

    4._____

5. Examples of risk mitigation include
    I. eliminating the cause of a risk
    II. using proven technology to reduce the probability that a loss will occur
    III. buying insurance
    IV. accepting a lower profit if a risk occurs

    5._____

A. I and II
B. I, II and III
C. II and III
D. I, II, III and IV

6. A person breaks into a physician's office at night and steals several bottles of medication. The offense that may have been committed is

A. theft
B. burglary
C. vandalism
D. robbery

7. "High-security" combination padlocks operate on a _____ rotation.

A. 4-3-2-1
B. 1-2-3-4
C. 3-2-1-2
D. 4-4-3-2

8. The "Standard Checklist Criteria for Business Recovery," published by the Federal Emergency Management Agency (FEMA), recommends that a company's business recovery plan (BRP) be updated every

A. month
B. six months
C. year
D. two years

9. A security team is assigning a criticality rating to a potential loss that would require a major change in investment policy and would have a major impact on the balance sheet assets. Usually, this kind of loss would be rated

A. fatal
B. very serious
C. moderately serious
D. relatively unimportant

10. Security inspections should
    I. be limited to hours of peak activity
    II. be conducted from the outside to the inside of a facility, activity, or area
    III. include both managerial and operational personnel
    IV. include readiness evaluations

A. I and II
B. I, II and III
C. II, III and IV
D. I, II, III and IV

11. A security officer is patrolling a private parking lot after hours and sees two people trespassing near a vehicle that is parked in the lot. The officer should FIRST

A. arrest them for trespassing
B. ask them what they are doing

C. prevent them from leaving and call the police
D. order them off the property without any questioning

12. The financial planning process at a security organization does NOT typically include

    A. predicting costs
    B. revenue projection
    C. the formation of separate planning staffs
    D. budgeting

13. The correct order of events in the analysis of a crime scene BEGINS with

    A. making a sketch
    B. dusting for fingerprints
    C. taking general measurements
    D. taking photographs

14. During an interview with an employee who is suspected of embezzlement, the questioner notes that the employee is a good actor who is giving no nonverbal behavior to interpret. The method the questioner should use to confront the employee's denial is

    A. selective interviewing
    B. bait-and-s witch
    C. cognitive interviewing
    D. the Reid model

15. An agency is using password protection to increase the security of its information network. Passwords in such a system should
    I. be at least eight characters in length
    II. be set to system defaults
    III. contain letters or numbers, but not both
    IV. be changed annually

    A. I only
    B. I and II
    C. II, III and IV
    D. I, II, III and IV

16. Each of the following is a potential security problem that might be overcome through the application of Crime Prevention Through Environmental Design (CPTED) principles, EXCEPT

    A. bleed-off parking
    B. through traffic in residential neighborhoods
    C. two-or three-way street systems
    D. major event facility parking areas

17. A security manager at a large private company is conducing job-satisfaction surveys. Typically, which of the following types of employees tend to be LEAST satisfied with their jobs?

    A. Older employees
    B. Employees who work together in small organizational units

C. Supervisors
D. Entry-level workers

18. In her investigative report, a security officer includes a description of several people involved in an incident. In describing a person in an investigative report, it is customary to FIRST provide the subject's

    A. gender
    B. race
    C. age
    D. height and weight

19. Which of the following documents is considered to be a "snapshot" of an organization at a particular point in time?

    A. Expense budget
    B. Income statement
    C. Balance sheet
    D. Cash flow statement

20. The specialized skills of a security manager working at a large proprietary business installation should include
    I. investigative capability with knowledge of proper evidentiary procedures
    II. writing skills consisting of factual documentation, brevity, and coerciveness
    III. motivational skills
    IV. analytical planning capabilities

    A. I, II and IV
    B. II, III and IV
    C. III and IV
    D. I, II, III and IV

21. A suspect in a crime is described by a forensic technologist as a "se-cretor." This means that the suspect has

    A. left fingerprints that are easily lifted because of a large amount of skin oils
    B. a tendency to perspire a lot during questioning
    C. left behind a good number of bodily fluids as evidence
    D. saliva and other bodily fluids, other than blood, that can be traced to a blood type

22. In a management scheme that follows Hertzberg's motivational model, _____ would serve as the strongest possible motivating factor for an employee.

    A. a sense of responsibility
    B. vacation time
    C. a retirement plan
    D. a clearly delineated set of tasks

23. The driving issue behind the formation of the American Society for Industrial Security (ASIS) in 1955 was the

    A. need for cooperation between private security and public law enforcement
    B. post World War II jobs draught for those with military training

C. dramatic increase in white-collar crime
D. Cold War expansion of the private defense industry

24. An employee is being questioned after a theft has occurred at the workplace. In forming an opinion of the employee's guilt, the questioning officer places great emphasis on how the subject responds to "yes" or "no" questions. Which of the following "NO" responses would be apt to generate suspicion?

    I. Saying "no" with unusual emphasis
    II. Hesitating before answering "no"
    III. Saying "no" and then immediately closing one's eyes
    IV. Saying "no" and then immediately fidgeting

    A. I and II
    B. II and III
    C. II, III and IV
    D. I, II, III and IV

25. Cooperative programs between private security and public law enforcement agencies are often "topic-specific." Which of the following is LEAST likely to be a topic around which such a relationship would be formed?

    A. High-tech crime
    B. Background investigations
    C. Narcotics
    D. Equipment

KEY (CORRECT ANSWERS)

1.	C	11.	B
2.	B	12.	C
3.	C	13.	D
4.	D	14.	A
5.	C	15.	A
6.	B	16.	C
7.	A	17.	D
8.	B	18.	A
9.	B	19.	C
10.	C	20.	D

21. D
22. A
23. A
24. D
25. C

TEST 2

DIRECTIONS: Each question or incomplete statement is followed by several suggested answers or completions. Select the one that BEST answers the question or completes the statement. *PRINT THE LETTER OF THE CORRECT ANSWER IN THE SPACE AT THE RIGHT.*

1. A security manager at a large defense-contracting firm is building a department from the ground up. Many of her employees will be former military personnel, and she has decided to adopt a traditional, bureaucratic organizational design. In order to achieve the maximum benefits of this design, the manager should

    A. base employment on technical qualifications
    B. require employees to report to more than one office head
    C. divide tasks along generalized lines
    D. establish informal, personal communication between employees

    1.____

2. Which of the following is a cognitive interviewing technique?

    A. Strongly asserting the subject's guilt in an attempt to elicit a confession
    B. Eliciting strongly emotional verbal responses
    C. Eliciting nonverbal responses
    D. Having the subject repeat a story from various starting points

    2.____

3. Which type of lock contains a spring latchbolt and provides additional security to a door's regular lock?

    A. Beveled
    B. Case ward
    C. Night latch
    D. Deadbolt

    3.____

4. A security officer receives a bomb threat call. The officer's FIRST duty is to

    A. hang up and call the fire department
    B. hang up and call the bomb squad
    C. try to keep the caller on the line and learn more information
    D. order an evacuation of the building

    4.____

5. Negative reinforcement occurs when an employee's behavior is

    A. accompanied by the removal of an unfavorable consequence
    B. ignored
    C. rewarded with a favorable consequence
    D. discouraged by an unfavorable consequence

    5.____

6. An employee is being questioned after a theft has occurred at the workplace. The questioning officer suspects that the employee was involved in the theft. During the earliest stages of the interview, the questioner will MOST likely want to

    A. induce undue stress and see how the employee responds
    B. solicit a "baseline" of specific responses to general, non-threatening questions
    C. confront the employee with his suspicions and see how the employee reacts
    D. ask the employee what he or she thinks of the crime that has been committed

    6.____

7. An organization is implementing an identification system to control access. Which of the following would NOT be a guideline to be followed in implementing an identification system?

    A. Digital cameras should be used to photograph employees for identification purposes
    B. ID badges should always be worn in clear view
    C. ID badges should include the employees' first and last names
    D. ID badges should include an encrypted employee number

8. The main disadvantage associated with most wireless alarm systems is that

    A. signals are easily duplicated
    B. they cannot protect outbuildings
    C. their transistor batteries do not have an inherent backup
    D. installation is significantly more difficult than hard-wired systems

9. The continued growth in demand for private security services is described in the Hallcrest Report as due to increases in each of the following factors, EXCEPT

    A. awareness of private security services
    B. workplace crime
    C. rate of government spending for public protection
    D. fear of crime

10. Which of the following steps in the budgetary process is usually performed FIRST?

    A. Planning activities in detail
    B. Combining unit budgets
    C. Outlining resource restraints
    D. Formulating performance targets

11. When questioning people on private property owned by his employer or client, a security officer's authority is usually
    I. the same as any other private citizen
    II. greater than other private citizens
    III. the same as the police
    IV. the same as the owner/client

    A. I only
    B. II only
    C. II and III
    D. III and IV

12. Management and labor at a security organization are in conflict on an issue. If the outcome is a win/lose situation, _____ has occurred.

    A. forced-choice ranking
    B. integrative bargaining
    C. collective bargaining
    D. distributive bargaining

13. The incident command system (ICS) framework relies on the principle of "unity of command." This principle states that in an emergency response,

    A. each member reports to the incident commander
    B. each member of the team reports to only one supervisor
    C. all team members share responsibility for decision-making
    D. each incident commander reports to the regional FEMA office

14. Attempts at liaison between private security organizations and public law enforcement are often hampered by major problems. Which of the following is NOT a significant problem?

    A. Isolation of jurisdictions/areas of operation
    B. Moonlighting policies for public police
    C. Lack of standards for private security personnel
    D. Lack of communication

15. Effective methods for security lighting include lighting
    I. boundaries and approaches
    II. areas and structures within property's general boundaries
    III. patrol routes
    IV. alarm control boxes and annunciators

    A. I and II
    B. I, II and III
    C. I and IV
    D. I, II, III and IV

16. In the investigation of a crime, an officer should return to re-interview a witness that could be described as _____ at the time of the first interview.

    A. unaware
    B. fearful
    C. talkative
    D. reluctant

17. Federal government documents that are marked FOR OFFICIAL USE ONLY
    I. may be stored in unlocked containers, desks or cabinets if government or government-contract security is provided
    II. may not be mailed
    III. must be stored at a minimum in a locked desk, file cabinet, or room if government or government-contract security is not provided
    IV. may be destroyed by discarding in a regular trash container

    A. I and III
    B. II and III
    C. III only
    D. I, II, III and IV

18. Prior to the commission of a violation, a security officer's role is

    A. observing and reporting
    B. apprehension and detention

C. prevention
D. watching and waiting

19. What is the most commonly used synthetic opiate?

    A. Methadone
    B. Demerol
    C. Heroin
    D. Diazepam

20. Management implications inherent in MacGregor's Theory Y of management do NOT include

    A. decentralization
    B. participative management
    C. tight controls
    D. performance appraisals

21. In writing an investigative report, an officer should AVOID

    A. composing the report in chronological order
    B. presenting a reasoned opinion about a suspect's guilt or innocence
    C. printing in block style
    D. writing in all capital letters

22. Information that an organization posts on one Web site may seem unimportant, but when combined with information from other Web sites it may form a larger and more complete picture that was neither intended nor desired by the organization. In the language of the military, this information is

    A. restricted data
    B. a trade secret
    C. confidential
    D. sensitive by aggregation

23. Which of the following is a Crime Prevention Through Environmental Design (CPTED) strategy?

    A. Dividing areas by planting tall hedges and screens
    B. Blending the perception of property and public space
    C. Obstructing lines of sight from loading zones to building entrances
    D. Minimizing the number of entry and exit points

24. The most appropriate process for conducting a crime scene search over a large area is the _____ method.

    A. zone
    B. strip
    C. spiral
    D. point

25. An organization has made the decision to accept a risk when it
    I. accepts the consequences of the risk
    II. develops a contingency plan to execute should the risk event occur
    III. transfers the risk to another party
    IV. reduces the probability of the risk event occurring

    A. I and II
    B. I, II and IV
    C. II and III
    D. I, II, III and IV

KEY (CORRECT ANSWERS)

1. A
2. D
3. C
4. C
5. A

6. B
7. C
8. C
9. C
10. C

11. B
12. D
13. B
14. A
15. A

16. A
17. A
18. C
19. A
20. C

21. B
22. D
23. D
24. C
25. A

TEST 3

DIRECTIONS: Each question or incomplete statement is followed by several suggested answers or completions. Select the one that BEST answers the question or completes the statement. *PRINT THE LETTER OF THE CORRECT ANSWER IN THE SPACE AT THE RIGHT.*

1. In most jurisdictions, a security officer has the same power to arrest as a(n) 1.____

    A. federal law enforcement agent
    B. state police officer
    C. regional or municipal police officer
    D. private citizen

2. A hard-wired security alarm system is experiencing numerous intermittent false alarms. The most likely cause is 2.____

    A. a short circuit
    B. an open circuit or defective switch
    C. no voltage to the control box
    D. a loose connection or broken wire

3. Title VII of the Civil Rights Act of 1964, as amended, prohibits discrimination based on race, color, religion, sex, or national origin in any term, condition, or privilege of employment. Which of the following types of organizations are EXEMPT from to the provisions of this legislation? 3.____

    A. All public and private educational institutions
    B. Private employers of 15 or fewer people
    C. Joint labor-management committees for apprenticeships and training
    D. Local governments

4. Defining a security problem involves an accurate assessment of the effect on the assets or on the enterprise responsible for the assets if the loss occurs. This assessment is known as 4.____

    A. loss event profile
    B. event criticality
    C. loss event frequency
    D. loss event probability

5. Which of the following is NOT an outward sign that would suggest amphetamine use? 5.____

    A. Compulsive scratching
    B. Sudden violent behavior
    C. Dilated pupils
    D. Paranoia

6. Practical examples of trade secrets may include 6.____
    I. internal testing procedures
    II. chemical formulas
    III. customer lists
    IV. software

    A. I and II
    C. II and IV
    B. I, II and IV
    D. I, II, III and IV

43

7. When an organization deflects or transfers risk to another party, risk _____ has been performed.

   A. mitigation
   B. analysis
   C. acceptance
   D. avoidance

8. On a case record, the code _____ indicates that the case was cleared by arrest.

   A. WPA
   B. COP
   C. ROR
   D. VCI

9. In risk management, a "trigger" is a(n)

   A. unexpected situation causing an identified risk event to occur
   B. unexpected situation causing an unidentified risk event to occur
   C. expected situation causing an unidentified risk event to occur
   D. warning sign that an identified risk event might have occurred

10. About 80 percent of internal security problems experienced by companies' information networks are caused by

    A. poorly chosen passwords
    B. outdated firewalls
    C. viruses
    D. inadequate encryption

11. In a high-crime urban housing facility, a security officer is talking with a resident about drug-related activities in the building. Because of several past events involving law enforcement officers, some residents regard the officer with suspicion. Which of the following nonverbal cues is usually NOT an indicator of mistrust on the part of a listener?

    A. Speaking with shoulders angled away from the speaker
    B. A clenched jaw
    C. Steady eye contact
    D. Crossing one's arms over the chest

12. False imprisonment is a civil liability for a security officer. Elements necessary to create liability for false imprisonment include
    I. detention
    II. unlawfulness of the detention
    III. physical restraint
    IV. unreasonable duration

    A. I only
    B. I and II
    C. I, II and III
    D. I, II, III and IV

13. The security manager of an organization, working in a proprietary system, is most likely to report to the

    A. chief executive officer
    B. chief operating officer
    C. ombudsperson
    D. administrative vice president

14. In an investigative report, a security officer describes an event that took place at 7:00 in the evening. The time recorded in the report should read

    A. 7:00 pm
    B. 7.5 pm
    C. 730
    D. 19:30

15. According to the Hallcrest Report on private security and investigation, employee theft accounts for about _____ percent of a private company's inventory losses.

    A. 10
    B. 30
    C. 60
    D. 90

16. A security manager is interviewing several employees who work in an area of an office building where a workstation has been hacked to allow some unauthorized access. In speaking with the employees, the manager should keep in mind that guilty people, when being interviewed, often scratch their

    A. head
    B. palms
    C. neck
    D. abdomen

17. A security manager wants to shape policies and practices through periodic departmental meetings during which the group will determine the organization's future. The manager is aware that this approach carries with it the risk of the phenomenon known as "groupthink." Symptoms of groupthink include
    I. self-censorship
    II. stereotyping
    III. internal arguments
    IV. high-risk decisions

    A. I only
    B. I and II
    C. II and IV
    D. I, II, III and IV

18. The first item to be mentioned in a court case after a workplace security incident is often, ironically, one of the first to be cut out of a company's budget. It is

    A. security personnel
    B. liaison efforts with local law enforcement
    C. employee training
    D. employee screening

19. A security manager wants to shape policies and practices through periodic departmental meetings during which the group will determine the organization's future. Each of the following statements about group and individual decision-making is true, EXCEPT

    A. Individuals are usually better than groups at establishing objectives, because of their ability to focus.
    B. The implementation of a decision is usually accomplished by individual managers.
    C. Groups tend to be better than individuals at evaluating alternatives, because of a wider range of viewpoints.
    D. Groups tend to accept greater risks than individuals when choosing alternatives.

20. While cooperative efforts between public law enforcement and private security are on the increase, many police officers still hold negative opinions about the work of security officers. These negative opinions are MOST likely to surface when a

    A. security officer makes an arrest
    B. police officer is responding to a criminal complaint or breach of police reported by security
    C. security officer is unarmed
    D. police officer attends a liaison function such as a plant tour or a luncheon

21. Of the following, the _____ electric release latch strike is MOST likely to provide a "fail-safe" unlocked door in the case of power failure or emergency.

    A. monitoring
    B. reverse action
    C. intermittent duty
    D. continuous duty

22. The _____ stage in the budgeting process typically involves the estimation of relevant cash inflows and outflows?

    A. development
    B. implementation
    C. identification
    D. selection

23. Within a large security organization, tactical or operational problems are primarily the responsibility of

    A. line officers
    B. low-level managers
    C. mid-level managers
    D. administrative heads

24. Under the incident command system (ICS) framework, any function not assigned by the incident commander   24.____

    A. is the responsibility of the incident commander
    B. is shared equally among battalion chiefs
    C. becomes the charge of the liaison officer
    D. becomes the charge of the safety officer

25. A bomb threat has been called in at a commercial workplace. The private security officer helps police to coordinate a bomb search. Which of the following may searchers use to communicate during their search?   25.____

    I. Whistles
    II. Runners
    III. Radios
    IV. Non-cellular telephones

    A. I and II
    B. I, III and IV
    C. II only
    D. I, II, III and IV

KEY (CORRECT ANSWERS)

1. D
2. D
3. B
4. B
5. B

6. D
7. A
8. A
9. B
10. A

11. C
12. B
13. D
14. D
15. D

16. C
17. B
18. C
19. A
20. B

21. B
22. A
23. C
24. A
25. B

EXAMINATION SECTION
TEST 1

DIRECTIONS: Each question or incomplete statement is followed by several suggested answers or completions. Select the one that BEST answers the question or completes the statement. *PRINT THE LETTER OF THE CORRECT ANSWER IN THE SPACE AT THE RIGHT.*

1. An effective emergency management plan includes
    I. a common terminology
    II. a modular scheme of organization
    III. distinct police and fire command posts
    IV. command functions that overlap jurisdictions

    A. I only
    B. I and III
    C. II and III
    D. I, II, III and IV

    1._____

2. Each of the following is a good rule for the use of radio in communications between security officers and managers or law enforcement officials, EXCEPT

    A. always use full names and locations
    B. use proper radio codes and terminology
    C. locate a good area for transmission
    D. be as brief as possible

    2._____

3. The majority of private computer systems breaches can be prevented by means of

    A. assigning a single IP address to the entire system
    B. installing correct software patches and security upgrades
    C. installing Carnivore or a similar online surveillance tool
    D. stricter authentication requirements

    3._____

4. Within a private security organization, a supervisor's span of control is LEAST likely to depend on the

    A. amount of personal contact between employees
    B. rate of change in the organization
    C. the number of potential relationships among employees
    D. supervisor's ability to delegate

    4._____

5. The Hallcrest Report II (Private Security trends) concludes that _____ is America's primary protective resource in terms of spending and employment.

    A. federal law enforcement
    B. state law enforcement
    C. regional/local law enforcement
    D. private security

    5._____

6. When taken from an automobile as evidence, paint chips can usually be used to identify the vehicle's
    I. year of manufacture

    6._____

49

    II. make
    III. model
    IV. speed at the time of impact

   A. I and II
   B. II and III
   C. II only
   D. I, II, III and IV

7. Hertzberg's model of employee motivation

   A. does not apply well to line workers
   B. demonstrates the powerful influence in intrinsic rewards
   C. tends to overemphasize the importance of pay and status as motivators
   D. does not involve universal classifications of motivators

8. The most common type of security lighting system is the _____ system.

   A. standby
   B. portable
   C. continuous
   D. emergency

9. The security manager of an organization, working in a proprietary system, should have a college degree in police science, but a degree in a _____ -related field is acceptable based on work experience.

   A. business
   B. mathematics
   C. science
   D. humanities

10. A security manager who adopts a "custodial" leadership style bases her decisions on

    A. partnership
    B. economic resources
    C. leadership
    D. sources of power

11. A security officer is helping in the investigation of a crime scene. If an item may contain relevant fingerprints, the officer should

    A. freeze it
    B. refrigerate it
    C. store it at room temperature
    D. dust the item for prints

12. Security lighting installed on the grounds of an industrial installation should
    I. shine inward
    II. silhouette an intruder
    III. be installed at the outer perimeter of the building
    IV. illuminate only the possible points of entry

A. I and II
B. I, II and III
C. II, III and IV
D. I, II, III and IV

13. In the last few decades, the perceived need for cooperation between private security and public law enforcement has increased because of the influence of several factors. Which of the following is NOT one of these factors?

    A. Public law enforcement's difficulty in handling increasing high-tech crimes
    B. Dwindling public resources for handling crime
    C. Increasing sophistication of some types of economic crimes
    D. Decreasing call rates for public law enforcement services

14. The Federal Emergency Management Agency (FEMA) has identified the typical stages or phases through which individuals respond to a disaster or emergency. The SECOND of these phases is
    A. inventory
    B. recovery
    C. impact
    D. response

15. Which of the following is NOT an advantage associated with internal recruitment for positions within a security organization?

    A. Increased internal morale due to upward mobility opportunities
    B. Good performance is rewarded
    C. Increased likelihood of new ideas being introduced
    D. Availability of reliable candidate information

16. A _____ locking bolt is protected by a device that will automatically block spring action after the door has shut, preventing jimmying of the bolt from the outside.

    A. deadbolt
    B. dead latch
    C. night latch
    D. bevel

17. The most important classifying characteristic of fiber evidence is its

    A. density
    B. mass
    C. refraction index
    D. volume

18. Within most organizations, the most successful use of the practice of job rotation is to

    A. create maximum flexibility through cross-training
    B. establish an employee development tool
    C. alleviate boredom with simple jobs
    D. improve organizational loyalty

19. Approximately what percentage of U.S. workers-according to federal studies-use dangerous drugs while on the job?

    A. 1-3
    B. 5-8
    C. 10-20
    D. 25-40

20. Log books, personal recognition, and ID cards are all a means to achieve

    A. access control
    B. documentary evidence
    C. traffic control
    D. perimeter protection

21. Which of the following lists street types in a sequence conforming to the traditional street hierarchy, which ranks roads ranging from private to interstate highway?

    A. limited access, service road, residential, sub-collector
    B. residential, sub-collector, arterial, service road
    C. arterial, collector, service road, limited access
    D. service road, residential, arterial, collector

22. During the interview of an employee, the employer representative's main responsibility is to

    A. protect the employee from legal liability for an act to which he has not confessed
    B. ensure that the employee is treated fairly
    C. ensure that no coercion is used to obtain a confession
    D. determine how a culpable employee will be treated and advise him of this treatment

23. What is the term for a risk response that involves eliminating a threat?

    A. Transfer
    B. Mitigation
    C. Avoidance
    D. Deflection

24. A security manager is interviewing several employees who work in an area of an office building where some expensive computer equipment has disappeared. The manager has a strong suspicion that one of the employees in the group is responsible. In an interview, a guilty person is most likely to confess to such an offense if the questioner

    A. places all of the suspected parties together in the same room during questioning
    B. asks directly and unemotionally why the person committed the offense
    C. begins talking as if it is already a proven assumption that the person is guilty
    D. offers hypothetical rationalizations for the offense

25. A felony arrest may be made by a(n)
    I. security officer
    II. federal law enforcement agent
    III. police officer
    IV. private citizen

A. I, II and III
B. II only
C. II and III only
D. I, II, III and IV

KEY (CORRECT ANSWERS)

1. D
2. A
3. B
4. C
5. D

6. A
7. B
8. C
9. A
10. B

11. C
12. B
13. D
14. A
15. C

16. B
17. C
18. B
19. C
20. A

21. B
22. B
23. C
24. D
25. D

TEST 2

DIRECTIONS: Each question or incomplete statement is followed by several suggested answers or completions. Select the one that BEST answers the question or completes the statement. *PRINT THE LETTER OF THE CORRECT ANSWER IN THE SPACE AT THE RIGHT.*

1. A security officer is arresting a suspect for suspicion of burglary. In most cases, when making the arrest, the officer should say
   I. You are under arrest for suspicion of burglary
   II. You have the right to remain silent
   III. I am making a citizen's arrest
   IV. Put your hands where I can see them

   A. I and II
   B. II only
   C. III and IV
   D. IV only

   1.____

2. Often, the earliest sign of a computer security breach will be

   A. server failure
   B. denial-of-service
   C. buggy application function
   D. altered file signatures

   2.____

3. At the turn of the 21st century, private security personnel in the United States

   A. numbered about half as many as all public law enforcement personnel (federal, state, local)
   B. numbered about the same as all public law enforcement personnel
   C. outnumbered all public law enforcement personnel, 3-to-1
   D. outnumbered local/municipal law enforcement personnel, 2-to-1

   3.____

4. In order for a private company to legally enforce its own information security policy, it must have a number of elements established. Which of the following is NOT one of these?

   A. A system of warnings and markings that advise of sensitivity and/or handling requirements
   B. A system to identify the specific information to be protected
   C. A specific and published hierarchy of proprietary information classifications
   D. Procedures for safeguarding and controlling the protected information

   4.____

5. Each of the following is a component of gunpowder residue, EXCEPT

   A. barium
   B. arsenic
   C. lead
   D. antimony

   5.____

54

6. MacGregor's Theory X of management can be described as a(n)

   A. autocratic and traditional set of assumptions
   B. focus on cooperation and interdependence
   C. humanistic and supportive set of assumptions
   D. an adaptation of Maslow's hierarchy of human needs

7. Pulsed-infrared motion detector systems are prone to false alarms caused by
   I. changes in humidity
   II. vibration
   III. the accumulation of dust on units
   IV. air motion

   A. I only
   B. I and IV
   C. II and III
   D. I, II, III and IV

8. Which of the following is an example of a vulnerability falling within the classification of "acts of God and conspiracy"?

   A. Fire
   B. Burglary
   C. Militant group destruction
   D. Industrial espionage

9. Of the following, an affidavit is most likely to be required for an evidentiary record for property that is

   A. seized by search warrant
   B. found
   C. recovered
   D. held for safekeeping

10. "Cross keying" is a term that refers to

    A. enabling two or more keys in a master system to operate the same lock
    B. the installation of two lock cylinders, as in safety-deposit boxes
    C. making cuts on both sides of the key blade
    D. milling pin-tumbler key cuts at an angle that will not only raise, but rotate pins

11. Which of the following organizational characteristics reflects the concept of centralization?

    A. Delegation of authority
    B. Broad span of control
    C. Low degree of specialization
    D. Separate service departments

12. The biggest disadvantage associated with hard-wired security alarm systems is that they

    A. are prone to numerous false alarms
    B. are not broadly applicable to different types of security problems

C. cannot easily accommodate the addition of smoke and fire sensors
D. involve wires that are vulnerable to tampering or attack

13. Problems inherent in managing a proprietary or contract security company for profit include a turnover rate that in the late 1990s and early 2000s averaged about _____ percent per year.

    A. 50
    B. 100
    C. 200
    D. 300

14. In a large office complex, a physical vulnerability assessment should include an analysis of
    I. hiring procedures
    II. parking permits
    III. shipping and receiving
    IV. contractor permits

    A. I and II
    B. II and III
    C. II, III and IV
    D. II and IV only

15. Which of the following crime scenes would most appropriately be searched using the zone method?

    A. Vacant lot
    B. Lake shore
    C. Shallow grave
    D. Private residence

16. A security officer is standing at his post when he hears the sound of glass breaking in the rear of the property. He then goes to investigate. This type of patrol is called

    A. reactive
    B. proactive
    C. directed
    D. random

17. An organization is practicing "active risk acceptance" when it

    A. develops a plan to minimize probability
    B. allocates additional resources
    C. creates contingency reserves in money and time
    D. develops a plan to minimize potential impact

18. The cognitive interview, a method for eliciting more complete and more accurate information from witnesses, is most successful with subjects who

    A. are good actors
    B. already have an alibi
    C. have psychiatric problems
    D. have memory problems

19. The security staff for a contract at a large university is experiencing a high turnover rate. Potential negative consequences of turnover include each of the following, EXCEPT

    A. reduced opportunities for internal promotion
    B. lowered employee morale
    C. increased costs
    D. a damaged reputation

20. Under the protocols of the incident command system (ICS) framework, an incident commander is responsible for
    I. gathering and assigning resources
    II. evaluating plan effectiveness
    III. coordinating the overall incident response
    IV. communicating with other officials within the system

    A. I and II
    B. I, III and IV
    C. III only
    D. I, II, III and IV

21. Most narcotics are derived from

    A. opium
    B. amphetamine
    C. hemp
    D. alcohol

22. A security manager who terminates a line officer as a result of _____ is adhering to the principle of "due cause."

    A. shop closure
    B. layoff
    C. retirement
    D. incompetence

23. The FIRST step in a comprehensive risk survey is typically to

    A. assign probability ratings
    B. identify the specific threats or risk
    C. describe the details that make occurrence of particular risks more or less probable
    D. measure criticality concept loss impact

24. When criminal charges are filed against a security officer, it is LEAST likely to be for

    A. false imprisonment
    B. assault
    C. discharging a firearm
    D. battery

25. As part of its emergency plan, a company has designated a crisis communications team room. Guidelines for the crisis center typically include each of the following, EXCEPT

    A. a room located far from key operational areas
    B. computers linked to the main system, e-mail, and Internet applications
    C. dedicated telephone lines that bypass the phone switch
    D. a speakerphone

25.____

KEY (CORRECT ANSWERS)

1.	C	11.	B
2.	D	12.	D
3.	C	13.	D
4.	C	14.	C
5.	B	15.	D
6.	A	16.	A
7.	C	17.	C
8.	A	18.	D
9.	B	19.	A
10.	A	20.	D

21. A
22. D
23. B
24. A
25. A

TEST 3

DIRECTION: Each question or incomplete statement is followed by several suggested answers or completions. Select the one that BEST answers the question or completes the statement. *PRINT THE LETTER OF THE CORRECT ANSWER IN THE SPACE AT THE RIGHT.*

1. The normal risk of doing business that carries opportunities for both gain and loss is called _____ risk.

    A. opportunity
    B. favorable
    C. pure
    D. dynamic

2. A security manager is interviewing several employees who were in or near a certain part of the office at the time some computer records were irretrievably altered. The manager asks each of the employees to describe what he or she saw at roughly the time of the offense. The employee who should be most strongly suspected would be the one who _____ during his or her description.

    A. coughs a lot
    B. looks left and down
    C. looks right and up
    D. closes his or her eyes

3. A security manager who adopts an "autocratic" leadership style bases her decisions on

    A. teamwork
    B. formal lines of authority
    C. creating a supportive atmosphere
    D. economic resources

4. When a security officer switches on a hard-wired security alarm system at the control box, the alarm sounds. The exit/entry delay does not delay. The MOST likely cause is

    A. a loose connection or broken wire
    B. no voltage to the control box
    C. an open circuit or defective switch
    D. a short circuit

5. Which of the following is classified as a "natural" security strategy?

    A. Window location
    B. Stationing guards
    C. Alarm systems
    D. Fences

6. Which of the following is NOT one of the three major components in an alarm system?

    A. Sensor
    B. Transformer

C. Annunciator
D. Transmitter

7. Most coding systems for master key combinations are based on differences in   7._____

   A. cut angles
   B. blade width
   C. tumbler depth
   D. keyway groove

8. An officer is circulating among the employees at a private workplace in order to report   8._____
   their activities to the employer. It would be illegal for the officer to report that

   A. two employees have become romantically involved
   B. an employee has just become pregnant
   C. some employees are beginning to talk informally about forming a union
   D. an employee is receiving treatment for drug addiction

9. The diversion of resources and assets for the purpose of lowering loss exposure is   9._____
   known as risk

   A. transfer
   B. abatement
   C. spreading
   D. reduction

10. Usually, the best place to get a sample of a person's signature is from the records at the   10._____

    A. county court
    B. state attorney general
    C. department of motor vehicles
    D. social security office

11. As part of its strategy to protect sensitive information, an office uses a paper shredder   11._____
    with a crosscut function. The optimum crosscut function should shred no larger than
    _____ inch.

    A. 1/8
    B. 1/4
    C. 1/2
    D. 3/4

12. A security officer is watching a suspect whom she suspects of having just committed a   12._____
    crime. The officer can't be sure a crime has been committed. The officer should

    A. notify the police and detain the suspect until they arrive
    B. search the suspect for evidence that can be used to arrest him
    C. arrest the suspect and explain after it has been determined whether a crime has
       been committed
    D. observe and report, without detention or arrest

13. New York's Area Police-Private Security Liaison (APPL) Program, in many ways an   13._____
    industry-wide model for interorganizational cooperation, implements _____ formal
    meetings between police commanders and security directors.

A. weekly
B. monthly
C. quarterly
D. annually

14. When using _____ detectors as a security device, the protected items must be electrically insulated.   14.____

    A. microwave
    B. proximity
    C. pulsed infrared
    D. ultrasonic

15. An evidentiary item's chain of custody is usually considered to have been initiated by the   15.____

    A. recovering or reporting officer
    B. party involved in the incident who is responsible for its location when found
    C. witness who first found it
    D. property or evidence specialist

16. One of the biggest advantages associated with the use of firewalls in computer network security is that   16.____

    A. access to the network is restricted to users within the building
    B. it allows remote access to a computer network
    C. the entire network presents only one IP address to the outside world
    D. encryption and authentication are flexibly managed

17. Of the following, the most compelling reason for a security manager to centralize authority within a department is to   17.____

    A. avoid duplicating functions
    B. encourage competitiveness among employees
    C. discourage supervisory delegation
    D. encouraging the development of professional managers from within

18. The bottom-up method of budgeting works well when   18.____

    A. unit managers have limited knowledge of the current situation
    B. first-line management is excluded from the process
    C. competitive pressures require a quick response
    D. there is a considerable degree of interdependence among units

19. In crime reconstruction, the FIRST step is typically to   19.____

    A. examine the physical evidence
    B. recreate the crime scene's physical appearance
    C. identify a suspect
    D. interpret eyewitness accounts

20. Of the following outward signs, which is MOST likely to suggest the use of cocaine?   20.____

    A. Facial contortions
    B. Slowed reaction time

C. Slurred speech
D. Persistently running nose

21. MacGregor's Theory Y of management assumes each of the following, EXCEPT that

    A. when conditions are favorable, the average person will seek responsibility
    B. commitment to goals is the function of available rewards
    C. the average person wants to be directed, and seeks security above all
    D. the intellectual potential of most workers is only partially utilized in most companies

22. In formulating or implementing a disaster response plan, an organization should NOT

    A. keep the media as informed as possible
    B. make public statements that the organization is "taking every precaution/doing everything possible to ensure the safety of our employees."
    C. provide elected officials with briefings on the situation
    D. assume a "worst-case" scenario when developing a plan

23. A security manager who encourages self-discipline among her employees is implementing an element of the _____ model of organizational behavior.

    A. autocratic
    B. collegial
    C. custodial
    D. supportive

24. In emergency planning, the determination of an event's probability and impact is known specifically as

    A. risk analysis
    B. vulnerability assessment
    C. risk management
    D. risk assessment

25. Which of the following is NOT a current trend that affects—or will likely affect—future cooperation between law enforcement and private security?

    A. Corporations' increasing need to prosecute crimes
    B. Changes in law enforcement's approach to work, including community- and problem-oriented policing
    C. Privatization of law enforcement functions
    D. Decreasing standards of professionalism in private security

KEY (CORRECT ANSWERS)

1.	D	11.	B
2.	C	12.	D
3.	B	13.	B
4.	C	14.	B
5.	A	15.	A
6.	B	16.	C
7.	C	17.	A
8.	C	18.	C
9.	C	19.	B
10.	C	20.	D

21. C
22. B
23. B
24. A
25. D

EXAMINATION SECTION
TEST 1

DIRECTIONS: Each question or incomplete statement is followed by several suggested answers or completions. Select the one that BEST answers the question or completes the statement. *PRINT THE LETTER OF THE CORRECT ANSWER IN THE SPACE AT THE RIGHT.*

1. Of the following, the MOST important single factor in any building security program is   1.____

    A. a fool-proof employee identification system
    B. an effective control of entrances and exits
    C. bright illumination of all outside areas
    D. clearly marking public and non-public areas

2. There is general agreement that the BEST criterion of what is a good physical security system in a large public building is   2.____

    A. the number of uniformed officers needed to patrol sensitive areas
    B. how successfully the system prevents rather than detects violations
    C. the number of persons caught in the act of committing criminal offenses
    D. how successfully the system succeeds in maintaining good public relations

3. Which one of the following statements most correctly expresses the CHIEF reason why women were originally made eligible for appointment to the position of officer?   3.____

    A. Certain tasks in security protection can be performed best by assigning women.
    B. More women than men are available to fill many vacancies in this position.
    C. The government wants more women in law enforcement because of their better attendance records.
    D. Women can no longer be barred from any government jobs because of sex.

4. The MOST BASIC purpose of patrol by officers is to   4.____

    A. eliminate as much as possible the opportunity for successful misconduct
    B. investigate criminal complaints and accident cases
    C. give prompt assistance to employees and citizens in distress or requesting their help
    D. take persons into custody who commit criminal offenses against persons and property

5. The highest quality of patrol service is MOST generally obtained by   5.____

    A. frequently changing the post assignments of each officer
    B. assigning officers to posts of equal size
    C. assigning problem officers to the least desirable posts
    D. assigning the same officers to the same posts

6. The one of the following requirements which is MOST essential to the successful performance of patrol duty by individual officers is their   6.____

    A. ability to communicate effectively with higher-level officers
    B. prompt signalling according to a prescribed schedule to insure post coverages at all times

65

C. knowledge of post conditions and post hazards
D. willingness to cover large areas during periods of critical manpower shortages

7. Officers on patrol are constantly warned to be on the alert for suspicious persons, actions, and circumstances.
With this in mind, a senior officer should emphasize the need for them to

   A. be cautious and suspicious when dealing officially with any civilian regardless of the latter's overt actions or the circumstances surrounding his dealings with the police
   B. keep looking for the unusual persons, actions, and circumstances on their posts and pay less attention to the usual
   C. take aggressive police action immediately against any unusual person or condition detected on their posts, regardless of any other circumstances
   D. become thoroughly familiar with the usual on their posts so as to be better able to detect the unusual

8. Of primary importance in the safeguarding of property from theft is a good central lock and key issuance and control system.
Which one of the following recommendations about maintaining such a control system would be LEAST acceptable?

   A. In selecting locks to be used for the various gates, building, and storage areas, consideration should be given to the amount of security desired.
   B. Master keys should have no markings that will identify them as such and the list of holders of these keys should be frequently reviewed to determine the continuing necessity for the individuals having them.
   C. Whenever keys for outside doors or gates or for other doors which permit access to important buildings and areas are misplaced, the locks should be immediately changed or replaced pending an investigation.
   D. Whenever an employee fails to return a borrowed key at the time specified, a prompt investigation should be made by the security force.

9. In a crowded building, a fire develops in the basement, and smoke enters the crowded rooms on the first floor. Of the following, the BEST action for an officer to take after an alarm is turned in is to

   A. call out a warning that the building is on fire and that everyone should evacuate because of the immediate danger
   B. call all of the officers together for an emergency meeting and discuss a plan of action
   C. immediately call for assistance from the local police station to help in evacuating the crowd
   D. tell everyone that there is a fire in the building next door and that they should move out onto the streets through available exits

10. Which of the following is in a key position to carry out successfully a safety program of an agency? The

    A. building engineer
    B. bureau chiefs
    C. immediate supervisors
    D. public relations director

11. It is GENERALLY considered that a daily roll call inspection, which checks to see that the officers and their equipment are in good order, is

    A. *desirable,* chiefly because it informs the superior officer what men will have to purchase new uniforms within a month
    B. *desirable,* chiefly because the public forms their impressions of the organization from the appearance of the officers
    C. *undesirable,* chiefly because this kind of daily inspection unnecessarily delays officers in getting to their assigned patrol posts
    D. *undesirable,* chiefly because roll call inspection usually misses individuals reporting to work late

12. A supervising officer in giving instructions to a group of officers on the principles of accident investigation remarked, "A conclusion that appears reasonable will often be changed by exploring a factor of apparently little importance".
    Which one of the following precautions does this statement emphasize as MOST important in any accident investigation?

    A. Every accident clue should be fully investigated.
    B. Accidents should not be too promptly investigated.
    C. Only specially trained officers should investigate accidents.
    D. Conclusions about accident causes are highly unreliable.

13. On a rainy day, a senior officer found that 9 of his 50 officers reported to work. What percentage of his officers was ABSENT?

    A. 18%   B. 80%   C. 82%   D. 90%

14. Officer A and Officer B work at the same post on the same days, but their hours are different. Officer A comes to work at 9:00 A.M. and leaves at 5:00 P.M., with a lunch period between 12:15 P.M. and 1:15 P.M. Officer B comes to work at 10:50 A.M. and works until 6:50 P.M., and he takes an hour for lunch between 3:00 P.M. and 4:00 P.M. What is the total amount of time between 9:00 A.M. and 6:50 P.M. that only ONE officer will be on duty?

    A. 4 hours
    B. 4 hours and 40 minutes
    C. 5 hours
    D. 5 hours and 40 minutes

15. An officer's log recorded the following attendance of 30 officers:

    Monday   20 present;   10 absent
    Tuesday   28 present;   2 absent
    Wednesday   30 present;   0 absent
    Thursday   21 present;   9 absent
    Friday   16 present;   14 absent
    Saturday   11 present;   19 absent
    Sunday   14 present;   16 absent

    On the average, how many men were present on the weekdays (Monday - Friday)?

    A. 21   B. 23   C. 25   D. 27

16. An angry woman is being questioned by an officer when she begins shouting abuses at him.
    The BEST of the following procedures for the officer to follow is to

    A. leave the room until she has cooled off
    B. politely ignore anything she says
    C. place her under arrest by handcuffing her to a fixed object
    D. warn her that he will have to use force to restrain her making remarks

17. Of the following, which is NOT a recommended practice for an officer placing a woman offender under arrest?

    A. Assume that the offender is an innocent and virtuous person and treat her accordingly.
    B. Protect himself from attack by the woman.
    C. Refrain from using excessive physical force on the offender.
    D. Make the public aware that he is not abusing the woman.

Questions 18-21.

DIRECTIONS: Questions 18 through 21 are to be answered SOLELY on the basis of the following passage.

Specific measures for prevention of pilferage will be based on careful analysis of the conditions at each agency. The most practical and effective method to control casual pilferage is the establishment of psychological deterrents.

One of the most common means of discouraging casual pilferage is to search individuals leaving the agency at unannounced times and places. These spot searches may occasionally detect attempts at theft but greater value is realized by bringing to the attention of individuals the fact that they may be apprehended if they do attempt the illegal removal of property.

An aggressive security education program is an effective means of convincing employees that they have much more to lose than they do to gain by engaging in acts of theft. It is important for all employees to realize that pilferage is morally wrong no matter how insignificant the value of the item which is taken. In establishing any deterrent to casual pilferage, security officers must not lose sight of the fact that most employees are honest and disapprove of thievery. Mutual respect between security personnel and other employees of the agency must be maintained if the facility is to be protected from other more dangerous forms of human hazards. Any security measure which infringes on the human rights or dignity of others will jeopardize, rather than enhance, the overall protection of the agency.

18. The $100,000 yearly inventory of an agency revealed that $50 worth of goods had been stolen; the only individuals with access to the stolen materials were the employees. Of the following measures, which would the author of the preceding paragraph MOST likely recommend to a security officer?

    A. Conduct an intensive investigation of all employees to find the culprit.
    B. Make a record of the theft, but take no investigative or disciplinary action against any employee.
    C. Place a tight security check on all future movements of personnel.
    D. Remove the remainder of the material to an area with much greater security.

19. What does the passage imply is the percentage of employees whom a security officer should expect to be honest?

   A. No employee can be expected to be honest all of the time
   B. Just 50%
   C. Less than 50%
   D. More than 50%

20. According to the passage, the security officer would use which of the following methods to minimize theft in buildings with many exits when his staff is very small?

   A. Conduct an inventory of all material and place a guard near that which is most likely to be pilfered.
   B. Inform employees of the consequences of legal prosecution for pilfering.
   C. Close off the unimportant exits and have all his men concentrate on a few exits.
   D. Place a guard at each exit and conduct a casual search of individuals leaving the premises.

21. Of the following, the title BEST suited for this passage is:

   A. Control Measures for Casual Pilfering
   B. Detecting the Potential Pilferer
   C. Financial losses Resulting from Pilfering
   D. The Use of Moral Persuasion in Physical Security

22. Of the following first aid procedures, which will cause the GREATEST harm in treating a fracture?

   A. Control hemorrhages by applying direct pressure
   B. Keep the broken portion from moving about
   C. Reset a protruding bone by pressing it back into place
   D. Treat the suffering person for shock

23. During a snowstorm, a man comes to you complaining of frostbitten hands. PROPER first aid treatment in this case is to

   A. place the hands under hot running water
   B. place the hands in lukewarm water
   C. call a hospital and wait for medical aid
   D. rub the hands in melting snow

24. While on duty, an officer sees a woman apparently in a state of shock. Of the following, which one is NOT a symptom of shock?

   A. Eyes lacking luster
   B. A cold, moist forehead
   C. A shallow, irregular breathing
   D. A strong, throbbing pulse

25. You notice a man entering your building who begins coughing violently, has shortness of breath, and complains of severe chest pains.
   These symptoms are GENERALLY indicative of

   A. a heart attack
   B. a stroke
   C. internal bleeding
   D. an epileptic seizure

26. When an officer is required to record the rolled fingerprint impressions of a prisoner on the standard fingerprint form, the technique recommended by the F.B.I, as MOST likely to result in obtaining clear impressions is to roll

    A. all fingers away from the center of the prisoner's body
    B. all fingers toward the center of the prisoner's body
    C. the thumbs away from and the other fingers toward the center of the prisoner's body
    D. the thumbs toward and the other fingers away from the center of the prisoner's body

27. The principle which underlies the operation and use of a lie detector machine is that

    A. a person who is not telling the truth will be able to give a consistent story
    B. a guilty mind will unconsciously associate ideas in a very indicative manner
    C. the presence of emotional stress in a person will result in certain abnormal physical reactions
    D. many individuals are not afraid to lie

Questions 28-32.

DIRECTIONS: Questions 28 through 32 are based SOLELY on the following diagram and the paragraph preceding this group of questions. The paragraph will be divided into two statements. Statement one (1) consists of information given to the senior officer by an agency director; *this information will detail the specific security objectives the senior officer has to meet.* Statement two (2) gives the resources available to the senior officer.

NOTE: The questions are correctly answered only when all of the agency's objectives have been met and when the officer has used all his resources efficiently (i.e., to their maximum effectiveness) in meeting these objectives. All X's in the diagram indicate possible locations of officers' posts. Each X has a corresponding number which is to be used when referring to that location.

DIAGRAM

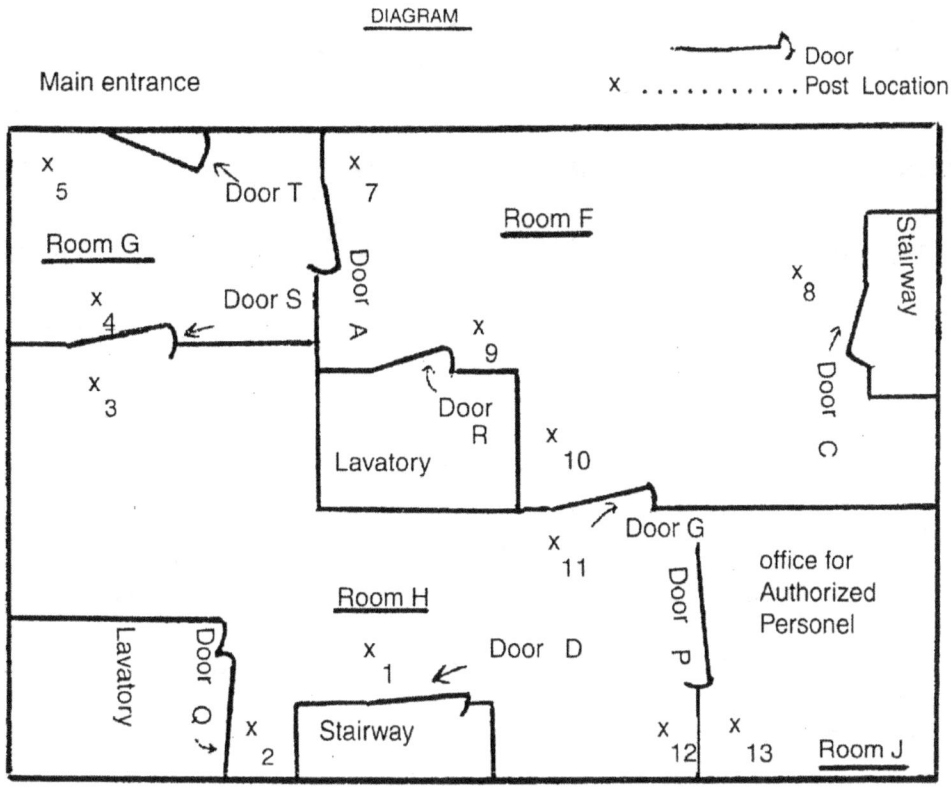

PARAGRAPH

PARAGRAPH

STATEMENT 1: Room G will be the public intake room from which persons will be directed to Room F or Room H; under no circumstances are they to enter the wrong room, and they are not to move from Room F to Room H or vice-versa. A minimum of two officers must be in each room frequented by the public at all times, and they are to keep unauthorized individuals from going to the second floor or into restricted areas. All usable entrances or exits must be covered.

STATEMENT 2: The senior officer can lock any door except the main entrance and stairway doors. He has a staff of five officers to carry out these operations.

NOTE: The senior officer is available for guard duty. Room J is an active office.

28. According to the instructions, how many officers should be assigned inside the office for authorized personnel (Room J)?

    A. 0   B. 1   C. 2   D. 3

29. In order to keep the public from moving between Room F and Room H, which door(s) can be locked without interfering with normal office operations? Door

    A. G   B. P   C. R and Q   D. S

8 (#1)

30. When placing officers in Room H, the only way the senior officer can satisfy the agency's objectives and his manpower limitations is by placing men at locations

    A. 1 and 3   B. 1 and 12   C. 3 and 11   D. 11 and 12

31. In accordance with the instructions, the LEAST effective locations to place officers in Room F are locations

    A. 7 and 9   B. 7 and 10   C. 8 and 9   D. 9 and 10

32. In which room is it MOST difficult for each of the officers to see all the movements of the public? Room

    A. G   B. F   C. H   D. J

33. According to its own provisions, the Penal Law of the State has a number of general purposes.
    It would be LEAST accurate to state that one of these general purposes is to

    A. give fair warning of the nature of the conduct forbidden and the penalties authorized upon conviction
    B. define the act or omission and accompanying mental state which constitute each offense
    C. regulate the procedure which governs the arrest, trial and punishment of convicted offenders
    D. insure the public safety by preventing the commission of offenses through the deterrent influence of the sentences authorized upon conviction

34. Officers must be well-informed about the meaning of certain terms in connection with their enforcement duties. Which one of the following statements about such terms would be MOST accurate according to the Penal Law of the State? A(n)

    A. offense is always a crime
    B. offense is always a violation
    C. violation is never a crime
    D. felony is never an offense

35. According to the Penal Law of the State, the one of the following elements which must ALWAYS be present in order to justify the arrest of a person for criminal assault is

    A. the infliction of an actual physical injury
    B. an intent to cause an injury
    C. a threat to inflict a physical injury
    D. the use of some kind of weapon

36. A recent law of the State defines who are police officers and who are peace officers. The official title of this law is: The

    A. Criminal Code of Procedure
    B. Law of Criminal Procedure
    C. Criminal Procedure Law
    D. Code of Criminal Procedure

37. If you are required to appear in court to testify as the complainant in a criminal action, it would be MOST important for you to

    A. confine your answers to the questions asked when you are testifying
    B. help the prosecutor even if some exaggeration in your testimony may be necessary
    C. be as fair as possible to the defendant even if some details have to be omitted from your testimony
    D. avoid contradicting other witnesses testifying against the defendant

38. A senior officer is asked by the television news media to explain to the public what happened on his post during an important incident.
    When speaking with departmental permission in front of the tape recorders and cameras, the senior officer can give the MOST favorable impression of himself and his department by

    A. refusing to answer any questions but remaining calm in front of the cameras
    B. giving a detailed report of the wrong decisions made by his agency for handling the particular incident
    C. presenting the appropriate factual information in a competent way
    D. telling what should have been done during the incident and how such incidents will be handled in the future

39. Of the following suggested guidelines for officers, the one which is LEAST likely to be effective in promoting good manners and courtesy in their daily contacts with the public is:

    A. Treat inquiries by telephone in the same manner as those made in person
    B. Never look into the face of the person to whom you are speaking
    C. Never give misinformation in answer to any inquiry on a matter on which you are uncertain of the facts
    D. Show respect and consideration in both trivial and important contacts with the public

40. Assume you are an officer who has had a record of submitting late weekly reports and that you are given an order by your supervisor which is addressed to all line officers. The order states that weekly reports will be replaced by twice-weekly reports.
    The MOST logical conclusion for you to make, of the following, is:

    A. Fully detailed information was missing from your past reports
    B. Most officers have submitted late reports
    C. The supervisor needs more timely information
    D. The supervisor is attempting to punish you for your past late reports

41. A young man with long hair and "mod" clothing makes a complaint to an officer about the rudeness of another officer.
    If the senior officer is not on the premises, the officer receiving the complaint should

    A. consult with the officer who is being accused to see if the youth's story is true
    B. refer the young man to central headquarters
    C. record the complaint made against his fellow officer and ask the youth to wait until he can locate the senior officer
    D. search for the senior officer and bring him back to the site of the complainant

42. During a demonstration, which area should ALWAYS be kept clear of demonstrators?

    A. Water fountains
    B. Seating areas
    C. Doorways
    D. Restrooms

43. During demonstrations, an officer's MOST important duty is to

    A. aid the agency's employees to perform their duties
    B. promptly arrest those who might cause incidents
    C. promptly disperse the crowds of demonstrators
    D. keep the demonstrators from disrupting order

44. Of the following, what is the FIRST action a senior officer should take if a demonstration develops in his area without advance warning?

    A. Call for additional assistance from the police department
    B. Find the leaders of the demonstrators and discuss their demands
    C. See if the demonstrators intend to break the law
    D. Inform his superiors of the event taking place

45. If a senior officer is informed in the morning that a demonstration will take place during the afternoon at his assigned location, he should assemble his officers to discuss the nature and aspects of this demonstration. Of the following, the subject which it is LEAST important to discuss during this meeting is

    A. making a good impression if an officer is called before the television cameras for a personal interview
    B. the known facts and causes of the demonstration
    C. the attitude and expected behavior of the demonstrators
    D. the individual responsibilities of the officers during the demonstration

46. A male officer has probable reason to believe that a group of women occupying the ladies' toilet are using illicit drugs.
    The BEST action, of the following, for the officer to take is to

    A. call for assistance and, with the aid of such assistance, enter the toilet and escort the occupants outside
    B. ignore the situation but recommend that the ladies' toilet be closed temporarily
    C. immediately rush into the ladies' toilet and search the occupants therein
    D. knock on the door of the ladies' toilet and ask their permission to enter so that he will not be accused of trying to molest them

47. Assume that you know that a group of demonstrators will not cooperate with your request to throw handbills in a waste basket instead of on the sidewalk. You ask one of the leaders of the group, who agrees with you, to speak to the demonstrators and ask for their cooperation in this matter.
    Your request of the group leader is

    A. *desirable,* chiefly because an officer needs civilians to control the public since the officer is usually unfriendly to the views of public groups
    B. *undesirable,* chiefly because an officer should never request a civilian to perform his duties
    C. *desirable,* chiefly because the appeal of an acknowledged leader helps in gaining group cooperation

D. *undesirable,* chiefly because an institutional leader is motivated to maneuver a situation to gain his own personal advantage

48. A vague letter received from a female employee in the agency accuses an officer of improper conduct.
The initial investigative interview by the senior officer assigned to check the accusation should GENERALLY be with the

    A. accused officer
    B. female employee
    C. highest superior about disciplinary action against the officer
    D. immediate supervisor of the female employee

48._____

Questions 49-50.

DIRECTIONS: Questions 49 and 50 are to be answered SOLELY on the basis of the information in the following paragraph.

The personal conduct of each member of the Department is the primary factor in promoting desirable police-community relations. Tact, patience, and courtesy shall be strictly observed under all circumstances. A favorable public attitude toward the police must be earned; it is influenced by the personal conduct and attitude of each member of the force, by his personal integrity and courteous manner, by his respect for due process of law, by his devotion to the principles of justice, fairness, and impartiality.

49. According to the preceding paragraph, what is the BEST action an officer can take in dealing with people in a neighborhood?

    A. Assist neighborhood residents by doing favors for them.
    B. Give special attention to the community leaders in order to be able to control them effectively.
    C. Behave in an appropriate manner and give all community members the same just treatment.
    D. Prepare a plan detailing what he, the officer, wants to do for the community and submit it for approval.

49._____

50. As used in the paragraph, the word *impartiality* means *most nearly*

    A. observant   B. unbiased
    C. righteousness   D. honesty

50._____

KEY (CORRECT ANSWERS)

1. B	11. B	21. A	31. D	41. C
2. B	12. A	22. C	32. C	42. C
3. A	13. C	23. B	33. C	43. D
4. A	14. D	24. D	34. C	44. D
5. D	15. B	25. A	35. A	45. A
6. C	16. B	26. D	36. C	46. A
7. D	17. A	27. C	37. A	47. C
8. C	18. B	28. A	38. C	48. B
9. D	19. D	29. A	39. B	49. C
10. C	20. B	30. B	40. C	50. B

TEST 2

DIRECTIONS: Each question or incomplete statement is followed by several suggested answers or completions. Select the one that BEST answers the question or completes the statement. *PRINT THE LETTER OF THE CORRECT ANSWER IN THE SPACE AT THE RIGHT.*

Questions 1-5.

DIRECTIONS: Questions 1 through 5 consist of short paragraphs. Each paragraph contains one word which is INCORRECTLY used because it is NOT in keeping with the meaning of the paragraph. Find the word in each paragraph which is INCORRECTLY used, and then select as the answer the suggested word which should be substituted for the incorrectly used word.

SAMPLE QUESTION

In determining who is to do the work in your unit, you will have to decide just who does what from day to day. One of your lowest responsibilities is to assign work so that everybody gets a fair share and that everyone can do his part well.
   A. new   B. old   C. important   D. performance

EXPLANATION

The word which is NOT in keeping with the meaning of the paragraph is "lowest". This is the INCORRECTLY used word. The suggested word "important" would be in keeping with the meaning of the paragraph and should be substituted for "lowest". Therefore, the CORRECT answer is Choice C.

1. If really good practice in the elimination of preventable injuries is to be achieved and held in any establishment, top management must refuse full and definite responsibility and must apply a good share of its attention to the task.

   A. accept   B. avoidable   C. duties   D. problem

1.____

2. Recording the human face for identification is by no means the only service performed by the camera in the field of investigation. When the trial of any issue takes place, a word picture is sought to be distorted to the court of incidents, occurrences, or events which are in dispute.

   A. appeals   B. description
   C. portrayed   D. deranged

2.____

3. In the collection of physical evidence, it cannot be emphasized too strongly that a haphazard systematic search at the scene of the crime is vital. Nothing must be overlooked. Often the only leads in a case will come from the results of this search.

   A. important   B. investigation
   C. proof   D. thorough

3.____

4. If an investigator has reason to suspect that the witness is mentally stable or a habitual drunkard, he should leave no stone unturned in his investigation to determine if the witness was under the influence of liquor or drugs, or was mentally unbalanced either at the time of the occurrence to which he testified or at the time of the trial.

   A. accused   B. clue   C. deranged   D. question

4.____

5. The use of records is a valuable step in crime investigation and is the main reason every department should maintain accurate reports. Crimes are not committed through the use of departmental records alone but from the use of all records, of almost every type, wherever they may be found and whenever they give any incidental information regarding the criminal.

   A. accidental B. necessary C. reported D. solved

Questions 6-8.

DIRECTIONS: Questions 6 through 8 are to be answered SOLELY on the basis of the following passage.

The mass media are an integral part of the daily life of virtually every American. Among these media, the youngest, television, is the most persuasive. Ninety-five percent of American homes have at least one television set, and on the average that set is in use for about 40 hours each week. The central place of television in American life makes this medium the focal point of a growing national concern over the effects of media portrayals of violence on the values, attitudes, and behavior of an ever increasing audience.

In our concern about violence and its causes, it is easy to make television a scapegoat. But we emphasise the fact that there is no simple answer to the problem of violence -- no single explanation of its causes, and no single prescription for its control. It should be remembered that America also experienced high levels of crime and violence in periods before the advent of television.

The problem of balance, taste, and artistic merit in entertaining programs on television are complex. We cannot countenance government censorship of television. Nor would we seek to impose arbitrary limitations on programming which might jeopardize television's ability to deal in dramatic presentations with controversial social issues. Nonetheless, we are deeply troubled by television's constant portrayal of violence, not in any genuine attempt to focus artistic expression on the human condition, but rather in pandering to a public preoccupation with violence that television itself has helped to generate.

6. According to the passage, television uses violence MAINLY

   A. to highlight the reality of everyday existence
   B. to satisfy the audience's hunger for destructive action
   C. to shape the values and attitudes of the public
   D. when it films documentaries concerning human conflict

7. Which one of the following statements is BEST supported by this passage?

   A. Early American history reveals a crime pattern which is not related to television.
   B. Programs should give presentations of social issues and never portray violent acts.
   C. Television has proven that entertainment programs can easily make the balance between taste and artistic merit a simple matter.
   D. Values and behavior should be regulated by governmental censorship.

8. Of the following, which word has the same meaning as countenance as it is used in the above passage?

   A. approve B. exhibit C. oppose D. reject

Questions 9-12.

DIRECTIONS: Questions 9 through 12 are to be answered SOLELY on the basis of the following graph relating to the burglary rate in the city, 2003 to 2008, inclusive.

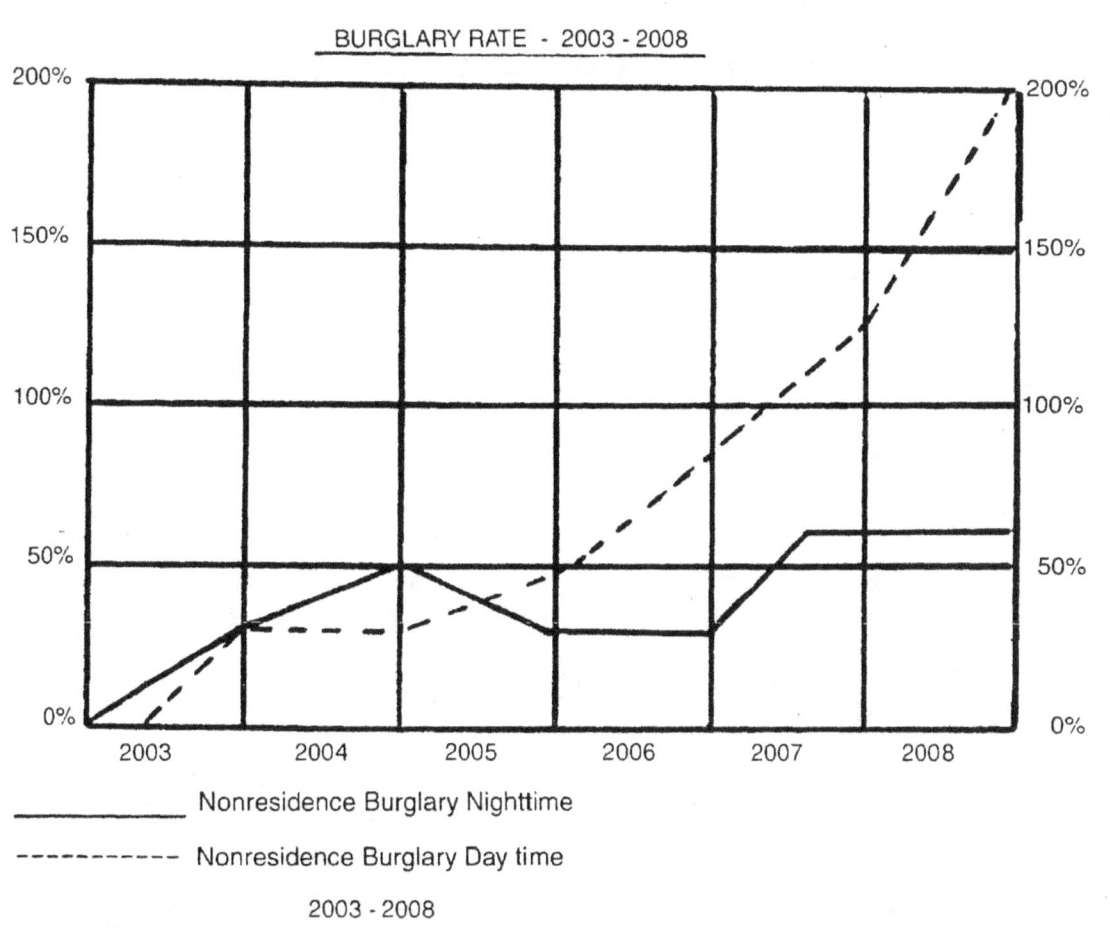

9. At the beginning of what year was the percentage increase in daytime and nighttime burglaries the SAME?

    A. 2004   B. 2005   C. 2006   D. 2008

10. In what year did the percentage of nighttime burglaries DECREASE?

    A. 2003   B. 2005   C. 2006   D. 2008

11. In what year was there the MOST rapid increase in the percentage of daytime non-residence burglaries?

    A. 2004   B. 2006   C. 2007   D. 2008

12. At the end of 2007, the actual number of nighttime burglaries committed

    A. was about 20%
    B. was 40%
    C. was 400
    D. cannot be determined from the information given

Questions 13-17.

DIRECTIONS: Questions 13 through 17 consist of two sentences numbered 1 and 2 taken from police officers' reports. Some of these sentences are correct according to ordinary formal English usage. Other sentences are incorrect because they contain errors in English usage or punctuation. Consider a sentence correct if it contains no errors in English usage or punctuation even if there may be other ways of writing the sentence correctly. Mark your answer to each question in the space at the right as follows:
- A. If only sentence 1 is correct, but not sentence 2
- B. If only sentence 2 is correct, but not sentence 1
- C. If sentences 1 and 2 are both correct
- D. If sentences 1 and 2 are both incorrect

SAMPLE QUESTION
1. The woman claimed that the purse was her's.
2. Everyone of the new officers was assigned to a patrol post.

EXPLANATION

Sentence 1 is INCORRECT because of an error in punctuation. The possessive words, "ours, yours, hers, theirs," do not have the apostrophe (').

Sentence 2 is CORRECT because the subject of the sentence is "Everyone" which is singular and requires the singular verb "was assigned".

Since only sentence 2 is correct, but not sentence 1, the CORRECT answer is B.

13.
1. Either the patrolman or his sergeant are always ready to help the public.
2. The sergeant asked the patrolman when he would finish the report.

14.
1. The injured man could not hardly talk.
2. Every officer had ought to hand in their reports on time.

15.
1. Approaching the victim of the assault, two large bruises were noticed by me.
2. The prisoner was arrested for assault, resisting arrest, and use of a deadly weapon.

16.
1. A copy of the orders, which had been prepared by the captain, was given to each patrolman.
2. It's always necessary to inform an arrested person of his constitutional rights before asking him any questions.

17.
1. To prevent further bleeding, I applied a tourniquet tothe wound.
2. John Rano a senior officer was on duty at the time of the accident.

Questions 18-25.

DIRECTIONS: Answer each of Questions 18 through 25 SOLELY on the basis of the statement preceding the questions.

18. The criminal is one whose habits have been erroneously developed or, we should say, developed in anti-social patterns, and therefore the task of dealing with him is not one of punishment, but of treatment.
The basic principle expressed in this statement is BEST illustrated by the

- A. emphasis upon rehabilitation in penal institutions
- B. prevalence of capital punishment for murder
- C. practice of imposing heavy fines for minor violations
- D. legal provision for trial by jury in criminal cases

19. The writ of habeas corpus is one of the great guarantees of personal liberty. Of the following, the BEST justification for this statement is that the writ of habeas corpus is frequently used to

    A. compel the appearance in court of witnesses who are outside the state
    B. obtain the production of books and records at a criminal trial
    C. secure the release of a person improperly held in custody
    D. prevent the use of deception in obtaining testimony of reluctant witnesses

20. Fifteen persons suffered effects of carbon dioxide asphyxiation shortly before noon recently in a seventh-floor pressing shop. The accident occurred in a closed room where six steam presses were in operation. Four men and one woman were overcome.
    Of the following, the MOST probable reason for the fact that so many people were affected simultaneously is that

    A. women evidently show more resistance to the effects of carbon dioxide than men
    B. carbon dioxide is an odorless and colorless gas
    C. carbon dioxide is lighter than air
    D. carbon dioxide works more quickly at higher altitudes

21. Lay the patient on his stomach, one arm extended directly overhead, the other arm bent at the elbow, and with the face turned outward and resting on hand or forearm.
    To the officer who is skilled at administering first aid, these instructions should IMMEDIATELY suggest

    A. application of artificial respiration
    B. treatment for third degree burns of the arm
    C. setting a dislocated shoulder
    D. control of capillary bleeding in the stomach

22. The soda and acid fire extinguisher is the hand extinguisher most commonly used by officers. The main body of the cylinder is filled with a mixture of water and bicarbonate of soda. In a separate interior compartment, at the top, is a small bottle of sulphuric acid. When the extinguisher is inverted, the acid spills into the solution below and starts a chemical reaction. The carbon dioxide thereby generated forces the solution from the extinguisher.
    The officer who understands the operation of this fire extinguisher should know that it is LEAST likely to operate properly

    A. in basements or cellars
    B. in extremely cold weather
    C. when the reaction is of a chemical nature
    D. when the bicarbonate of soda is in solution

23. Suppose that, at a training lecture, you are told that many of the men in our penal institutions today are second and third offenders.
    Of the following, the MOST valid inference you can make SOLELY on the basis of this statement is that

    A. second offenders are not easily apprehended
    B. patterns of human behavior are not easily changed
    C. modern laws are not sufficiently flexible
    D. laws do not breed crimes

24. In all societies of our level of culture, acts are committed which arouse censure severe enough to take the form of punishment by the government. Such acts are crimes, not because of their inherent nature, but because of their ability to arouse resentment and to stimulate repressive measures.
Of the following, the MOST valid inference which can be drawn from this statement is that

    A. society unjustly punishes acts which are inherently criminal
    B. many acts are not crimes but are punished by society because such acts threaten the lives of innocent people
    C. only modern society has a level of culture
    D. societies sometimes disagree as to what acts are crimes

24.___

25. Crime cannot be measured directly. Its amount must be inferred from the frequency of some occurrence connected with it; for example, crimes brought to the attention of the police, persons arrested, prosecutions, convictions, and other dispositions, such as probation or commitment. Each of these may be used as an index of the amount of crime.
SOLELY on the basis of the foregoing statement, it is MOST correct to state that

    A. the incidence of crime cannot be estimated with any accuracy
    B. the number of commitments is usually greater than the number of probationary sentences
    C. the amount of crime is ordinarily directly correlated with the number of persons arrested
    D. a joint consideration of crimes brought to the attention of the police and the number of prosecutions undertaken gives little indication of the amount of crime in a locality

25.___

KEY (CORRECT ANSWERS)

1.	B	11.	D
2.	A	12.	D
3.	D	13.	D
4.	C	14.	D
5.	D	15.	B
6.	B	16.	C
7.	A	17.	A
8.	A	18.	A
9.	A	19.	C
10.	B	20.	B

21. A
22. B
23. B
24. D
25. C

EXAMINATION SECTION
TEST 1

DIRECTIONS: Each question or incomplete statement is followed by several suggested answers or completions. Select the one that BEST answers the question or completes the statement. *PRINT THE LETTER OF THE CORRECT ANSWER IN THE SPACE AT THE RIGHT.*

1. Which of the following is the LEAST important factor to consider in surveying the physical layout of a building for traffic flow?

    A. Location of windows
    B. Number of entrances
    C. Number of exits
    D. Location of first aid rooms

2. The major purpose of any security program in a large organization is to prevent unlawful acts.
   If adequate patrol coverage is provided at a given location, it is MOST likely that

    A. crimes will not be committed
    B. undesirables will not enter the building
    C. unlawful acts will increase in the long run
    D. there will be less opportunity to commit a crime

3. The MOST frequent cause of fires in public facilities is

    A. incinerators   B. vandalism
    C. electrical sources   D. smoking on the job

4. After bomb threats are received, it is sometimes necessary to evacuate a facility. How long BEFORE the threatened time of explosion should a facility be evacuated?
   At least _____ minutes.

    A. 15   B. 25   C. 50   D. 60

5. Once a facility is evacuated because of a bomb threat, how much time should pass before the public and employees are allowed to enter the building?
   _____ minutes.

    A. 10   B. 20   C. 40   D. 60

6. Of the following locations in public buildings, the one which is the LEAST likely place for bombs to be planted is in

    A. storerooms   B. bathrooms
    C. cafeterias   D. waste receptacles

7. The one of the following that is the surest means of establishing positive identification of someone entering a facility is by

    A. personal recognition   B. I.D. badge
    C. social security card   D. driver's license

8. The one of the following which most probably would NOT be included in a police record report concerning an incident at a facility is the

    A. name of complainant or injured party
    B. name of the investigating officer
    C. statement of each witness
    D. religion of complainant or injured party

9. Preventing trouble is one of the primary concerns of special officers.
   When dealing with unruly groups of people who threaten to become violent, which of the following is a measure which should NOT be taken?

    A. Maintain close surveillance of such groups
    B. Try to contact the leaders of the group regardless of their militancy
    C. Keep the officer force alerted
    D. Have the officer force deal aggressively with provocations

10. Of the following, the MOST important factor to consider in the deployment of officers dealing with a client population is the officers' ability to

    A. remain calm
    B. look stern
    C. evaluate personality
    D. take a firm stand

11. Assume that an offender is struggling with a group of officers who are trying to arrest him.
    What force, if any, can be used to overcome this resistance?

    A. The amount of force acceptable to the public
    B. The amount of force necessary to restrain the offender and protect the officers
    C. Any amount of force that is acceptable to the officers at the scene
    D. No force may be used until the police arrive

12. Assume that a fire is discovered at your work location. The one of the following actions which would be INAPPROPRIATE for you to take is to

    A. notify the telephone operator
    B. station a reliable person at the entrance
    C. open all windows and doors in the area
    D. start evacuating the area

13. If a person has an object caught in his throat or air passage but is breathing adequately, which one of the following should you do?

    A. Probe for the object
    B. Force him to drink water
    C. Lay him over your arm and slap him between the shoulder blades
    D. Allow him to cough and to assume the position he finds most comfortable

14. The one of the following methods which should NOT be used to report a fire is to

    A. call 911
    B. pull the handle in the red box on the street corner
    C. call the fire department county numbers listed in each county directory
    D. call 411

15. Assume that an officer, alone in a building at night, smells the strong odor of cooking or heating gas. In addition to airing the building and making sure that he is not overcome, it would be BEST for the officer to call

   A. his superior at his home and ask for instructions
   B. for a plumber from the department of public works
   C. 911 for police and fire help
   D. the emergency number at Con Edison

16. Of the following situations, the one that is MOST dangerous for an officer is when he

   A. investigates suspicious persons and circumstances
   B. finds a burglary in progress or pursues burglary suspects
   C. attempts an arrest or finds a robbery in progress
   D. patrols on the overnight shift

17. An officer on security patrol generally should spend MOST of his time

   A. checking doors and locks
   B. helping the public and answering questions
   C. chasing criminals and looking for clues
   D. writing reports on unusual incidents

18. The one of the following that is an ACCEPTABLE way to arrest a person is to

   A. tell him to report to the nearest police precinct
   B. send a summons to his permanent address
   C. tell him in person that he is under arrest
   D. show him handcuffs and ask him to come along

19. A carbon dioxide fire extinguisher is BEST suited for extinguishing _____ fires.

   A. paper   B. rag   C. rubbish   D. grease

20. A pressurized water or soda-acid fire extinguisher is BEST suited for extinguishing _____ fires.

   A. wood   B. gasoline
   C. electrical   D. magnesium

21. The one of the following statements that does NOT apply to the use of handcuffs is that they

   A. are used as temporary restraining devices
   B. eliminate the need for vigilance
   C. cannot be opened without keys
   D. are used to secure a violent person

22. The one of the following that is GENERALLY a crime against the person is

   A. trespass   B. burglary   C. robbery   D. arson

23. Of the following, the SAFEST way of escape from an office in a burning building is generally the

     A. stairway
     B. rooftop
     C. passenger elevator
     D. freight elevator

24. In attempting to control a possible riot situation, an officer pushed his way into a crowd gathered outside the building and tried to cause confusion by arguing with members of the group.
    This procedure NORMALLY is considered

     A. *desirable;* any violence that occurs will remain outside the building
     B. *desirable;* the crowd will break into smaller groups and disperse
     C. *undesirable;* to maintain control of the situation, the officer must not become part of the crowd
     D. *undesirable;* the supervisor should stay clear of the scene

25. Which one of the following is MOST effective in making officers more safety-minded?

     A. Maintaining an up-to-date library of the latest safety literature
     B. Reading daily safety bulletins at roll-call
     C. Holding informal group safety meetings periodically
     D. Offering prizes for good safety slogans and displays

KEY (CORRECT ANSWERS)

1.	A	11.	B
2.	D	12.	C
3.	C	13.	D
4.	A	14.	D
5.	D	15.	D
6.	C	16.	C
7.	A	17.	A
8.	D	18.	C
9.	D	19.	D
10.	A	20.	A

21.	B
22.	C
23.	A
24.	C
25.	C

TEST 2

DIRECTIONS: Each question or incomplete statement is followed by several suggested answers or completions. Select the one that BEST answers the question or completes the statement. *PRINT THE LETTER OF THE CORRECT ANSWER IN THE SPACE AT THE RIGHT.*

1. Assume that an angry crowd of some 75 to 100 people has built up in one of the hallways of a center and that only one superior officer and two subordinate officers are on duty in the building. A glass panel in one of the stairway doors has just been broken under the pressure of the crowd and a bench has been hurled down a flight of stairs. The one of the following actions that the superior officer SHOULD take in this situation is to

    A. push his way into the crowd and try to reason with them
    B. order the two other officers to try to quiet the crowd
    C. call the police on 911 and meet them outside the building
    D. do nothing at this point in order to avoid a riot

    1.____

2. One of the duties and responsibilities of a supervisor is to test the knowledge of the officers concerning their post conditions.
   This should be done if the officer's assignment is

    A. fixed only
    B. roving only
    C. roving only in a troublesome spot
    D. either fixed or roving

    2.____

3. An officer discovers early one morning that an office in the building he guards has been burglarized.
   Of the following, it is important for the officer to FIRST

    A. go through the building and look for suspects
    B. call the police and protect the area and whatever evidence exists until they arrive
    C. allow people into their offices as they come to work
    D. examine, sort, and handle all evidence before the police get there

    3.____

4. Assume that two officers are interrogating one suspect. How should these officers position themselves during the interrogation?

    A. One officer should stand on either side of the suspect.
    B. One officer should stand to the right of the suspect, and the other officer should stand behind the suspect.
    C. Both officers should stand to the right of the suspect.
    D. One officer should stand to the right of the suspect, and the other officer should stand in front of the suspect.

    4.____

5. A witness who takes an oath to testify truly and who states as true any matter which he knows to be false is guilty of

    A. perjury   B. libel   C. slander   D. fraud

    5.____

89

6. An officer checking a substance suspected of containing narcotics should GENERALLY

   A. taste it in small amounts
   B. send it to a laboratory for analysis
   C. smell it for its distinctive odor
   D. examine it for its unusual texture

7. A certain center is situated in an area where frequent outbreaks of hostilities seem to be focused on the center itself.
   Which of the following BEST explains why the center may be a target for hostile acts?
   It

   A. serves community needs
   B. represents governmental authority
   C. represents all ethnic groups
   D. serves as a neutral battlefield

8. An officer often deals with people who might be addicted to drugs.
   The one of the following symptoms which is NOT generally an indication of drug addiction is

   A. dilation of the eye pupils
   B. frequent yawning and sneezing
   C. a deep, rasping cough
   D. continual itching of the arms and legs

9. In emergency situations, panic will MOST probably occur when people are

   A. unexpectedly confronted with a terrorizing condition from which there appears to be no escape
   B. angry and violent
   C. anxious about circumstances which are not obvious, easily visible or within the immediate area
   D. familiar with the effects of the emergency

10. The one of the following actions on the part of a person that would NOT be considered *resisting arrest* is

    A. retreating and running away
    B. saying, *You can't arrest me*
    C. pushing the officer aside
    D. pulling away from an officer's grasp

11. Which of the following items would NOT be considered an APPROPRIATE item of uniform for an officer to wear while on duty?

    A. Reefer type overcoat
    B. Leather laced shoes with flat soles
    C. White socks
    D. Cap cover with cap device displayed

12. What can happen to an officer if the leather thong on his night stick is NOT twisted correctly?
    The

    A. baton may be taken out of the officer's hand
    B. officer's wrist may be broken
    C. leather will tear more easily
    D. officer's arm may be injured

13. The one of the following kinds of information which SHOULD be included in the log book is

    A. any important matter of police information
    B. an item noted in Standard Operating Procedures only
    C. everything of general interest
    D. a crime or offense only

14. While on patrol at your work location, you receive a call that an assault has taken place. Upon your arrival at the scene, the victim, who has severe lacerations, informs you that the assailant ran into a nearby basement.
    After apprehending the suspect, the type of search you should conduct is a _____ search.

    A. wall   B. frisk   C. body   D. strip

15. A tactical force is valuable in MOST emergency situations PRIMARILY because of its

    A. location   B. morale
    C. flexibility   D. size

16. An officer should be encouraged to talk easily and frankly when he is dealing with his superior.
    In order to encourage such free communication, it would be MOST appropriate for a superior to behave in a(n)

    A. *sincere* manner; assure the officer that you will deal with him honestly and openly
    B. *official* manner; you are a superior officer and must always act formally with subordinates
    C. *investigative* manner; you must probe and question to get to a basis of trust
    D. *unemotional* manner; the officer's emotions and background should play no part in your dealings with him

17. Research findings show that an increase in free communication within an agency GENERALLY results in which one of the following?

    A. Improved morale and productivity
    B. Increased promotional opportunities
    C. An increase in authority
    D. A spirit of honesty

18. Assume that you are a superior officer and your superiors have given you a new arrest procedure to be followed. Before passing this information on to your subordinates, the one of the following actions that you should take FIRST is to

    A. ask your superiors to send out a memorandum to the entire staff
    B. clarify the procedure in your own mind
    C. set up a training course to provide instructions on the new procedure
    D. write a memorandum to your subordinates

19. Communication is necessary for an organization to be effective.
    The one of the following which is LEAST important for most communication systems is that

    A. messages are sent quickly and directly to the person who needs them to operate
    B. information should be conveyed understandably and accurately
    C. the method used to transmit information should be kept secret so that security can be maintained
    D. senders of messages must know how their messages were received and acted upon

20. Which one of the following is the CHIEF advantage of listening willingly to subordinate officers and encouraging them to talk freely and honestly?
    It

    A. reveals to superiors the degree to which ideas that are passed down are accepted by subordinates
    B. reduces the participation of subordinates in the operation of the department
    C. encourages officers to try for promotion
    D. enables officers to learn about security leaks on the part of officials

21. A superior may be informed through either oral or written reports.
    Which one of the following is an ADVANTAGE of using oral reports?

    A. There is no need for a formal record of the report.
    B. An exact duplicate of the report is not easily transmitted to others.
    C. A good oral report requires little time for preparation.
    D. An oral report involves two-way communication between a subordinate and his superior.

22. Of the following, the MOST important reason why officers should communicate effectively with the public is to

    A. improve the public's understanding of information that is important for them to know
    B. establish a friendly relationship
    C. obtain information about the kinds of people who come to the center
    D. convince the public that services are adequate

23. Officers should generally NOT use phrases like *too hard, too easy,* and *a lot* principally because such phrases

    A. may be offensive to some minority groups
    B. are too informal

C. mean different things to different people
D. are difficult to remember

24. The ability to communicate clearly and concisely is an important element in effective leadership.
Which of the following statements about oral and written communication is GENERALLY true?

A. Oral communication is more time-consuming.
B. Written communication is more likely to be misinterpreted.
C. Oral communication is useful only in emergencies.
D. Written communication is useful mainly when giving information to fewer than twenty people.

24.____

25. Rumors can often have harmful and disruptive effects on an organization.
Which one of the following is the BEST way to prevent rumors from becoming a problem?

A. Refuse to act on rumors, thereby making them less believable
B. Increase the amount of information passed along by the *grapevine*
C. Distribute as much factual information as possible
D. Provide training in report writing

25.____

KEY (CORRECT ANSWERS)

1. C		11. C	
2. D		12. A	
3. B		13. A	
4. B		14. A	
5. A		15. C	
6. B		16. A	
7. B		17. A	
8. C		18. B	
9. A		19. C	
10. B		20. A	

21. D
22. A
23. C
24. B
25. C

EXAMINATION SECTION
TEST 1

DIRECTIONS: Each question or incomplete statement is followed by several suggested answers or completions. Select the one that BEST answers the question or completes the statement. *PRINT THE LETTER OF THE CORRECT ANSWER IN THE SPACE AT THE RIGHT.*

1. As a superior officer, you have the responsibility of deciding whether some of your duties should be delegated to subordinate officers.
   The delegation of certain duties to subordinates is GENERALLY considered

   A. *inadvisable;* subordinates should not share your responsibilities
   B. *advisable;* this will help to prevent you from getting bogged down with minor details and problems
   C. *inadvisable;* you can probably do all parts of your job better than anyone else can
   D. *advisable;* more time can therefore be devoted to day-to-day operations and less to long-range planning

2. Assume that you are a superior officer and that one of your subordinates is careless in the performance of his job.
   Of the following, it would be MOST important for you, when helping this employee, to realize that

   A. punitive methods produce better long-term results than non-punitive methods
   B. most problem officers require strict supervision rather than counseling and training
   C. the superior can often play a large part in changing employee patterns of work
   D. if orders are given in detail, carelessness will be eliminated

3. One of the key qualities of a good superior officer is his ability to balance his work load against the time available to him to complete the job.
   Of the following, the BEST procedure for a superior to follow in establishing his work priorities is to

   A. organize tasks according to urgency without regard to importance
   B. undertake all important, difficult tasks in any order and delegate the routine work to subordinates
   C. assign all work to various subordinates and guide their handling of the problems
   D. delegate those problems that can be solved by others and personally handle the difficult, most pressing issues first

4. It is generally CORRECT to state that the planning process within an organization

   A. is a management responsibility and should not involve the participation of operating personnel
   B. should include long-range programs and goals, and should not include activities which can be carried out within a few weeks or months
   C. is to be used in order to develop and improve practices and procedures but is not to be used in applying these procedures in actual operations
   D. should be used at all supervisory levels since each superior officer must determine how to accomplish tasks and what resources are needed

5. Assume you are a superior officer and one of your subordinates, who has a low performance rating, has made a good suggestion that will make his job easier.
The BEST course of action for you to take in this situation is to

   A. disregard his suggestion, since he is only trying to do as little work as possible
   B. use his suggestion, since it is a positive suggestion and could motivate him to do better work
   C. use his suggestion, but transfer him to a position where he will not benefit from it
   D. disregard his suggestion, and have a talk with him about his poor performance

6. The use of different criteria to rate employees in different jobs is GENERALLY considered

   A. *desirable,* chiefly because people should be treated as individuals with varying strengths and weaknesses
   B. *undesirable,* chiefly because the use of different criteria results in unfair evaluations
   C. *desirable,* chiefly because people in different jobs cannot always be rated on the basis of the same criteria
   D. *undesirable,* chiefly because ratings that are standardized cannot be compared

7. In preparing an annual division budget for equipment and supplies, the one of the following methods that is MOST appropriate to use is to

   A. combine the previous year's division budget with the estimate of any additional or reduced needs for the coming year
   B. determine what amount the department will approve and use that figure
   C. overestimate division needs by 10% because the department will automatically reduce the figure that is first submitted
   D. underestimate division needs because a reduction in the budget indicates increased efficiency

8. All of the following are objectives of in-service training EXCEPT

   A. discovering and developing skills
   B. providing better service to the public
   C. raising the status of the service
   D. eliminating the need for performance evaluations

9. From a management point of view, the one of the following that is the MOST important advantage of regular personnel performance appraisals is that they

   A. help an officer to prepare for promotion examinations
   B. pinpoint an officer's personality weaknesses
   C. provide an opportunity for regular discussions, including counseling, between an officer and his superior
   D. provide the setting to explain the reasons for disciplinary actions which an officer might not understand

10. Assume that an officer arrests a man for assaulting a woman in the building he is guarding. Later, while the suspect is being searched, the officer finds a switchblade knife, four bags of heroin, and three hypodermic syringes in his clothing.
In these circumstances, the possession of which of the following items might indicate a violation of some law?

    A. Only the heroin
    B. The heroin, the hypodermic syringes, but not the switchblade knife
    C. The switchblade knife, the heroin, but not the hypodermic syringes
    D. The switchblade knife, the heroin, and the hypodermic syringes

11. Upon arriving at the scene of a serious crime, a superior officer SHOULD instruct his subordinates to

    A. protect the crime scene
    B. collect, mark, and evaluate evidence
    C. brief the news media on the status of the crime
    D. prevent medical personnel from entering the crime scene

12. In standard police terminology, the term *fugitive warrant* refers to

    A. any type of warrant that is not a local warrant
    B. a written request for the detention of a suspect
    C. a warrant for a person who leaves his local jurisdiction and commits an offense in another jurisdiction
    D. a type of booking made when a person wanted by an out-of-state jurisdiction is arrested by local officers

13. The one of the following actions with respect to an offender that an officer should NOT take when an infraction has been committed is to

    A. inform the offender of his rights
    B. punish the offender
    C. warn the offender of possible consequences
    D. apprehend the offender using appropriate force

14. Perimeter barriers, intrusion devices, protective lighting, and a personnel identification system are used for good physical security of a building.
An objective of personnel identification and control is to

    A. exempt authorized personnel from compliance with annoying entry and departure procedures
    B. detect unauthorized persons who attempt to gain entry
    C. eliminate the need for expensive perimeter barriers and intrusion alarms
    D. allow an increased number of gates and perimeter entrances to be operated at the same time during peak activity hours

15. A true copy of the testimony taken in a criminal action is known as a(n)

    A. verdict
    B. transcript
    C. judgment
    D. indictment

16. The process of gathering information during an investigation usually involves interviewing or interrogating witnesses.
Interviews or interrogations are *primarily* used for all of the following purposes EXCEPT to

   A. establish the facts of a possible crime to provide the investigator with leads
   B. verify information already known to the police
   C. secure evidence that may establish the guilt or complicity of a suspect
   D. prevent the person questioned from giving an account of the incident under investigation to newspapers

17. Of the following, the BEST reason to apprehend a narcotics violator out of view of the public is to

   A. prevent the drug user from becoming violent
   B. allow the suspect to *save face* with his friends
   C. prevent the knowledge of his apprehension from reaching any collaborators
   D. keep the suspect from disposing of evidence

18. Assume that you, a superior officer, are planning the physical security operation at a facility. One of the problems you are faced with is that of casual thievery by staff.
Of the following, the BEST means of discouraging such thievery is by establishing

   A. an aggressive security education program
   B. adequate inventory control measures
   C. spot search procedures
   D. an effective key control system

19. Under an officer's scope of authority, all of the following actions would be proper EXCEPT

   A. apprehending persons attempting to gain unauthorized access to any work location
   B. enforcing the traffic control rules applicable to the work location
   C. removing persons suspected of theft with a warning to them not to return
   D. responding to protective alarm signals and other warning devices

20. One of the ways of deploying an officer force at the scene of a demonstration is called *strength in reserve.* This procedure involves having only a few officers police the demonstration while most are being held in reserve. Which one of the following is a DISADVANTAGE of this type of deployment?
It

   A. permits the demonstrators to estimate the number of officers available
   B. might result in a delay between a violent outbreak and the arrival of enough officers to handle the situation
   C. prevents the superior officer from deploying his forces
   D. does not permit rotation of the officers confronting the demonstrators

21. Of the following, the MOST important principle to keep in mind when making arrests is that   21.____

    A. the absence of force will discourage resistance on the part of the offender
    B. the arresting officer should assume, for his own safety, that the person to be arrested is dangerous
    C. once the offender is arrested he should be kept at the scene of the arrest and questioned
    D. in order to prevent violence, it is better to have too few officers making arrests than too many

22. Of the following steps, the one that an officer should take FIRST upon discovering a broken electrical power line while on duty is to   22.____

    A. notify his supervisor
    B. notify the electrical company
    C. determine whether it is a live wire
    D. take measures to protect and barricade the area

23. Assume you are a superior officer interrogating a suspect. The FIRST question you ask him should usually pertain to   23.____

    A. his name and address
    B. a package which he may be carrying
    C. where he has been
    D. where he is going

24. Which one of the following statements concerning the interrogation of a juvenile is INCORRECT?   24.____

    A. The juvenile should be advised of his rights.
    B. The juvenile should be told as little as possible about the case.
    C. A bond of mutual interest should be established with the juvenile.
    D. The juvenile should be encouraged to ask the interrogator questions.

25. Assume that an intoxicated man has wandered into a center and is begging for money and harassing clients. Of the following, the MOST effective action to take in this situation would be to   25.____

    A. call immediately for police assistance
    B. take the man aside quietly and try to persuade him to move along
    C. ask two or three male clients to help you take the man outside
    D. arrest the man at once so that drunks will know they should stay away

KEY (CORRECT ANSWERS)

1. B
2. C
3. D
4. D
5. B

6. C
7. A
8. D
9. C
10. D

11. A
12. D
13. B
14. B
15. B

16. D
17. C
18. C
19. C
20. B

21. B
22. D
23. A
24. D
25. B

TEST 2

DIRECTIONS: Each question or incomplete statement is followed by several suggested answers or completions. Select the one that BEST answers the question or completes the statement. *PRINT THE LETTER OF THE CORRECT ANSWER IN THE SPACE AT THE RIGHT.*

1. Assume that you, a superior officer, have received a communication from one of your subordinates that his center has just received a *ticking* package.
   Of the following steps, the one that he should take FIRST is to

   A. notify the Police Department
   B. remove the package and soak it in water
   C. check the contents of the package
   D. evacuate the area

   1._____

2. Assume that an individual suspected of drug abuse is apprehended. The suspect produces a prescription which he claims is for the drug found on his person.
   Which of the following actions should be taken NEXT?

   A. The prescription should be disregarded and the suspect should be arrested.
   B. Release the individual, but confiscate the drug in order to have a laboratory check its composition.
   C. The opinion of a medical doctor should be obtained.
   D. The suspect should be released since he has a prescription.

   2._____

3. A mob has been defined as a group of individuals who commit lawless acts under the stimulus of intense excitement or agitation.
   All of the following are generally considered characteristics of a mob EXCEPT

   A. some degree of organization
   B. one or more leaders
   C. a common motive for action
   D. unemotional behavior

   3._____

4. Which of the following would be IMPROPER for an officer to do while apprehending a suspect?

   A. Maintain a quiet voice and manner
   B. Remove the person from the scene as soon as possible in order to avoid conflict with the suspect and bystanders
   C. Allow the suspect to realize that the officer does not like persons who commit crimes
   D. Direct and accompany the person to an appropriate location

   4._____

5. Which of the following is MOST appropriate for an officer to do while testifying as a witness in court?

   A. State the facts only of your own knowledge
   B. Argue with the defense attorney in order to show that your actions were proper
   C. Deny that you have discussed the case outside of court even if you have done so only with close friends
   D. Use as much technical language as possible in order to impress the jury with your knowledge

   5._____

6. It is sometimes inadvisable to arrest the leaders of an unlawful demonstration immediately.
   Of the following, the BEST reason to delay arresting the leaders of a demonstration is to

   A. permit them to restrain their followers who might threaten violence
   B. avoid unfavorable coverage by the press
   C. determine whether there is more than one charge involved
   D. let them get deeper in trouble so they will receive longer sentences when convicted

7. The one of the following approaches which would BEST foster good human relations when dealing with the public is for an officer to

   A. act very self-assured, thus gaining respect
   B. learn how to appeal to the biases and prejudices of others
   C. treat everyone in exactly the same way since everyone has the same needs
   D. appeal to the positive interests of others

8. The causes of many job complaints come not just from wages and working conditions but also from contacts with people on and off the job and from the officer's background and outlook on life.
   Because of this, the BEST of the following ways for a superior officer to handle a complaint from a subordinate is generally to

   A. talk to the officer for the purpose of getting him to withdraw his complaint
   B. get as much information as possible to try to determine the real causes of the complaint
   C. postpone action on the complaint since conditions change so rapidly that it is useless to try to act quickly on a complaint
   D. handle each complaint as quickly as possible without looking into the motives for the complaint

9. In every unit certain officers are more cooperative than others.
   The one of the following that is MOST likely to occur with regard to supervising such cooperative officers is that they

   A. are more easily intimidated
   B. are often assigned to difficult jobs
   C. are unfriendly to the general public
   D. assume a supervisor's position in dealing with others

10. Assume that you are a superior officer and that one of your subordinate officers comes to you with a complaint about an officer under his command. After listening to a few of the details, you suspect that his complaint is not justified.
    Considering this, you should do all of the following during this initial conversation EXCEPT

    A. listen with interest until the subordinate officer finishes making his complaint
    B. tell the subordinate officer that you will investigate the matter further
    C. inform the subordinate that his complaint is invalid
    D. ask the subordinate officer further questions about his complaint

11. As a superior officer, you may receive complaints about the department or individual officers from the public.
    Of the following, the PROPER attitude to take with regard to such complaints is that they

    A. are often helpful in determining how to give the public better service
    B. cause poor morale in the service and should not be revealed to subordinates
    C. are useful as a basis for disciplining officers who have been troublesome in the past
    D. take up too much of an officer's time and should not be accepted

12. One of the people present at a local parent-teacher organization meeting complained about the time it took for him to be taken care of at an agency office. A superior officer, present at the meeting, stood up and explained to the person and the group that there was no personal discrimination involved because the normal procedures took a while and that everyone spent about the same amount of time in the office.
    In this situation, the action of the superior officer was

    A. *proper,* mainly because it will show the group how much he knows about agency operations
    B. *improper,* mainly because he should tell the man who complained to check first with the agency before complaining
    C. *proper,* mainly because he helped to clear up a misunderstanding
    D. *improper,* mainly because the officer should not discuss his agency in public

13. Assume that you are a superior officer and that you have begun a campaign to encourage your subordinates to be prompt in reporting for work. One of your subordinates requests that he be allowed to arrive a half hour late in the morning while his wife is in the hospital as a maternity patient.
    Of the following actions, it would be BEST in this situation for you to

    A. *refuse* the request, claiming it would be unfair to others to make an exception
    B. *grant* the request, telling your other subordinates the reason for this exception
    C. *refuse* the request, blaming the central office for having inflexible rules
    D. *grant* the request, making it clear to all that this will be the last exception

14. Authorities agree that keeping rumors to a minimum is one of the goals of communication.
    Which of the following is NOT consistent with this goal?

    A. Distribute information that will tend to make rumors unnecessary
    B. Reduce the social distance between top management and the lower supervisors
    C. Stress the development of downward rather than upward channels of communication
    D. Understand the emotional elements that cause stress

15. Of the following, the MOST important factor in determining the success or failure of communication between officers and the public is the

    A. attitude of the public toward the officers prior to and during the communication
    B. use of proper channels of communication within the organization
    C. use of the mass media to change the public's attitude from negative to positive
    D. increase in opportunities for personal contact between the officers and the public

16. Assume that you are a superior officer concerned with the effective use of praise and criticism to motivate your subordinates.
    Of the following statements, the one that is EQUALLY TRUE of praise and criticism is that both should generally be

    A. directed mainly toward the act instead of the person
    B. given often and with no restrictions
    C. given in public for the greatest effect
    D. directed toward group efforts rather than individual efforts

17. Which of the following actions on the part of a superior officer is MOST likely to improve upward communication between his subordinates and himself?

    A. Delay acting on undesirable working conditions until complaints from subordinates have reached top management
    B. Make the time to listen to subordinates' ideas
    C. Resist becoming involved with the personal problems of subordinates
    D. Discourage communications that indicate which policies may have resulted in poor performance

18. Assume that you are a recently appointed superior officer and are told that one of your subordinates is a chronic complainer.
    In this situation, which of the following steps should you take FIRST?

    A. Report your subordinate to higher authority
    B. Discipline your subordinate for his poor performance
    C. Change your subordinate's tour of duty
    D. Ask your subordinate for a list of his complaints

19. In addition to formal supervision, every group of officers soon develops informal leaders who influence the other members of the group.
    Of the following statements about informal leaders, the one that is GENERALLY correct is that they

    A. provide supervision when the regular supervisor is absent
    B. are entitled to special benefits for their services
    C. can be used to help settle disputes between employees
    D. prevent the rapid transmission of orders

20. The grapevine is a frequently used means of informal communication in any work location.
    The one of the following statements that BEST describes the attitude a superior officer should take in relation to the grapevine is that it is

    A. unreliable and should not be trusted
    B. useful and should be recognized
    C. valuable and should be the chief method of transmitting orders
    D. insignificant and should be ignored

21. As a supervising officer, it may be useful for you to conduct periodic interviews with each of your subordinates to discuss his job performance in broad perspective.
All of the following are ground rules to follow during such an interview EXCEPT

   A. showing him how he compares in work performance with other supervisors in your district
   B. giving him a chance to talk
   C. focusing on what can be learned from any mistakes discussed rather than on the mistakes themselves
   D. avoiding a discussion of personalities

22. When you, as a superior officer, are correcting the errors of a supervisor in your district, which of the following is NOT a good point to keep in mind?

   A. Find something on which to compliment the supervisor before you correct him
   B. Watch yourself carefully to avoid the mistake of overcorrecting
   C. Correct the supervisor at the same time as you correct other supervisors who make similar mistakes
   D. Induce the supervisor to correct himself if possible

23. Following are four steps to be used when instructing a subordinate in the performance of his job:
   I. Observe the subordinate doing the job
   II. Compare his performance to established standards
   III. Explain the purpose of the job to the subordinate
   IV. Demonstrate each step of the job

   Which of the following choices lists the CORRECT order in which the above steps should be taken?

   A. III, IV, I, II   B. IV, III, I, II
   C. III, IV, II, I   D. IV, III, II, I

24. Of the following leadership characteristics, the one that is generally considered PRIMARY for a supervisor is the ability to

   A. achieve good working relations with fellow supervisors
   B. get subordinates to air their personal problems
   C. take action to get the job done
   D. plan his work efficiently

25. A recently appointed supervising officer is placed in charge of a district which includes several senior employees. He finds that while these subordinates are able to learn new tasks and methods, some of them tend to take longer to learn procedural changes than newer, younger workers.
Of the following, the MAIN reason for this is that senior workers

   A. are embarrassed by younger workers' intelligence
   B. have to *unlearn* what was taught them in the past
   C. form learning blocks when they are supervised by a younger person
   D. are more interested in doing the work than in academic discussion

KEY (CORRECT ANSWERS)

1.	D	11.	A
2.	C	12.	C
3.	D	13.	B
4.	C	14.	C
5.	A	15.	A
6.	A	16.	A
7.	D	17.	B
8.	B	18.	D
9.	B	19.	C
10.	C	20.	B

21. A
22. C
23. A
24. C
25. B

———

EXAMINATION SECTION
TEST 1

DIRECTIONS: Each question or incomplete statement is followed by several suggested answers or completions. Select the one that BEST answers the question or completes the statement. *PRINT THE LETTER OF THE CORRECT ANSWER IN THE SPACE AT THE RIGHT.*

1. Although some kinds of instructions are best put in written form, a supervisor can give many instructions verbally.
   In which one of the following situations would verbal instructions be MOST suitable?
   A. Furnishing an employee with the details to be checked in doing a certain job
   B. Instructing an employee on the changes necessary to update the office manual used in your unit
   C. Informing a new employee where different kinds of supplies and equipment that he might need are kept
   D. Presenting an assignment to an employee who will be held accountable for following a series of steps

2. You may be asked to evaluate the organization structure of your unit.
   Which one of the following questions would you NOT expect to take up in an evaluation of this kind?
   A. Is there an employee whose personal problems are interfering with his or her work?
   B. Is there an up-to-date job description for each position in this section?
   C. Are related operations and tasks grouped together and regularly assigned together?
   D. Are responsibilities divided as far as possible, and is this division clearly understood by all employees?

3. In order to distribute and schedule work fairly and efficiently, a supervisor may wish to make a work distribution study. A simple way of getting the information necessary for such a study is to have everyone for one week keep track of each task doe and the time spent on each.
   Which one of the following situations showing up in such study would MOST clearly call for corrective action?
   A. The newest employee takes longer to do most tasks than do experienced employees.
   B. One difficult operation takes longer to do than most other operations carried out by the section.
   C. A particular employee is very frequently assigned tasks that are not similar and have no relationship to each other.
   D. The most highly skilled employee is often assigned the most difficult jobs.

4. The authority to carry out a job can be delegated to a subordinate, but the supervisor remains responsible for the work of the section as a whole.
As a supervisor, which of the following rules would be the BEST one for you to follow in view of the above statement?
   A. Avoid assigning important tasks to your subordinates, because you will be blamed if anything goes wrong
   B. Be sure each subordinate understands the specific job he has been assigned, and check at intervals to make sure assignments are done properly
   C. Assign several people to every important job so that responsibility will be spread out as much as possible
   D. Have an experienced subordinate check all work done by other employees so that there will be little chance of anything going wrong

5. The human tendency to resist change is often reflected in higher rates of turnover, absenteeism, and errors whenever an important change is made in an organization. Although psychologists do not fully understand the reasons why people resist change, they believe that the resistance stems from a threat to the individual's security, that it is a form of fear of the unknown.
In light of this statement, which one of the following approaches would probably be MOST effective in preparing employees for a change in procedure in their unit?
   A. Avoid letting employees know anything about the change until the last possible moment
   B. Sympathize with employees who resent the change and let them know you share their doubts and fears
   C. Promise the employees that if the change turns out to be a poor one, you will allow them to suggest a return to the old system
   D. Make sure that employees know the reasons for the change and are aware of the benefits that are expected from it

6. Each of the following methods of encouraging employee participation in work planning has been used effectively with different kinds and sizes of employee groups.
Which one of the following methods would be MOST suitable for a group of four technically skilled employees?
   A. Discussions between the supervisor and a representative of the group
   B. A suggestion program with semi-annual awards for outstanding suggestions
   C. A group discussion summoned whenever a major problem remains unsolved for more than a month
   D. Day-to-day exchange of information, opinions, and experience

7. Of the following, the MOST important reason why a supervisor is given the authority to tell subordinates what work they should do, how they should do it, and when it should be done is that usually
   A. most people will not work unless there is someone with authority standing over them

B. work is accomplished more effectively if the supervisor plans and coordinates it
C. when division of work is left up to subordinates, there is constant arguing, and very little work is accomplished
D. subordinates are not familiar with the tasks to be performed

8. Fatigue is a factor that affects productivity in all work situations. However, a brief rest period will ordinarily serve to restore a person from fatigue.
According to this statement, which one of the following techniques is MOST likely to reduce the impact of fatigue on overall productivity in a unit?
   A. Scheduling several short breaks throughout the day
   B. Allowing employees to go home early
   C. Extending the lunch period an extra half hour
   D. Rotating job assignments every few weeks

8.____

9. After giving a new task to an employee, it is a good idea for a supervisor to ask specific questions to make sure that the employee grasps the essentials of the task and sees how it can be carried out. Questions which ask the employee what he thinks or how he feels about an important aspect of the task are particularly effective.
Which one of the following questions is NOT the type of question which would be useful in the foregoing situation?
   A. Do you feel there will be any trouble meeting the 4:30 deadline?
   B. How do you feel about the kind of work we do here?
   C. Do you think that combining those two steps will work all right?
   D. Can you think of any additional equipment you may need for this process?

9.____

10. Of the following, the LEAST important reason for having a *continuous* training program is that
    A. employees may forget procedures that they have already learned
    B. employees may develop shortcuts on the job that result in inaccurate work
    C. the job continue to change because of new procedures and equipment
    D. training is one means of measuring effectiveness and productivity on the job

10.____

11. In training a new employee, it is usually advisable to break down the job into meaningful parts and have the new employee master one part before going on to the next.
Of the following, the BEST reason for using this technique is to
    A. let the new employee know the reason for what he is doing and thus encourage him to remain in the unit
    B. make the employee aware of the importance of the work and encourage him to work harder
    C. show the employee that the work is easy so that he will be encouraged to work faster
    D. make it more likely that the employee will experience success and will be encouraged to continue learning the job

11.____

12. You may occasionally find a serious error in the work of one of your subordinates.
    Of the following, the BEST time to discuss such an error with an employee usually is
    A. immediately after the error is found
    B. after about two weeks, since you will also be able to point out some good things that the employee has accomplished
    C. when you have discovered a pattern of errors on the part of this employee so that he will not be able to dispute your criticism
    D. after the error results in a complaint by your own supervisor

13. For very important announcements to the staff, a supervisor should usually use both written and oral communications. For example, when a new procedure is to be introduced, the supervisor can more easily obtain the group's acceptance by giving his subordinates a rough draft of the new procedure and calling a meeting of all his subordinates.
    The LEAST important benefit of this technique is that it will better enable the supervisor to
    A. explain why the change is necessary
    B. make adjustments in the new procedure to meet valid staff objections
    C. assign someone to carry out the new procedure
    D. answer questions about the new procedure

14. Assume that, while you are interviewing an individual to obtain information, the individual pauses in the middle of an answer.
    The BEST of the following actions for you to take at that time is to
    A. correct any inaccuracies in what he has said
    B. remain silent until he continues
    C. explain your position on the matter being discussed
    D. explain that time is short and that he must complete his story quickly

15. When you are interviewing someone to obtain information, the BEST of the following reasons for you to repeat certain of his exact words is to
    A. assure him that appropriate action will be taken
    B. encourage him to switch to another topic of discussion
    C. assure him that you agree with his point of view
    D. encourage him to elaborate on a point he has made

16. Generally, when writing a letter, the use of precise words and concise sentences is
    A. *good*, because less time will be required to write the letter
    B. *bad*, because it is most likely that the reader will think the letter is unimportant and will not respond favorably
    C. *good*, because it is likely that your desired meaning will be conveyed to the reader
    D. *bad*, because your letter will be too brief to provide adequate information

17. In which of the following cases would it be MOST desirable to have two cards for one individual in a single alphabetic file?
The individual has
   A. a hyphenated surname
   B. two middle names
   C. a first name with an unusual spelling
   D. a compound first name

17.____

18. Of the following, it is MOST appropriate to use a form letter when it is necessary to answer many
   A. requests or inquiries from a single individual
   B. follow-up letters from individuals requesting additional information
   C. request or inquiries about a single subject
   D. complaints from individuals that they have been unable to obtain various types of information

18.____

19. Assume that you are asked to make up a budget for your section for the coming year, and you are told that the most important function of the budget is its "control function."
Of the following, "control" in this context implies MOST NEARLY that
   A. you will probably be asked to justify expenditures in any category when it looks as though these expenditures are departing greatly from the amount budgeted
   B. your section will probably not be allowed to spend more than the budgeted amount in any given category, although it is always permissible to spend less
   C. your section will be required to spend the exact amount budgeted in every category
   D. the budget will be filed in the Office of the Comptroller so that when a year is over the actual expenditures can be compared with the amounts in the budget

19.____

20. In writing a report, the practice of taking up the LEAST important points *first* and the most important points *last* is a
   A. *good* technique, since the final points made in a report will make the greatest impression on the reader
   B. *good* technique, since the material is presented in a more logical manner and will lead directly to the conclusions
   C. *poor* technique, since the reader's time is wasted by having to review irrelevant information before finishing the report
   D. *poor* technique, since it may cause the reader to lose interest in the report and arrive at incorrect conclusions about the report

20.____

21. Typically, when the technique of "supervision by results" is practiced, higher management sets down, either implicitly or explicitly, certain performance standards or goals that the subordinate is expected to meet. So long as these standards are met, management interferes very little.
The MOST likely result of the use of this technique is that it will

21.____

A. lead to ambiguity in terms of goals
B. be successful only to the extent that close direct supervision is practiced
C. make it possible to evaluate both employee and supervisory effectiveness
D. allow for complete dependence on the subordinate's part

22. When making written evaluations and reviews of the performance of subordinates, it is usually ADVISABLE to
    A. avoid informing the employee of the evaluation if it is critical because it may create hard feelings
    B. avoid informing the employee of the evaluation whether critical or favorable because it is tension-producing
    C. to permit the employee to see the evaluation but not to discuss it with him because the supervisor cannot be certain where the discussion might lead
    D. to discuss the evaluation openly with the employee because it helps the employee understand what is expected of him

22.____

23. There are a number of well-known and respected human relations principles that successful supervisors have been using for years in building good relationships with their employees.
    Which of the following does NOT illustrate such a principle?
    A. Give clear and complete instructions
    B. Let each person know how he is getting along
    C. Keep an open-door policy
    D. Make all relationships personal ones

23.____

24. Assume that it is necessary for you to give an unpleasant assignment to one of your subordinates. You expect this employee to raise some objections to this assignment.
    The MOST appropriate of the following actions for you to take FIRST is to issue the assignment
    A. *orally*, with the further statement that you will not listen to any complaints
    B. *in writing*, to forestall any complaints by the employee
    C. *orally*, permitting the employee to express his feelings
    D. *in writing*, with a note that any comments should be submitted in writing

24.____

25. Suppose you have just announced at a staff meeting with your subordinates that a radical reorganization of work will take place next week. Your subordinates at the meeting appear to be excited, tense, and worried.
    Of the following, the BEST action for you to take at that time is to
    A. schedule private conferences with each subordinate to obtain his reaction to the meeting
    B. close the meeting and tell your subordinates to return immediately to their work assignments
    C. give your subordinates some time to ask questions and discuss your announcement
    D. insist that your subordinates do not discuss your announcement among themselves or with other members of the agency

25.____

KEY (CORRECT ANSWERS)

1.	C	11.	D
2.	A	12.	A
3.	C	13.	C
4.	B	14.	B
5.	D	15.	D
6.	D	16.	C
7.	B	17.	A
8.	A	18.	C
9.	B	19.	A
10.	D	20.	D

21.	C
22.	D
23.	D
24.	C
25.	C

TEST 2

DIRECTIONS: Each question or incomplete statement is followed by several suggested answers or completions. Select the one that BEST answers the question or completes the statement. *PRINT THE LETTER OF THE CORRECT ANSWER IN THE SPACE AT THE RIGHT.*

1. Of the following, the BEST way for a supervisor to increase employees' interest in their work is to
   A. allow them to make as many decisions as possible
   B. demonstrate to them that he is as technically competent as they
   C. give each employee a difficult assignment
   D. promptly convey to them instructions from higher management

   1.____

2. The one of the following which is LEAST important in maintaining a high level of productivity on the part of employees is the
   A. provision of optimum physical working conditions for employees
   B. strength of employees' aspirations for promotion
   C. anticipated satisfactions which employees hope to derive from their work
   D. employees' interest in their jobs

   2.____

3. Of the following, the MAJOR advantage of group problem-solving, as compared to individual problem-solving, is that groups will more readily
   A. abide by their own decisions
   B. agree with agency management
   C. devise new policies and procedures
   D. reach conclusions sooner

   3.____

4. The group problem-solving conference is a useful supervisory method for getting people to reach solutions to problems.
   Of the following, the reason that groups usually reach more realistic solutions than do individuals is that
   A. individuals, as a rule, take longer than do groups in reaching decisions and are, therefore, more likely to make an error
   B. bringing people together to let them confer impresses participants with the seriousness of problems
   C. groups are generally more concerned with the future in evaluating organizational problems
   D. the erroneous opinions of group members tend to be corrected by the other members

   4.____

5. A competent supervisor should be able to distinguish between human and technical problems.
   Of the following, the MAJOR difference between such problems is that serious human problems, in comparison to ordinary technical problems
   A. are remedied more quickly
   B. involve a lesser need for diagnosis
   C. are more difficult to define
   D. become known through indications which are usually the actual problem

   5.____

6. Of the following, the BEST justification for a public agency establishing an alcoholism program for its employees is that
   A. alcoholism has traditionally been looked upon with a certain amused tolerance by management and thereby ignored as a serious illness
   B. employees with drinking problems have twice as many on-the-job accidents, especially during the early years of the problem
   C. excessive use of alcohol is associated with personality instability hindering informal social relationships among peers and subordinates
   D. the agency's public reputation will suffer despite an employee's drinking problem being a personal matter of little public concern

7. Assume you are a manager and you find a group of maintenance employees assigned to your project drinking and playing cards for money in an incinerator room after their regular working hours.
   The one of the following actions it would be BEST for you to take is to
   A. suspend all employees immediately if there is no question in your mind as to the validity of the charges
   B. review the personnel records of those involved with the supervisor and make a joint decision on which employees should sustain penalties of loss of annual leave or fines
   C. ask the supervisor to interview each violator and submit written reports to you and thereafter consult with the supervisor about disciplinary actions
   D. deduct three days of annual leave from each employee involved if he pleads guilty in lieu of facing more serious charges

8. Assume that as a manager you must discipline a subordinate, but all of the pertinent facts necessary for a full determination of the appropriate action to take are not yet available. However, you fear that a delay in disciplinary action may damage the morale of other employees.
   The one of the following which is MOST appropriate for you to do in this matter is to
   A. take immediate disciplinary action as if all the pertinent facts were available
   B. wait until all pertinent facts are available before reaching a decision
   C. inform the subordinate that you know he is guilty, issue a stern warning, and then let him wait for your further action
   D. reduce the severity of the discipline appropriate for the violation

9. There are two standard dismissal procedures utilized by most public agencies. The first is the "open back door" policy, in which the decision of a supervisor in discharging an employee for reasons of inefficiency cannot be cancelled by the central personnel agency. The second is the "closed back door" policy, in which the central personnel agency can order the supervisor to restore the discharged employee to his position.
   Of the following, the major DISADVANTAGE of the "closed back door" policy as opposed to the "open back door" policy is that central personnel agencies are
   A. likely to approve the dismissal of employees when there is inadequate justification

B. likely to revoke dismissal actions out of sympathy for employees
   C. less qualified than employing agencies to evaluate the efficiency of employees
   D. easily influenced by political, religious, and racial factors

10. The one of the following for which a formal grievance-handling system is LEAST useful is in
    A. reducing the frequency of employee complaints
    B. diminishing the likelihood of arbitrary action by supervisors
    C. providing an outlet for employee frustrations
    D. bringing employee problems to the attention of higher management

11. The one of the following managers whose leadership style involves the GREATEST delegation of authority to subordinates is the one who presents to subordinates
    A. his ideas and invites questions
    B. his decision and persuades them to accept it
    C. the problem, gets their suggestions, and makes his decision
    D. a tentative decision which is subject to change

12. Which of the following is MOST likely to cause employee productivity standards to be set too high?
    A. Standards of productivity are set by first-line supervisors rather than by higher level managers.
    B. Employees' opinions about productivity standards are sought through written questionnaires.
    C. Initial studies concerning productivity are conducted by staff specialists.
    D. Ideal work conditions assumed in the productivity standards are lacking in actual operations.

13. The one of the following which states the MAIN value of an organization chart for a manager is that such charts show the
    A. lines of formal authority
    B. manner in which duties are performed by each employee
    C. flow of work among employees on the same level
    D. specific responsibilities of each position

14. Which of the following BEST names the usual role of a line unit with regard to the organization's programs?
    A. Seeking publicity
    B. Developing
    C. Carrying out
    D. Evaluating

15. Critics of promotion *from within* a public agency argue for hiring *from outside* the agency because they believe that promotion from within leads to
    A. resentment and consequent weakened morale on the part of those not promoted
    B. the perpetuation of outdated practices and policies
    C. a more complex hiring procedure than hiring from outside the agency
    D. problems of objectively appraising someone already in the organization

16. The one of the following management functions which usually can be handled MOST effectively by a committee is the
    A. settlement of interdepartmental disputes
    B. planning of routine work schedules
    C. dissemination of information
    D. assignment of personnel

16._____

17. Assume that you are serving on a committee which is considering proposals in order to recommend a new maintenance policy. After eliminating a number of proposals by unanimous consent, the committee is deadlocked on three proposals.
    The one of the following which is the BEST way for the committee to reach agreement on a proposal they could recommend is to
    A. consider and vote on each proposal separately by secret ballot
    B. examine and discuss the three proposals until the proponents of two of them are persuaded they are wrong
    C. reach a synthesis which incorporates the significant features of each proposals
    D. discuss the three proposals until the proponents of each one concede those aspects of the proposals about which there is disagreement

17._____

18. A commonly used training and development method for professional staff is the case method, which utilizes the description of a situation, real or simulated, to provide a common base for analysis, discussion, and problem-solving.
    Of the following, the MOST appropriate time to use the case method is when professional staff needs
    A. insight into their personality problems
    B. practice in applying management concepts to their own problems
    C. practical experience in the assignment of delegated responsibilities
    D. to know how to function in many different capacities

18._____

19. The incident process is a training and development method in which trainees are given a very brief statement of an event or o a situation presenting a job incident or an employee problem of special significance.
    Of the following, it is MOST appropriate to use the incident process when
    A. trainees need to learn to review and analyze facts before solving a problem
    B. there are a large number of trainees who require the same information
    C. there are too many trainees to carry on effective discussion
    D. trainees are not aware of the effect of their behavior on others

19._____

20. The one of the following types of information about which a clerical employee is usually LEAST concerned during the orientation process is
    A. his specific job duties
    B. where he will work
    C. his organization's history
    D. who his associates will be

20._____

21. The one of the following which is the MOST important limitation on the degree to which work should be broken down into specialized tasks is the point at which
    A. there ceases to be sufficient work of a specialized nature to occupy employees
    B. training costs equal the half-yearly savings derived from further specialization
    C. supervision of employees performing specialized tasks becomes more technical than supervision of general employees
    D. it becomes more difficult to replace the specialist than to replace the generalist who performs a complex set of functions

22. When a supervisor is asked for his opinion of the suitability for promotion of a subordinate, the supervisor is actually being asked to predict the subordinate's future behavior in a new role.
    Such a prediction is MOST likely to be accurate if the
    A. higher position is similar to the subordinate's current one
    B. higher position requires intangible personal qualities
    C. new position has had little personal association with the subordinate away from the job

23. In one form of the non-directive evaluation interview, the supervisor communicates his evaluation to the employee and then listens to the employee's response without making further suggestions.
    The one of the following which is the PRINCIPAL danger of this method of evaluation is that the employee is MOST likely to
    A. develop an indifferent attitude towards the supervisor
    B. fail to discover ways of improving his performance
    C. become resistant to change in the organization's structure
    D. place the blame for his shortcomings on his co-workers

24. In establishing rules for his subordinates, a superior should be PRIMARILY concerned with
    A. creating sufficient flexibility to allow for exceptions
    B. making employees aware of the reasons for the rules and the penalties for infractions
    C. establishing the strength of his own position in relation to his subordinates
    D. having his subordinates know that such rules will be imposed in a personal manner

25. The practice of conducting staff training sessions on a periodic basis is generally considered
    A. *poor*; it takes employees away from their work assignments
    B. *poor*; all staff training should be done on an individual basis
    C. *good*; it permits the regular introduction of new methods and techniques
    D. *good*; it ensures a high employee productivity rate

KEY (CORRECT ANSWERS)

1.	A	11.	C
2.	A	12.	D
3.	A	13.	A
4.	D	14.	C
5.	C	15.	B
6.	B	16.	A
7.	C	17.	C
8.	B	18.	B
9.	C	19.	A
10.	A	20.	C

21.	A
22.	A
23.	B
24.	B
25.	C

EXAMINATION SECTION
TEST 1

DIRECTIONS: Each question or incomplete statement is followed by several suggested answers or completions. Select the one that BEST answers the question or completes the statement. *PRINT THE LETTER OF THE CORRECT ANSWER IN THE SPACE AT THE RIGHT.*

1. Following are three statements concerning on-the-job training:
   I. On-the-job training is rarely used as a method of training employees.
   II. On-the-job training is often carried on with little or no planning.
   III. On-the-job training is often less expensive than other types.
   Which of the following BEST classifies the above statements into those that are correct and those that are not?
   A. I is correct, but II and III are not.
   B. II is correct but I and III are not.
   C. I and II are correct, but III is not.
   D. II and III are correct, but I is not.

   1.____

2. The one of the following which is NOT a valid principle for a supervisor to keep in mind when talking to a subordinate about his performance is:
   A. People frequently know when they deserve criticism.
   B. Supervisors should be prepared to offer suggestions to subordinates about how to improve their work.
   C. Good points should be discussed before bad points.
   D. Magnifying a subordinate's faults will get him to improve faster.

   2.____

3. In many organizations information travels quickly through the grapevine. Following are three statements concerning the *grapevine*:
   I. Information a subordinate does not want to tell her supervisor may reach the supervisor through the *grapevine*.
   II. A supervisor can often do her job better by knowing the information that travels through the *grapevine*.
   III. A supervisor can depend on the *grapevine* as a way to get accurate information from the employees on his staff.
   Which one of the following CORRECTLY classifies the above statements into those which are generally correct and those which are not?
   A. II is correct, but I and III are not.
   B. III is correct, but I and II are not.
   C. I and II are correct, but III is not.
   D. I and III are correct, but II is not.

   3.____

4. Following are three statements concerning supervision:
   I. A supervisor knows he is doing a good job if his subordinates depend upon him to make every decision.
   II. A supervisor who delegates authority to his subordinates soon finds that his subordinates begin to resent him.
   III. Giving credit for good work is frequently an effective method of getting subordinates to work harder

   4.____

Which one of the following CORRECTLY classifies the above statements into those that are correct and those that are not?
- A. I and II are correct, but III is not.
- B. II and III are correct, but I is not.
- C. II is correct, but I and III are not.
- D. III is correct, but I and II are not.

5. Of the following, the LEAST appropriate action for a supervisor to take in preparing a disciplinary case against a subordinate is to
   - A. keep careful records of each incident in which the subordinate has been guilty of misconduct or incompetency, even though immediate disciplinary action may not be necessary
   - B. discuss with the employee each incident of misconduct as it occurs so the employee knows where he stands
   - C. accept memoranda from any other employees who may have been witnesses to acts of misconduct
   - D. keep the subordinate's personnel file confidential so that he is unaware of the evidence being gathered against him

6. Praise by a supervisor can be an important element in motivating subordinates. Following are three statements concerning a supervisor's praise of subordinates:
   I. In order to be effective, praise must be lavish and constantly restated.
   II. Praise should be given in a manner which meets the needs of the individual subordinate.
   III. The subordinate whose work is praised should believe that the praise is earned.
   Which of the following CORRECTLY classifies the above statements into those that are correct and those that are not?
   - A. I is correct, but II and III are not.
   - B. II and III are correct, but I is not.
   - C. III is correct, but I and II are not.
   - D. I and II are correct, but III is not.

7. A supervisor feels that he is about to lose his temper while reprimanding a subordinate.
   Of the following, the BEST action for the supervisor to take is to
   - A. postpone the reprimand for a short time until his self-control is assured
   - B. continue the reprimand because a loss of temper by the supervisor will show the subordinate the seriousness of the error he made
   - C. continue the reprimand because failure to do so will show that the supervisor does not have complete self-control
   - D. postpone the reprimand until the subordinate is capable of understanding the reason for the supervisor's loss of temper

8. Following are three statements concerning various ways of giving orders to subordinates:
   I. An implied order or suggestion is usually appropriate for the inexperienced employee.
   II. A polite request is less likely to upset a sensitive subordinate than a direct order.
   III. A direct order is usually appropriate in an emergency situation.

Which of the following CORRECTLY classifies the above statements into those that are correct and those that are not?
- A. I is correct, but II and III are not.
- B. II and III are correct, but I is not.
- C. III is correct, but I and II are not.
- D. I and II are correct, but III is not.

9. The one of the following which is NOT an acceptable reason for taking disciplinary action against a subordinate guilty of serious violations of the rules is that
    - A. the supervisor can *let off steam* against subordinates who break rules frequently
    - B. a subordinate whose work continues to be unsatisfactory may be terminated
    - C. a subordinate may be encouraged to improve his work
    - D. an example is set for other employees

10. At the first meeting with your staff after appointment as a supervisor, you find considerable indifference and some hostility among the participants.
    Of the following, the MOST appropriate way to handle this situation is to
    - A. disregard the attitudes displayed and continue to make your presentation until you have completed it
    - B. discontinue your presentation but continue the meeting and attempt to find out the reasons for their attitudes
    - C. warm up your audience with some good-natured statements and anecdotes and then proceed with your presentation
    - D. discontinue the meeting and set up personal interviews with the staff members to try to find out the reason for their attitude

11. Use a written rather than oral communication to amend any previous written communication.
    Of the following, the BEST justification for this statement is that
    - A. oral changes will be considered more impersonal and thus less important
    - B. oral changes will be forgotten or recalled indifferently
    - C. written communications are clearer and shorter
    - D. written communications are better able to convey feeling tone

12. Assume that a certain supervisor, when writing important communications to his subordinates, often repeats certain points in different words.
    This technique is GENERALLY
    - A. *ineffective*; it tends to confuse rather than help
    - B. *effective*; it tends to improve understanding by the subordinates
    - C. *ineffective*; it unnecessarily increases the length of the communication and may annoy the subordinates
    - D. *effective*; repetition is always an advantage in communications

13. In preparing a letter or a report, a supervisor may wish to persuade the reader of the correctness of some idea or course of action.
    The BEST way to accomplish this is for the supervisor to
    - A. encourage the reader to make a prompt decision
    - B. express each idea in a separate paragraph

C. present the subject matter of the letter in the first paragraph
D. state the potential benefits for the reader

14. Effective communications, a basic necessity for successful supervision is a two-way street. A good supervisor needs to listen to, as well as disseminate, information and he must be able to encourage his subordinates to communicate with him.
Which of the following suggestions will contribute LEAST to improving the *listening power* of a supervisor?
    A. Don't assume anything; don't anticipate, and don't let a subordinate think you know what he is going to say
    B. Don't interrupt; let him have his full say even if it requires a second session that day to get the full story
    C. React quickly to his statements so that he knows you are interested, even if you must draw some conclusions prematurely
    D. Try to understand the real need for his talking to you even if it is quite different from the subject under discussion

15. Of the following, the MOST useful approach for the supervisor to take toward the informal employee communications network known as the *grapevine* is to
    A. remain isolated from it, but not take any active steps to eliminate it
    B. listen to it, but not depend on it for accurate information
    C. use it to disseminate confidential information
    D. eliminate it as diplomatically as possible

16. If a supervisor is asked to estimate the number of employees that he believes he will need in his unit in the coming fiscal year, the supervisor should FIRST attempt to learn the
    A. nature and size of the workload his unit will have during that time
    B. cost of hiring and training new employees
    C. average number of employee absences per year
    D. number of employees needed to indirectly support or assist his unit

17. An important supervisory responsibility is coordinating the operations of the unit. This may include setting work schedules, controlling work quality, establishing interim due dates, etc. In order to handle this task, it has been divided into the following five stages:
    I. <u>Determine the steps</u> or sequence required for the tasks to be performed.
    II. <u>Give the orders</u>, either written or oral, to begin work on the tasks.
    III. <u>Check up</u> by following each task to make sure it is proceeding according to plan.
    IV. <u>Schedule the jobs</u> by setting a time for each task of operation to begin and end.
    V. <u>Control the process</u> by correcting conditions which interfere with the plan.
    The MOST logical sequence in which these planning steps should be performed is:
    A. I, II, III, IV, V   B. II, I, V, III, IV   C. I, IV, II, III, V   D. IV, I, II, III, V

18. Assume that a supervisor calls a meeting with the staff under his supervision in order to discuss several proposals. After some discussion, he realizes that he strongly disagrees with one proposal that four of the staff have rather firmly favored.
    At this point, he could BEST handle the situation by saying:
    A. *I have the responsibility for this decision, and I must disagree.*
    B. *I am just reminding you that I have had a great deal more experience in these matters.*
    C. *You have presented some good points, but perhaps we could look at it another way.*
    D. *The only way that this proposal can be disposed of is to defer it for further discussion.*

19. As far as the social activities and groups of his subordinates are concerned, a supervisor in a large organization can BEST strengthen his tools of leadership by
    A. emphasizing the organization as a whole and forbidding the formation of groups
    B. ignoring the groups as much as possible and dealing with each subordinate as an individual
    C. learning about the status structure of employee groups and their values
    D. avoiding any relationship with groups

20. If a subordinate asks you, his superior, for advice in planning his career in the department, you should
    A. encourage him to feel that he can easily reach the top of his occupational ladder
    B. discourage him from setting his hopes too high
    C. discuss career opportunities realistically with him
    D. explain that you have no control over his opportunities for advancement

21. A supervisor's evaluation of an employee is usually based upon a combination of objective facts and subjective judgments or opinions.
    Which of the following aspects of an employee's work or performance is MOST likely to be subjectively evaluated?
    A. Quantity   B. Accuracy   C. Attitude   D. Attendance

22. Of the following possible characteristics of supervisors, the one MOST likely to lead to failure as a supervisor is
    A. a tendency to seek several opinions before making decisions in complex matters
    B. lack of a strong desire to advance to a top position in management
    C. little formal training in human relations skills
    D. poor relations with subordinates and other supervisory personnel

23. People who break rules do so for a number of reasons. However, employees will break rules LESS often if
    A. the supervisor uses his own judgment about work methods
    B. the supervisor pretends to act strictly, but isn't really serious about it
    C. they greatly enjoy their work
    D. they have completed many years of service

24. Assume that an employee under your supervision has become resentful and generally non-cooperative after his request for transfer to another office closer to his place of residence was denied. The request was denied primarily because of the importance of his current assignment. The employee has been a valued worker, but you are now worried that his resentful attitude will have a detrimental effect.
    Of the following, the MOST desirable way for you to handle this situation is to
    A. arrange for the employee's transfer to the office he originally requested
    B. arrange for the employee's transfer to another office, but not the one he originally requested
    C. attempt to re-focus the employee's attention on those aspects of his current assignment which will be most rewarding and satisfying to him
    D. explain to the employee that, while you are sympathetic to his request, department rules will not allow transfers for reasons of personal convenience

25. Of the following, it would be LEAST advisable for a supervisor to use his administrative authority to affect the behavior and activities of his subordinates when he is trying to
    A. change the way his subordinates perform a particular task
    B. establish a minimum level of conformity to established rules
    C. bring about change in the attitudes of his subordinates
    D. improve the speed with which his subordinates respond to his orders

26. Assume that a supervisor gives his subordinate instructions which are appropriate and clear. The subordinate thereupon refuses to follow these instructions.
    Of the following, it would then be MOST appropriate for the supervisor to
    A. attempt to find out what it is that the employee objects to
    B. take disciplinary action that same day
    C. remind the subordinate about supervisory authority and threaten him with discipline
    D. insist that the subordinate carry out the order immediately

27. Of the following, the MOST effective way to identify training needs resulting from gradual changes in procedure is to
    A. monitor on a continuous basis the actual jobs performed and the skills required
    B. periodically send out a written questionnaire asking personnel to identify their needs
    C. conduct interviews at regular intervals with selected employees
    D. consult employees' personnel records

28. Assume that you, as a supervisor, have had a new employee assigned to you. If the duties of his position can be broken into independent parts, which of the following is usually the BEST way to train this new employee?
Start with
    A. the easiest duties and progressively proceed to the most difficult
    B. something easy; move to something difficult; then back to something easy
    C. something difficult; move to something easy; then to something difficult
    D. the most difficult duties and progressively proceed to the easiest

29. The oldest and most commonly used training technique is on-the-job training. Instruction is given to the worker by his supervisor or by another employee. Such training is essential in most jobs, although it is not always effective when used alone.
This technique, however, can be effectively used alone if
    A. the skills involved can be learned quickly
    B. a large number of people are to be trained at one time
    C. other forms of training have not been previously used with the people involved
    D. the skills to be taught are mental rather than manual

30. It is generally agreed that the learning process is facilitated in proportion to the amount of feedback that the learner is given about his performance.
Following are three statements concerning the learning process:
    I. The more specific the learner's knowledge of how he performed, the more rapid his improvement and the higher his level of performance
    II. Giving the learner knowledge of his results does not affect his motivation to learn.
    III. Learners who are not given feedback will set up subjective criteria and evaluate their own performance.
Which of the following choices lists ALL of the above statements that are generally CORRECT?
    A. I and II only   B. I and III only   C. II and III only   D. I, II, and III

KEY (CORRECT ANSWERS)

1.	D	11.	B	21.	C
2.	D	12.	B	22.	D
3.	C	13.	D	23.	C
4.	D	14.	C	24.	C
5.	D	15.	B	25.	C
6.	B	16.	A	26.	A
7.	A	17.	C	27.	A
8.	B	18.	C	28.	A
9.	A	19.	C	29.	A
10.	D	20.	C	30.	B

TEST 2

DIRECTIONS: Each question or incomplete statement is followed by several suggested answers or completions. Select the one that BEST answers the question or completes the statement. *PRINT THE LETTER OF THE CORRECT ANSWER IN THE SPACE AT THE RIGHT.*

Questions 1-6.

DIRECTIONS: Questions 1 through 6 are to be answered SOLELY on the basis of the information given in the following paragraph.

The use of role-playing as a training technique was developed during the past decade by social scientists, particularly psychologists, who have been active in training experiments. Originally, this technique was applied by clinical psychologists who discovered that a patient appears to gain understanding of an emotionally disturbing situation when encouraged to act out roles in that situation. As applied in government and business organizations, the purpose of role-playing is to aid employees to understand certain work problems involving interpersonal relations and to enable observers to evaluate various reactions to them. Thus, for example, on the problem of handling grievances, two individuals from the group might be selected to act out extemporaneously the parts of subordinate and supervisor. When this situation is enacted by various pairs among the class and the techniques and results are discussed, the members of the group are presumed to reach conclusions about the most effective means of handling similar situations. Often the use of role reversal, where participants take parts different from their actual work roles, assists individuals to gain more insight into other people's problems and viewpoints. Although role-playing can be a rewarding training device, the trainer must be aware of his responsibilities. If this technique is to be successful, thorough briefing of both actors and observers as to the situation in question, the participants' roles, and what to look for, is essential.

1. The role-playing technique was FIRST used for the purpose of
    A. measuring the effectiveness of training programs
    B. training supervisors in business organizations
    C. treating emotionally disturbed patients
    D. handling employee grievances

2. When role-playing is used in private business as a training device, the CHIEF aim is to
    A. develop better relations between supervisor and subordinate in the handling of grievances
    B. come up with a solution to a specific problem that has arisen
    C. determine the training needs of the group
    D. increase employee understanding of the human relation factors in work situations

3. From the above passage, it is MOST reasonable to conclude that when role-playing is used, it is preferable to have the roles acted out by
    A. only one set of actors   B. no more than 2 sets of actors
    C. several different sets of actors   D. the trainer or trainers of the group

4. Based on the above passage, a trainer using the technique of role reversal in a problem of first-line supervision should assign a senior employee to play the part of a(n)
   A. new employee
   B. senior employee
   C. principal employee
   D. angry citizen

4.____

5. It can be inferred from the above passage that a limitation of role-play as a training method is that
   A. many work situations do not lend themselves to role-play
   B. employees are not experienced enough as actors to play the roles realistically
   C. only trainers who have psychological training can use it successfully
   D. participants who are observing and not acting do not benefit from it

5.____

6. To obtain good results from the use of role-playing in training, a trainer should give participants
   A. a minimum of information about the situation so that they can act spontaneously
   B. scripts which illustrate the best method for handling the situation
   C. a complete explanation of the problem and the roles to be acted out
   D. a summary of work problems which involve interpersonal relations

6.____

7. Of the following, the MOST important reason for a supervisor to prepare good written reports is that
   A. a supervisor is rated on the quality of his reports
   B. decisions are often made on the basis of the reports
   C. such reports take less time for superiors to review
   D. such reports demonstrate efficiency of department operations

7.____

8. Of the following, the BEST test of a good report is whether it
   A. provides the information needed
   B. shows the good sense of the writer
   C. is prepared according to a proper format
   D. is grammatical and neat

8.____

9. When a supervisor writes a report, he can BEST show that he has an understanding of the subject of the report by
   A. including necessary facts and omitting non-essential details
   B. using statistical data
   C. giving his conclusions but not the data on which they are based
   D. using a technical vocabulary

9.____

10. Suppose you and another supervisor on the same level are assigned to work together on a report. You disagree strongly with one of the recommendations the other supervisor wants to include in the report but you cannot change his views.
    Of the following, it would be BEST that
    A. you refuse to accept responsibility for the report
    B. you ask that someone else be assigned to this project to replace you

10.____

C. each of you state his own ideas about this recommendation in the report
D. you give in to the other supervisor's opinion for the sake of harmony

11. Standardized forms are often provided for submitting reports.
Of the following, the MOST important advantage of using standardized forms for reports is that
    A. they take less time to prepare than individually written reports
    B. necessary information is less likely to be omitted
    C. the responsibility for preparing these reports can be delegated to subordinates
    D. the person making the report can omit information he considers unimportant

11._____

12. A report which may BEST be classed as a *periodic* report is one which
    A. requires the same type of information at regular intervals
    B. contains detailed information which is to be retained in permanent records
    C. is prepared whenever a special situation occurs
    D. lists information in graphic form

12._____

13. Which one of the following is NOT an important reason for keeping accurate records in an office?
    A. Facts will be on hand when decisions have to be made.
    B. The basis for past actions can be determined.
    C. Information needed by other bureaus can be furnished.
    D. Filing is easier when records are properly made out.

13._____

14. Suppose you are preparing to write a report recommending a change in a certain procedure. You learn that another supervisor made a report a few years ago suggesting a change in this same procedure, but that no action was taken.
Of the following, it would be MOST desirable for you to
    A. avoid reading the other supervisor's report so that you will write with a more up-to-date point of view
    B. make no recommendation since management seems to be against any change in the procedure
    C. read the other report before you write your report to see what bearing it may have on your recommendations
    D. avoid including in your report any information that can be obtained by referring to the other report

14._____

15. If a report you are preparing to your superior is going to be a very long one, it would be DESIRABLE to include a summary of your basic conclusions
    A. at the end of the report
    B. at the beginning of the report
    C. in a separate memorandum
    D. right after you present the supporting data

15._____

16. Suppose that some bureau and department policies must be very frequently applied by your subordinates while others rarely come into use.
    As a supervising employee, a GOOD technique for you to use in fulfilling your responsibility of seeing to it that policies are adhered to is to
    A. ask the director of the bureau to issue to all employees an explanation in writing of all policies
    B. review with your subordinates every week those policies which have daily application
    C. follow up on and explain at regular intervals the application of those policies which are not used very often by your subordinates
    D. recommend to your superiors that policies rarely used be changed or dropped

17. The BASIC purpose behind the principle of delegation of authority is to
    A. give the supervisor who is delegating a chance to acquire skills in higher level functions
    B. free the supervisor from routine tasks in order that he may do the important parts of his job
    C. prevent supervisors from overstepping the lines of authority which have been established
    D. place the work delegated in the hands of those employees who can perform it best

18. A district commander can BEST assist management in long-range planning by
    A. reporting to his superiors any changing conditions in the district
    B. maintaining a neat and efficiently run office
    C. scheduling work so that areas with a high rate of non-compliance get more intensive coverage
    D. properly training new personnel assigned to his district

19. Suppose that new quarters have been rented for your district office.
    Of the following, the LEAST important factor to be considered in planning the layout of the office is the
    A. need for screening confidential activities from unauthorized persons
    B. relative importance of the various types of work
    C. areas of noise concentration
    D. convenience with which communication between sections of the office can be achieved

20. Of the following, the MOST basic effect of organizing a department so that lines of authority are clearly defined and duties are specifically assigned is to
    A. increase the need for close supervision
    B. decreases the initiative of subordinates
    C. lessen the possibility of duplication of work
    D. increase the responsibilities of supervisory personnel

21. An accepted management principle is that decisions should be delegated to the lowest point in the organization at which they can be made effectively.
The one of the following which is MOST likely to be a result of the application of this principle is that
    A. no factors will be overlooked in making decisions
    B. prompt action will follow the making of decisions
    C. decisions will be made more rapidly
    D. coordination of decisions that are made will be simplified

22. Suppose you are a supervisor and need some guidance from a higher authority. In which one of the following situations would it be PERMISSIBLE for you to bypass the regular upward channels of communication in the chain of command?
    A. In an emergency when your superior is not available
    B. When it is not essential to get a quick reply
    C. When you feel your immediate superior is not understanding of the situation
    D. When you want to obtain information that you think your superior does not have

23. Of the following, the CHIEF limitation of the organization chart as it is generally used in business and government is that the chart
    A. makes lines of responsibility and authority undesirably definite and formal
    B. is often out of date as soon as it is completed
    C. does not show human factors and informal working relationships
    D. is usually too complicated

24. The *span of control* for any supervisor is the
    A. number of tasks he is expected to perform himself
    B. amount of office space he and his subordinates occupy
    C. amount of work he is responsible for getting out
    D. number of subordinates he can supervise effectively

25. Of the following duties performed by a supervising employee, which would be considered a LINE function rather than a staff function?
    A. Evaluation of office personnel
    B. Recommendations for disciplinary action
    C. Initiating budget requests for replacement of equipment
    D. Inspections, at irregular times, of conditions and staff in the field

KEY (CORRECT ANSWERS)

1.	C	11.	B
2.	D	12.	A
3.	C	13.	D
4.	A	14.	C
5.	A	15.	B
6.	C	16.	C
7.	B	17.	B
8.	A	18.	A
9.	A	19.	B
10.	C	20.	C

21. B
22. A
23. C
24. D
25. D

EXAMINATION SECTION
TEST 1

DIRECTIONS: Each question or incomplete statement is followed by several suggested answers or completions. Select the one that BEST answers the question or completes the statement. *PRINT THE LETTER OF THE CORRECT ANSWER IN THE SPACE AT THE RIGHT.*

1. Assume that you are interviewing a witness who is telling a story crucial to your investigation. It is important that you get all the facts being related by this witness.
   In order to secure this vital information, the BEST of the following techniques is to
   A. quietly interrupt the witness's story and request him to speak with deliberation to that you can record his statement
   B. guide the witness during his recital so that all important points are validated
   C. confine your activities during the story to brief note-taking; and after the information has been secured, request a full written statement
   D. inform the witness that he must relate all the facts as truthfully and concisely as possible

1.____

2. The statement of any witness obtained by an investigator in an interview should GENERALLY be considered
   A. as a lead requiring substantiation by additional evidence
   B. accurate if the witness appears honest and is cooperative
   C. unreliable if the witness has been involved in similar investigations
   D. as a fact admissible under the rules of evidence

2.____

3. During an important interview, an investigator takes notes from time to time but very rarely looks at the subject being questioned.
   Such action on the part of the investigator is
   A. *unacceptable*, chiefly because during the actual interview an investigator should pay more attention to the witness's manner of giving the information rather than to the content of his statement
   B. *acceptable*, chiefly because data should be recorded at the earliest opportunity and important data should be noted meticulously
   C. *unacceptable*, chiefly because it inhibits the person being interviewed and is not conducive to a give-and-take discussion
   D. *acceptable*, chiefly because focusing attention on note-taking and not on the person being interviewed creates an impression of professional objectivity

3.____

4. The BEST source with which to check the credit rating of a business you are investigating is
   A. the Better Business Bureau   B. Standard and Poor's
   C. Dun and Bradstreet, Inc.   D. the State Attorney General's Office

4.____

5. Since he must, in the course of his investigations, interview persons with various personalities and attitudes, an investigator should GENERALLY adopt a method of interviewing that
   A. is uniformly applicable to all types so that discrepancies in the accounts of individuals may be readily detected
   B. can be adjusted to the persons whom he interviews
   C. is based on the premise that most witnesses tend to be uncooperative
   D. requires the investigator to spend as little time as possible in questioning witnesses

6. An investigator finds that X, Y, and Z are eyewitnesses to an incident under investigation. He interviews X, who gives him a complete and very detailed statement about the incident. X also informs the investigator that he has discussed the matter with Y and Z, and that each of them completely agrees with him as to what had occurred.
   Under these circumstances, it would be MOST appropriate for the investigator to
   A. interview Y and Z before assessing the value of the statements made by the three witnesses
   B. interview Y and Z and accept their versions if they both disagree with the story given by witness X
   C. interview either Y or Z and close the investigation if the statement of either witness agrees with the story given by witness X
   D. close the investigation on the basis of his interview with witness X since there is no reason to assume that Y and Z will tell a different story

7. Which one of the following is a legal requirement for the admissibility of evidence in a legal procedure?
   A. Weight   B. Sufficiency   C. Competency   D. Recency

8. Of the following diagrams, which one represents the CORRECT utilization of the ABC Method of Surveillance?
   Note: S identifies the suspect's position
   X identifies the positions of investigators
   Arrow indicates direction in which suspect is moving

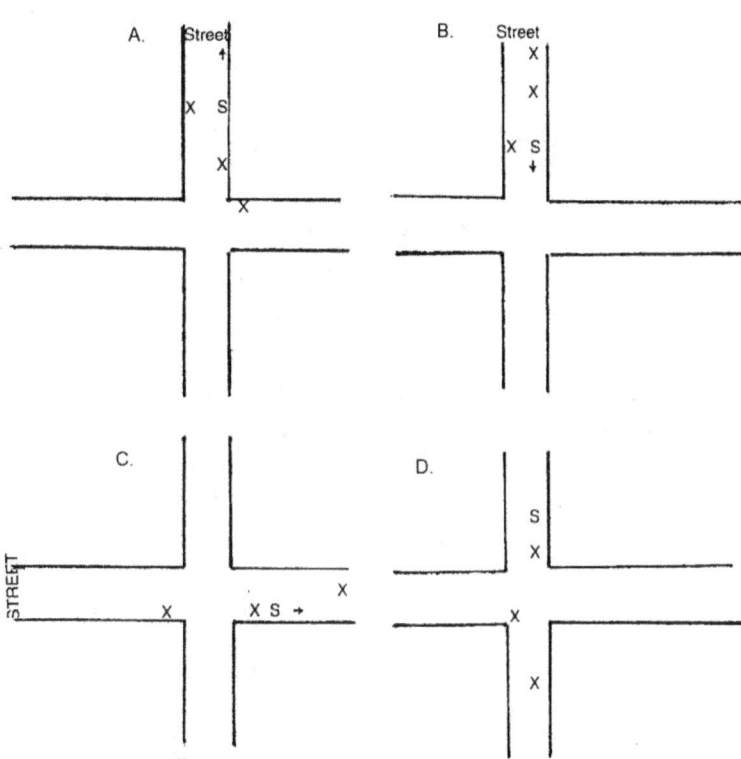

9. During an interview, an interviewee makes the following statement: *I have given the problem of getting a job a great deal of thought. I am looking primarily for an opportunity to grow and develop—to find the type of job that will provide the greatest challenge and bring out the best that is in me. Security probably ranks at the bottom of my list since I feel that I can always make a living somewhere.*
From an analysis of this statement, an investigator would be LEAST likely to conclude that the interviewee is
   A. capable of analytical thought
   B. looking for job satisfaction
   C. seeking self-improvement
   D. trying to cover for his lack of self-confidence

10. One of the more difficult tasks facing an investigator in an interview is to control the tendency of witnesses to ramble when giving information.
Of the following, the BEST technique for keeping a witness's comments pertinent is to
   A. ask questions which indicate the desired answer
   B. insist on *yes* and *no* answers to his questions
   C. construct questions that restrict the range of information which the witness can give in response
   D. ask precise questions so that the answers of the witness will necessarily be brief

11. The BASIC purpose of producing evidence in legal proceedings is to
    A. provide a permanent official record for legal action
    B. screen out confusing issues of law and fact
    C. determine the truth of a matter in issue
    D. insure that hearsay statements will be excluded

12. An investigator is handling a case involving an individual and find that the case is proving very difficult because he has run out of leads to follow up.
    Of the following, the BEST way for the investigator to deal with this case is FIRST to
    A. prepare a report of the case indicating that no further action can be taken
    B. place himself in the position of the person being investigated
    C. re-interview all those affected by the case until a new clue is revealed
    D. wait for the first break in the case which will give a substantial lead

13. Assume that you need to interview a person who is suspected of collaborating with the subject under investigation.
    Of the following, the interviewing procedure that is MOST appropriate for handling this situation is to
    A. conduct a casual interview with the person on a pretext different from the actual purpose of the interview
    B. interview the person intensively by means of the *team* method until he breaks down and gives information
    C. insist that the suspected person cooperate
    D. plan to review every statement made by the person until he realizes that no fact will be overlooked

14. Assume that two disinterested individuals had directly witnessed the same event. An investigator who interviewed them received two distinctly different versions of this event.
    Which of the following assumptions PROBABLY accounts for the difference in the two versions?
    A. The event must have consisted of so many separate happenings that no one could understand everything that occurred.
    B. Each individual was selective in his perception of the event.
    C. The interviewing technique used by the investigator was instrumental in eliciting different facts from each individual.
    D. One of the individuals wishes to cooperate with the investigator, but the other did not.

15. During interviews, a certain investigator phrases follow-up questions mentally during pauses while the subject is still answering the previous question.
    This practice is GENERALLY
    A. *desirable*, chiefly because it gives the impression that the investigator is well-acquainted with all the facts
    B. *undesirable*, chiefly because the investigator cannot know whether such questions will be appropriate

C. *desirable*, chiefly because it enables the investigator to pose new questions without significant breaks in the discussion
D. *undesirable*, chiefly because it subjects the person being interviewed to a barrage of questions

16. Generally, a professional investigator's practice of training himself to give the impression of telling the truth during court appearances is considered
    A. *desirable*, chiefly because only by such practice can he perfect his ability to give accurate testimony
    B. *undesirable*, chiefly because any deviation from the unadulterated truth by using a pretension constitutes perjury
    C. *desirable*, chiefly because such training lessens the possibility of his appearing nervous and timid while testifying, which might convey the impression that he is evasive or lying
    D. *undesirable*, chiefly because all testimony should be given in a natural manner, including hesitations, to avoid the court's suspicion that the witness has been coached

16.____

17. Assume that prior to an interview, a person makes a spontaneous declaration relating to his case in the presence of an investigator.
    According to a rule of evidence, the person's statement is GENERALLY
    A. *admissible*, only if the investigator testifies to the declaration and his testimony is corroborated by another person
    B. *inadmissible*, chiefly because it constitutes a hearsay declaration against the person's interest
    C. *admissible*, chiefly because it was not the product of the person's deliberation and reflection
    D. *inadmissible*, chiefly because the person was under duress when the exclamation was made

17.____

18. In order to break down the communication barriers between an interviewer and his subject, the interviewer should GENERALLY ask introductory questions which
    A. focus on the individual's job status
    B. can be answered in a *yes-or-no* fashion
    C. focus directly on official business
    D. are likely to be of mutual interest to the two parties

18.____

19. To introduce as evidence a set of business books prepared by a person other than the individual under investigation, preliminary evidence pertaining to the content of the books must first be established.
    Which of the following does NOT constitute a fact which must be established before such books may be admitted as evidence?
    A. entries were made in the regular course of business at or about the time of the transactions involved
    B. books have been audited and certified as correct
    C. books are the regular books used for making business entries
    D. entries in the books were made by persons required to make them in the course of their regular duties

19.____

20. A person who is suffering from a mental disability is not necessarily disqualified from testifying as a witness in a legal proceeding PROVIDED that such person
    A. has the ability to recall and describe past events pertaining to the case
    B. is not an inmate of a mental institution
    C. is attended by a qualified psychiatrist at all times while in the courtroom
    D. swears that he knows the difference between right and wrong

21. Of the following public records, which is the BEST single source of information on the personal history and background of a subject?
    A. Birth or baptismal certificate
    B. Marriage license application
    C. Discharge certificate from the military services
    D. Income tax return

22. When it is necessary to prove the contents of a written instrument concerning a matter in dispute, the *best evidence rule* provides that
    A. the contents of written instruments must be subscribed and sworn to before a notary public to be admissible in legal proceedings
    B. no evidence outside the instrument itself shall be used to alter the wording of the instrument
    C. a witness who qualifies as an expert in handwriting identification shall first testify on the genuineness of the instrument
    D. the original instrument itself must be produced in court if it is available

23. Public documents, if otherwise competent, are admissible as evidence of the facts recorded therein, without the testimony of the officers who entered the facts, CHIEFLY because
    A. public records are subject to such strict security that the entries therein cannot be altered or falsified
    B. all such documents require further corroboration before they are admissible as proof of any facts recorded therein
    C. entries in these documents are made by officers who have sworn to perform their duties in the public interest
    D. hearsay evidence may not be admitted to prove a fact in dispute without the testimony of the officer who recorded it

24. One of the following ways in which an investigator might ordinarily detect an inconsistency in an interviewee's story is by
    A. having a third party present during the interview
    B. requesting the subject to speak more slowly
    C. observing the subject's manner of dress or attire
    D. watching the subject's facial expressions and mannerisms

25. The use of small talk or conversation about extraneous topics such as sports, the weather, or current events at the start of a routine interview designed to elicit information is GENERALLY considered
    A. *desirable*, chiefly because it gives the subject a chance to relax and relieve himself of the tension that normally develops before an interview

B. un*desirable*, chiefly because it wastes the valuable time of subjects with matters that are unrelated to the purpose of the interview
C. *desirable*, chiefly because it is the only way the interviewer is able to ascertain whether he and the subject will be able to develop rapport
D. un*desirable*, chiefly because it is possible to obtain more information about the subject if he is unaware of the purpose of the interview

26. Assume that your superior assigns you to interview an individual who, he warns, seems to be highly *introverted*.
    You should be aware that, during an interview, such a person is likely to
    A. hold views which are highly controversial in nature
    B. be domineering and try to control the direction of the interview
    C. resist answering personal questions regarded his background
    D. give information which is largely fabricated

27. The one of the following persons who is MOST likely to be willing to give information leading to the apprehension of a suspect is someone who is
    A. friendly with the suspect
    B. afraid of the subject
    C. interested in law enforcement
    D. seeking revenge against the suspect

28. During the course of a routine interview, the BEST tone of voice for an interviewer to use is
    A. authoritative   B. uncertain   C. formal   D. conversational

29. It is recommended that interviews which inquire into the personal background of an individual should be held in private.
    The BEST reason for this practice is that privacy
    A. allows the individual to talk freely about the details of his background
    B. induces contemplative thought on the part of the interviewed individual
    C. prevents any interruptions by departmental personnel during the interview
    D. most closely resembles the atmosphere of the individual's personal life

30. Of the following, the MOST preferable way for an investigator to make a reference check on a subject's previous employment in the area is to
    A. write to the employer and ask him to fill out a standard employee evaluation form
    B. call the employer and conduct a telephone interview
    C. write to the employer and request a personal interview
    D. telephone the employer and ask him to submit a written evaluation

31. Of the following, the BEST way for an investigator to prepare himself for a court appearance as a witness is generally by
    A. memorizing every detail of the case in order to give an exact recital of the information
    B. reviewing his notes and trying to fix in his mind the highlights of the case

C. consulting with his superiors in order to ascertain which aspects of the case should be emphasized
D. studying all aspects of the case and writing out in detail the testimony he intends to give under oath

32. When an investigator is called as a witness to relate a series of incidents, his testimony should GENERALLY consist of
    A. a background narrative, followed by important facts and a concluding statement
    B. important facts, followed by a background narrative and a concluding statement
    C. details personally observed followed by any undeveloped leads
    D. a simple chronological account of the events he has observed

33. Of the following, an individual who smokes heavily during interrogation or an interview is LEAST likely to experience a(n)
    A. decrease in mental efficiency
    B. decrease in physical efficiency
    C. state of high emotion during questioning
    D. emotional release during questioning

34. The BEST way for an investigator to handle a situation in which the person interviewed asks a few slightly personal questions is generally to
    A. give quick, evasive answers and continue with the interview
    B. tell the person such questions are irrelevant and objectionable
    C. inquire fully into the person's reasons for wanting such information
    D. answer the questions briefly and truthfully

35. The CHIEF purpose of using surveillance in an investigation is to
    A. obtain information about persons and activities
    B. cause suspected persons to feel continuously uneasy
    C. maintain a close watch over hostile witnesses
    D. induce subjects to volunteer information

36. A *surreptitious* recording of an interview is one which is made
    A. whenever the information is highly technical
    B. to conceal the identity of the interviewee
    C. without the knowledge of the subject
    D. to encourage a subject to be more informative

37. All the means by which any alleged matter of fact, the truth of which is submitted to investigation, is established or disproved is the legal definition of
    A. proof   B. burden of proof
    C. evidence   D. admissibility of evidence

38. That section of an affidavit in which an officer empowered to administer an oath certifies that this document was sworn to before him is called a(n)
    A. affirmation   B. jurat
    C. acknowledgement   D. verification

39. In legal terminology, a *bailee* is a person who
    A. lawfully holds property belonging to another
    B. deposits cash or property for the release of an arrested person
    C. has been released from arrest on a bond that guarantees his court appearance
    D. deposits personal property as collateral for a debt

40. A specimen of handwriting of known authorship which can be used by an investigator for making a comparison with a questioned or suspected writing is called a(n)
    A. inscription   B. precis   C. coordinate   D. exemplar

41. The attorney felt that his client would be *exonerated*.
    In this sentence, *exonerated* means MOST NEARLY
    A. unwilling to testify   B. declared blameless
    C. severely punished   D. placed on probation

42. The two witnesses were suspected of *collusion*.
    In this sentence, the word *collusion* means MOST NEARLY
    A. a conflict of interest   B. an unintentional error
    C. an illegal secret agreement D. financial irregularities

43. Many of the subject's answers during the interview were *redundant*.
    In this sentence, *redundant* means MOST NEARLY
    A. uninformative   B. thoughtful   C. repetitious   D. argumentative

44. He was assigned to investigate an individual who was *insolvent*.
    In this sentence, *insolvent* means MOST NEARLY
    A. unable to pay debts   B. extremely disrespectful
    C. difficult to understand   D. frequently out of work

45. In his report, the investigator described several *covert* business transactions.
    In this sentence, *covert* means MOST NEARLY
    A. unauthorized   B. joint   C. complicated   D. secret

KEY (CORRECT ANSWERS)

1.	C	11.	C	21.	B	31.	B	41.	B
2.	A	12.	B	22.	D	32.	D	42.	C
3.	C	13.	A	23.	C	33.	C	43.	C
4.	C	14.	B	24.	D	34.	D	44.	A
5.	B	15.	C	25.	A	35.	A	45.	D
6.	A	16.	C	26.	C	36.	C		
7.	C	17.	C	27.	D	37.	C		
8.	C	18.	D	28.	D	38.	B		
9.	D	19.	B	29.	A	39.	A		
10.	C	20.	A	30.	A	40.	D		

TEST 2

DIRECTIONS: Each question or incomplete statement is followed by several suggested answers or completions. Select the one that BEST answers the question or completes the statement. *PRINT THE LETTER OF THE CORRECT ANSWER IN THE SPACE AT THE RIGHT.*

Questions 1-5.

DIRECTIONS: Questions 1 through 5 consist of two sentences which may or may not contain errors in word usage or sentence structure, punctuation, or capitalization. Consider a sentence correct although there may be other correct ways of expressing the same thought.
Mark your answer:
A. If only Sentence I is correct;
B. If only sentence II is correct;
C. If Sentences I and II are both correct;
D. If Sentences I and II are both incorrect.

1. I. Being locked in his desk, the investigator felt sure that the records would be safe.
   II. The reason why the witness changed his statement was because he had been threatened.

2. I. The investigation had just began then an important witness disappeared.
   II. The check that had been missing was located and returned to its owner, Harry Morgan, a resident of Suffolk County, New York.

3. I. A supervisor will find that the establishment of standard procedures enables his staff to work more efficiently.
   II. An investigator hadn't ought to give any recommendations in his report if he is in doubt.

4. I. Neither the investigator nor his supervisor is ready to interview the witnesses.
   II. Interviewing has been and always will be an important asset in investigation.

5. I. One of the investigator's reports has been forwarded to the wrong person.
   II. The investigator stated that he was not familiar with those kind of cases.

Questions 6-8.

DIRECTIONS: Questions 6 through 8 are to be answered SOLELY on the basis of the following passage.

As investigators, we are more concerned with the utilitarian than the philosophical aspects of ethics and ethical standards, procedures, and conduct. As a working consideration, we might view ethics as the science of doing the right thing at the right time in the right manner in conformity with the normal, everyday standards imposed by society; and in conformity with the judgment society would be expected to make concerning the rightness or wrongness of what we have done.

An ethical code might be considered a basic set of rules and regulations to which we must conform in the performance of investigative duties. Ethical standards, procedures, and conduct might be considered the logical workings of our ethical code in its everyday application to our work. Ethics also necessarily involves morals and morality. We must eventually answer the self-imposed question of whether or not we have acted in the right way in conducting our investigative activities in their individual and total aspects.

6. Of the following, the MOST suitable title for the above passage is 6._____
    A. The Importance of Rules for Investigators
    B. The Basic Philosophy of a Lawful Society
    C. Scientific Aspects of Investigations
    D. Ethical Guidelines For the Conduct of Investigations

7. According to the above passage, ethical considerations for investigators involve 7._____
    A. special standards that are different from those which apply to the rest of society
    B. practices and procedures which cannot be evaluated by others
    C. individual judgments by investigators of the appropriateness of their own actions
    D. regulations which are based primarily upon a philosophical approach

8. Of the following, the author's PRINCIPAL purpose in writing the above passage seems to have been to 8._____
    A. emphasize the importance of self-criticism in investigative activities
    B. explain the relationship that exists between ethics and investigative conduct
    C. reduce the amount of unethical conduct in the area of investigations
    D. seek recognition by his fellow investigators for his academic treatment of the subject matter

Questions 9-11.

DIRECTIONS: Questions 9 through 11 are to be answered SOLELY on the basis of the following passage.

The investigator must remember that acts of omission can be as effective as acts of commission in affecting the determination of disputed issues. Acts of omission, such as failure to obtain available information or failure to verify dubious information, manifest themselves in miscarriages of justice and erroneous adjudications. An incomplete investigation is an erroneous investigation because a conclusion predicated upon inadequate facts is based on quicksand.

When an investigator throws up his hands and admits defeat, the reason for this action does not necessarily lie in his possible laziness and ineptitude. It is more likely that the investigator has made his conclusions after exhausting only those avenues of investigation of which he is aware. He has exercised good faith in his belief that nothing else can be done.

This tendency must be overcome by all investigators if they are to operate at top efficiency. If no suggestion for new or additional action can be found in any authority, an investigator should use his own initiative to cope with a given situation. No investigator should ever hesitate to set precedents. It is far better in the final analysis to attempt difficult solutions, even if the chances of error are obviously present, than it is to take refuge in the spinless adage: If you don't do anything, you don't do it wrong.

9. Of the following, the MOST suitable title for the above passage is
   A. The Need For resourcefulness in Investigations
   B. Procedures For Completing an Investigation
   C. The Development of Standards For Investigators
   D. The Causes of Incomplete Investigations

10. Of the following, the author of this passage considers that the LEAST important consideration in developing new investigative methods is
    A. efficiency   B. caution
    C. imagination   D. thoroughness

11. According to this passage, which of the following statements is INCORRECT?
    A. Lack of creativity may lead to erroneous investigations.
    B. Acts of omission are sometimes as harmful as acts of commission.
    C. Some investigators who give up on a case are lazy or inept.
    D. An investigator who gives up on a case is usually not acting in good faith.

Questions 12-15.

DIRECTIONS: Questions 12 through 15 are to be answered SOLELY on the basis of the following passage.

Perpetrators of crimes are often described by witnesses or victims in terms of salient facial features. The Bertillon System of Identification, which preceded the widespread use of fingerprints, was based on body measurements. Recently, there have been developments in the quantification of procedures used in the classification and comparison of facial characteristics. Devices are now available which enable a trained operator, with the aid of a witness, to form a composite picture of a suspect's face and to translate that composite into a numerical code. Further developments in this area are possible, using computers to develop efficient sequences of questions so that witnesses may quickly arrive at the proper description.

Recent studies of voice analysis and synthesis, originally motivated by problems of efficient telephone transmission, have led to the development of the audio-frequency profile or "voice print." Each voice print may be sufficiently unique to permit development of a classification system that will make possible positive identification of the source of a voice print. This method of identification, using an expert to identify the voice patterns, has been introduced in more than 40 cases by 15 different police departments. As with all identification systems that rely on experts to perform the identification, controlled laboratory tests are needed to establish with care the relative frequency of errors of omission and commission made by experts.

4 (#2)

12. The MOST appropriate title for the above passage is   12._____
    A. Technology in Modern Investigative Detection
    B. Identification By Physical Features
    C. Verification of Identifications By Experts
    D. The Use of Electronic Identification Techniques

13. According to the above passage, computers may be used in conjunction with   13._____
    which of the following identification techniques?
    A. Fingerprints   B. Bertillon System
    C. Voice prints   D. Composite facial pictures

14. According to the above passage, the ability to identify individuals based on   14._____
    facial characteristics has improved as a result of
    A. an increase in the number of facial types which can be shown to witnesses
    B. information which is derived from other body measurements
    C. coded classification and comparison techniques
    D. greater reliance upon experts to make the identifications

15. According to the above passage, it is CORRECT to state that audio-frequency   15._____
    profiles or voice prints
    A. have been decisive in many prosecutions
    B. reduce the number of errors made by experts
    C. developed as a result of problems in telephonic communications
    D. are unlikely to result in positive identifications

Questions 16-20.

DIRECTIONS: Questions 16 through 20 are to be answered SOLELY on the basis of the following graph.

EMPLOYMENT APPLICATION INFORMATION
CHECKED BY INVESTIGATORS IN DEPARTMENT Z
CENTRAL CITY

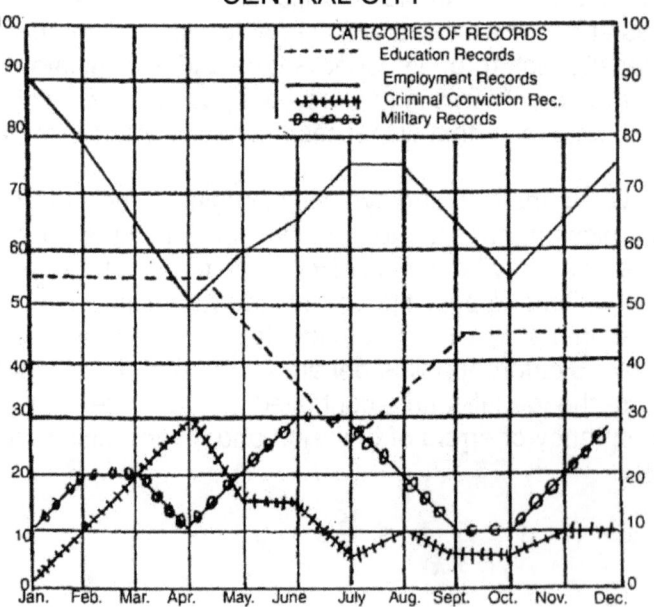

16. The category for which the SMALLEST number of record checks was made in _____ records.
    A. education
    B. employment
    C. criminal conviction
    D. military

17. In which of the following months did the combined number of criminal conviction record checks and military record checks EXCEED the number of education record checks?
    A. March
    B. April
    C. May
    D. June

18. During which of the following months was the total number of records checked LARGEST?
    A. March
    B. April
    C. September
    D. November

19. Which of the following statements is INCORRECT according to the graph?
    A. Employment records checked each month always exceeded 45.
    B. Education records checked in February did not equal the number of education records checked in November.
    C. Military records checked per month increased from October to December.
    D. Criminal conviction records checked in any given month never exceeded the number of military records checked.

20. Of the total number of records checked in March, the percentage that were education records was MOST NEARLY
    A. 13%
    B. 25%
    C. 34%
    D. 41%

Questions 21-25.

DIRECTIONS: Questions 21 through 25 are to be answered SOLELY on the basis of the information contained in the following tables.

STATUS OF TAX CASES ASSIGNED TO INVESTIGATORS, FISCAL YEAR, CENTRAL CIT, DEPARTMENT Y

Investigator	Cases Assigned	Cases Completed	Cases Pending at End of Fiscal Year
Albert	70	50	20
Bennett	90	60	30
Gordon	82	50	32
Nolton	70	40	30
Paxton	75	50	25
Rich	80	60	20

STATUS OF MISCELLANEOUS CASES ASSIGNED TO INVESTIGATORS
FISCAL YEAR, CENTRAL CITY, DEPARTMENT Y

Investigator	Cases Assigned	Cases Completed	Cases Pending at End of Fiscal Year
Albert	25	20	5
Bennett	20	15	5
Gordon	18	13	5
Nolton	30	23	7
Paxton	17	17	0
Rich	32	24	6

21. Of the following, the investigator who completed the GREATEST percentage of his assigned tax cases in the fiscal year was
    A. Albert   B. Gordon   C. Paxton   D. Rich

22. The total number of the tax cases assigned in the fiscal year EXCEEDED the total number of miscellaneous cases assigned by
    A. 142   B. 325   C. 400   D. 467

23. Of the following, the two investigators who completed the SAME percentage of the miscellaneous cases assigned to them were
    A. Albert and Gordon
    B. Gordon and Nolton
    C. Nolton and Paxton
    D. Bennett and Rich

24. The average number of cases (both tax and miscellaneous) pending per investigator at the end of the fiscal year was MOST NEARLY
    A. 31   B. 28   C. 26   D. 5

25. Assume that the total number of miscellaneous cases pending at the end of the fiscal year is equal to 25% of the number of cases pending at the end of the previous fiscal year.
    What was the TOTAL number of miscellaneous cases pending at the end of the previous fiscal year?
    A. 28   B. 56   C. 74   D. 112

26. The head of an agency, in addressing a group of investigators, stated, *Whenever possible, do all you can to satisfy the needs of members of the public.*
    Which of the following is the LEAST acceptable procedure for investigators to use in implementing this policy?
    A. Handle public grievances and frustrations before they can accumulate.
    B. Satisfy public demands even though organizational goals may be compromised.
    C. Interpret rules and regulations reasonably.
    D. Use mass media to enlist support of programs to win public cooperation.

27. Of the following, the MOST important purpose of having a citizen advisory committee in a public agency is to
    A. make both the citizen groups and the public agency more responsive to the total public interest
    B. prevent fraud and mismanagement within the administration of the agency
    C. improve efficiency and encourage greater diligence on the part of agency personnel
    D. prevent the spread of unfavorable publicity about the agency's activities

28. Of the following, the term *public relations* in its application to any public agency is BEST defined as
    A. all the publicity received by the agency
    B. all the direct and indirect contacts between the agency itself and the clientele it deals with
    C. the sum total of efforts which the agency directs toward performing its functions
    D. de-emphasis of the agency's basic obligations which are not popular with its clientele

29. Assume that you receive a phone call from a man who refuses to identify himself and insists that he *knows for a fact* that an investigator on the staff of your agency has destroyed incriminating records upon receipt of a bribe.
    The MOST appropriate action for you to take would be to
    A. refuse to discuss the matter unless the caller gives you his name and additional identification
    B. ask the caller for the facts and the name of the suspected investigator
    C. advise the caller that such a serious charge should be reported immediately to the police department
    D. politely advise the caller to report the facts in a letter to your agency head

30. In a public agency, the FIRST step in adopting a system which will give citizens an opportunity to make complaints against the agency's staff members is to
    A. establish an adequate complaint procedure
    B. design a citizen complaint report form
    C. establish physical facilities where complaints to the agency may be received
    D. initiate a public relations campaign informing the public that they may file complaints

31. Which of the following kinds of information is NOT found in the Official Directory of the City (Green Book)?
    A. The number of persons employed in each city agency
    B. A listing of police station houses and fire engine companies in each borough
    C. The names and addresses of all public high schools and city hospitals in each borough
    D. The names and addresses of federal, state, and city courts located within the city

32. An investigator should contact the State Department of Health to obtain information about persons who are licensed or qualified to practice as
    A. x-ray technicians
    B. physiotherapists
    C. chiropractors
    D. pharmacists

33. An employee complains that the city has refused to pay him some back salary for services he performed last year.
    This employee may bring legal action in the Small Claims Part if the amount of his claim does NOT exceed
    A. $1,000   B. $1,500   C. $300   D. $100

34. Experienced investigators have found that using the question-and-answer method in interviewing a witness, instead of allowing the witness to tell his own story freely and without interruption, MOST often tends to _____ the accuracy of the information given by the witness.
    A. *increase* both the scope and
    B. *increase* the scope but *decrease*
    C. *decrease* both the scope and
    D. *decrease* the scope but *increase*

35. Of the following, the STRONGEST indication that the signature on an important document is a forgery is that the suspected signature
    A. is partly illegible
    B. shows a noticeable trembling in certain letters
    C. shows that the writer retouched several letters
    D. is identical in all respects with a signature known to be genuine

36. Prior to writing the complete and final report at the conclusion of an important case, some investigators prepare an outline or blueprint of the investigative data compiled.
    All of the following are important advantages of preparing such an outline or blueprint EXCEPT that it
    A. results in the omission of less important or minor facts
    B. helps in achieving logical arrangement of the materials
    C. lessens chances of omitting essential details
    D. aids in recognizing irrelevant details

37. In determining the validity of a document, the use of oblique lighting renders certain kinds of alterations visible.
    Which of the following alterations would NOT be exposed by use of the oblique lighting technique?
    A. Abrasions and erasures made in order to change some significant part of a document
    B. Rubber-stamp impressions intended to violate a document but made from a non-genuine stamp
    C. Tears, mutilations, or excessive foldings made deliberately in order to conceal or obscure some damaging feature of the document
    D. Traced writing or writing taken from some pattern or model of genuine writing

38. When an investigator takes the witness stand for the prosecution, he must realize that the opposing counsel will GENERALLY endeavor to portray him as a(n)
    A. individual whose moral character is questionable and whose veracity therefore should be doubted
    B. disinterested collector and retailer of facts
    C. interested party who is trying to convict his client on the basis of insufficient evidence
    D. unprejudiced official with competent professional experience

39. Assume that on a certain day, an investigator finds that he has an excessive number of appointments for interviews and believes that he will be unable to keep them all during the course of the day.
    Of the following, the BEST action he could take is to
    A. ask a fellow investigator to help him conduct a group interview
    B. interview the maximum number that can be interviewed properly and reschedule the others for a future date
    C. proceed according to the established schedule
    D. shorten the length of time spent interviewing each person in order to insure that everyone is interviewed

40. There has been a tendency in recent times to publicize the use of instrumentation such as lie detectors, electronic eavesdropping devices, special cameras, and other technical devices in civil and criminal investigations.
    Of the following statements, the one which expresses a MAJOR weakness which results from relying too much on instrumentation as an investigative aid is:
    A. The use of these technical devices invariably violates the constitutional rights of persons subject to investigations
    B. Excessive publicity in the mass media about the success of these mechanical devices in solving difficult cases destroys their value as investigative aids
    C. These technical devices have a very limited value in cases where abundant physical evidence is available
    D. Inexperienced investigators are prone to place their faith in technical methods to the neglect of the more basic investigative procedures

KEY (CORRECT ANSWERS)

1. D	11. D	21. D	31. A
2. B	12. B	22. B	32. A
3. A	13. D	23. D	33. B
4. C	14. C	24. A	34. B
5. A	15. C	25. D	35. D
6. D	16. C	26. B	36. A
7. C	17. D	27. A	37. B
8. B	18. A	28. B	38. C
9. A	19. D	29. B	39. B
10. B	20. C	30. A	40. D

EXAMINATION SECTION
TEST 1

DIRECTIONS: Each question or incomplete statement is followed by several suggested answers or completions. Select the one that BEST answers the question or completes the statement. *PRINT THE LETTER OF THE CORRECT ANSWER IN THE SPACE AT THE RIGHT.*

1. During an interview with a witness, the investigator should carefully observe the witness's gestures and facial expressions.
   To interpret the meaning of these actions, the investigator should do all of the following EXCEPT to

   A. try to *read* the situation in which a puzzling gesture is used
   B. ask questions that relate specifically to the gesture
   C. take an educated guess based on past experience
   D. rely on the standard meaning of the gesture

   1.____

2. Of the following, the MOST important skill for a supervisor of investigators to possess is the ability to

   A. communicate effectively
   B. obtain the respect of his staff
   C. remain calm in pressure situations
   D. develop high morale among his subordinates

   2.____

3. Following are three statements concerning the preparation by an investigator of a written statement taken from a witness:
   I. Have each page initialed by the witness
   II. Correct and initial any mistakes in grammar that are made by the witness
   III. Leave space between paragraphs to facilitate the addition of notes and comments.

   Which of the following correctly classifies the above statements into those that are valid and those that are not?

   A. I is valid, but II and III are not.
   B. II and III are valid, but I is not.
   C. III is valid, but I and II are not.
   D. I and II are valid, but III is not.

   3.____

4. Assume, as an investigator, you are questioning an employee of your agency suspected of misstating previous work experience on his employment application. You notice that the employee is reluctant to admit that his previous statements were inaccurate.
   The one of the following that is the BEST method of obtaining the truth from this employee would be for you to

   A. tell him that his job is not in jeopardy
   B. make him feel he is not being criticized
   C. have him discuss the matter with your supervisor
   D. allow him to correct any inaccuracies on his employment application

   4.____

5. If several witnesses describing the same occurrence agree on most details, the investigator should then

   A. determine whether or not these witnesses were in communication with each other
   B. assume that such agreement means that the recollection was correct
   C. assume that the witnesses' observations were incorrect since two or more people usually will not agree on the same details
   D. question the witnesses again, concentrating on the details on which they differ

6. In trying to obtain a statement from a hospitalized individual who is unable to receive visitors, it would be BEST for an investigator

   A. draw up a statement from his own knowledge of the case and ask a hospital staff member to have the patient sign the statement when he is well
   B. contact the patient's family and arrange for an appointment to see the patient as soon as his condition permits
   C. leave a message at the hospital for the patient to contact him when he is available to receive visitors
   D. appear at the hospital with proper identification and request official permission from the hospital administrator to speak with the patient

7. Among employment specialists, it is generally agreed that the value of character references on employment applications is

   A. *limited,* chiefly because such references are written only by personal friends of the applicant
   B. *significant,* chiefly because information they transmit is unavailable from other sources
   C. *limited,* chiefly because they tend to give only favorable information
   D. *significant,* chiefly because they have direct knowledge of the applicant's abilities

8. The MOST important requirement of a person who is testifying about a criminal act that he witnessed is that he

   A. was conscious and attentive during the crime
   B. is a respected and trustworthy member of the community
   C. is without a prior criminal record
   D. gives a consistent account of the details of the crime

9. Assume that, after taking a written statement from Employee A, an investigator is about to obtain his signature. He wants to ask Employee B, a co-worker, to witness the signing but Employee B is not available at that time.
   To expedite the investigation, it would be MOST desirable for the investigator to

   A. have Employee A sign the statement and obtain Employee B's signature at a later time
   B. ask an available disinterested party to witness Employee A's signature
   C. witness Employee A's signature himself
   D. have Employee A sign when Employee B is available

10. Witnesses are usually MOST willing to discuss an event when they are

    A. disinterested in the subsequent investigation
    B. interviewed immediately following the event
    C. interviewed for the first time
    D. known by the investigator

11. To determine the former addresses of a person who has moved several times within the same locality, it would be BEST to contact

    A. the Post Office   B. insurance companies
    C. public utilities   D. banking institutions

12. The one of the following that is CHARACTERISTIC of the interview as compared with the observation approach to investigation is that an interview generally

    A. requires more time to complete adequately
    B. is more likely to result in incomplete information
    C. is less applicable to the study of an individual's beliefs and values
    D. is less costly to conduct

13. The use of slang on the part of an investigator when questioning subjects is generally

    A. *inadvisable*; chiefly because it leads to misinterpretations
    B. *advisable*; chiefly because it will insure objective responses
    C. *inadvisable*; chiefly because it can compromise the investigator's dignity
    D. *advisable*; chiefly because it can promote ease of speech and understanding

14. Assume that a job applicant claims on his employment application that he has just recently become a United States citizen.
    Of the following, it would be MOST appropriate for you, in verifying this matter, to consult the

    A. Department of State   B. Treasury Department
    C. Immigration and Naturalization Service   D. Department of Justice

15. If an investigator receives an anonymous phone call from a person claiming to have knowledge of criminal behavior in an agency which is currently being investigated, the investigator should

    A. listen politely and make notes on the important facts given by the informant
    B. tell the informant what has already been discovered and ask if he has anything to add
    C. question the informant to obtain all the information he has
    D. ask the informant to submit his information in writing

16. When interviewing a child, an investigator should keep in mind the fact that children

    A. are psychologically incapable of giving an accurate statement
    B. usually have faulty perception
    C. are easily led into making incorrect statements since they tend to agree with the questioner
    D. will often make statements which are pure fantasy because they are not as observant as adults

17. Following are three statements concerning the use of an investigator's notebook in court:
    I. A looseleaf-type notebook creates a more favorable impression in the courtroom than a bound notebook because the former permits the removal of pages unrelated to the case in question
    II. An investigator's notebook should be written in ink, not pencil, because of the need for permanence
    III. The notebook should ideally contain the notes of only one investigation so that its scrutiny will not involve the disclosure of information relating to other investigations

    Which of the following CORRECTLY classifies the above statements into those which are valid and those which are not valid?

    A. I and III are valid, but II is not.
    B. I and II are valid, but III is not.
    C. I is valid, but II and III are not.
    D. II and III are valid, but I is not.

18. The first three digits of a social security number are coded for the

    A. age of the cardholder when the card was issued
    B. cardholder's initials
    C. year the card was issued
    D. area in which the card was issued

19. Two methods of obtaining personal background information are the personal interview and the telephone inquiry.
    As compared with the latter, the personal type of interview USUALLY _____ flexibility in questioning _____ frankness.

    A. permits; but discourages
    B. restricts; but encourages
    C. permits; and encourages
    D. restricts; and discourages

20. One of the important functions of investigators is to perform surveillances without the knowledge of the subject. If a subject thinks he is being followed, he is LEAST likely to react by

    A. reversing his course to see whether anyone else does likewise
    B. boarding a subway car and getting off just before it pulls out
    C. attempting to pass the surveillant several times to view him face-to-face
    D. using the services of a *convoy* to observe whether he is being followed

21. Assume that you are conducting an interview with a prospective employee who is of limited mental ability and low socio-economic status.
    Of the following, it is MOST likely that asking him many open-ended questions about his work experience would cause him to respond

    A. articulately
    B. reluctantly
    C. comfortably
    D. aggressively

22. Assume, as an investigator, you want a witness to sign a statement. Which of the following phrases is MOST likely to secure his signature?

    A. I would appreciate it if you would sign the statement at this time.
    B. Sign the statement where indicated.
    C. Sign the statement when you get the chance.
    D. If the statement is generally correct, please sign it.

23. During an interview, a subject makes statements an investigator knows to be false. Of the following, it would be MOST appropriate for the investigator to

    A. point out each inconsistency in the subject's story as soon as the investigator detects it
    B. interrupt the subject and request that he submit to a polygraph test
    C. allow the subject to continue talking until he becomes enmeshed in his lies and then confront him with his falsehoods
    D. allow the subject to finish what he has to say and then explicitly inform him that it is a crime to lie to a government employee

24. One of the major objectives of a pre-employment interview is to get the interviewee to respond freely to inquiries. The one of the following actions that would be MOST likely to restrict the conversation of the interviewee would be for the investigator to

    A. keep a stenographic record of the interviewee's statements
    B. ask questions requiring complete explanations
    C. pose direct, specific questions to the interviewee
    D. allow the interviewee to respond to questions at his own pace

25. A list of the names, addresses, and titles of city employees is made available to the public by the

    A. civil service commission
    B. comptroller's office
    C. mayor's office
    D. municipal reference and research center

KEY (CORRECT ANSWERS)

1. D		11. C
2. A		12. D
3. A		13. D
4. B		14. C
5. A		15. C
6. B		16. C
7. C		17. D
8. A		18. D
9. B		19. C
10. B		20. C

21. B
22. B
23. C
24. A
25. D

EXAMINATION SECTION
TEST 1

DIRECTIONS: Each question or incomplete statement is followed by several suggested answers or completions. Select the one that BEST answers the question or completes the statement. *PRINT THE LETTER OF THE CORRECT ANSWER IN THE SPACE AT THE RIGHT.*

1. Which amendments to the Constitution limit the power of the federal government to discriminate in employment?

    A. 2nd and 12th
    B. 3rd and 8th
    C. 4th and 9th
    D. 5th and 14th

2. In sexual harassment investigations involving co-workers, the investigator should look most closely at the

    A. presumption of knowledge on the part of the co-worker
    B. nature of the behavior
    C. overall effect of the co-worker's behavior on the workplace atmosphere
    D. relative power of the co-worker compared to the plaintiff

3. Which of the following causes of action may be indicated if an HIV-infected individual knowingly exposes another person to the disease without forewarning?
    I. Negligence
    II. Battery
    III. Intentional Infliction of Emotional Distress
    IV. Fraud

    The CORRECT answer is:

    A. I, II   B. II, III   C. III, IV   D. I, IV

4. Which of the following is NOT a federal requirement involving child labor?

    A. Children attending school and at least 14 years old are permitted to work outside of school hours provided they work no more than 3 hours on a school day.
    B. Under no conditions may a student in grades up to 12 work in jobs declared hazardous by the Secretary of Labor.
    C. Children attending school and at least 14 years old are prohibited from working more than 8 hours on a non-school day.
    D. Work may not begin before 7 A.M. or end after 7 P.M. during the school year.

5. Which of the following federal laws established the Equal Employment Opportunity Commission (EEOC)?
   The

    A. Fair Labor Standards Act of 1938
    B. Landrum-Griffin Act of 1959
    C. Civil Rights Act of 1964
    D. Age Discrimination in Employment Act of 1967

6. The *new construction* requirements of the Americans with Disabilities Act (ADA) of 1990 apply to buildings which were first occupied after

    A. March 11, 1990
    B. August 11, 1991
    C. January 26, 1993
    D. November 4, 1995

7. Workers who believe they have been terminated as a result of a *whistleblower* who reported unsafe workplace conditions can generally file a complaint with OSHA within _____ of the alleged incident.

    A. 30 days   B. 90 days   C. 180 days   D. 1 year

8. In general, a landlord is entitled to reject a rental application for each of the following reasons EXCEPT

    A. insufficient income
    B. past negative behavior such as property damage
    C. marital status or cohabitation that conflicts with the landlord's moral principles
    D. bad credit history

9. Under the terms of the Employee Retirement Income Security Act (ERISA) of 1974, employers have several options for granting vesting rights to employees. Which of the following is not one of these?

    A. Ten-year vesting
    B. Five-year vesting
    C. Graded vesting
    D. 50% vesting when the total of an employee's age and length of employment equals 45 years

10. Regardless of whether the EEOC has completed its own investigation, an employee who wants to bring a private civil suit against an employer is entitled to do so _____ days after filing the complaint.

    A. 30   B. 60   C. 180   D. 300

11. To which of the following actions, performed by an owner, landlord, or tenant seeking a roommate, do the discrimination provisions of the Federal Fair Housing Act apply?
    I. Refuse to negotiate for housing
    II. Set different terms, conditions or privileges for sale or rental of a dwelling
    III. Persuade owners to sell or rent
    IV. Provide different housing services or facilities
    The CORRECT answer is:

    A. I, III
    B. II, IV
    C. II, III
    D. I, II, III, IV

12. Each of the following is an eligibility requirement for an employee seeking benefits under the Family Medical Leave Act (FMLA) of 1993 EXCEPT that he or she must

    A. have worked for the covered employer for a total of at least 12 months
    B. not be classified as an agricultural worker
    C. have worked for a minimum of 1,250 hours in the previous 12 months
    D. work at a location within the United States or its territories or possessions

13. Which of the following types of immigrants is NOT protected by the discrimination provisions of federal immigration legislation?

    A. Refugees
    B. Permanent residents
    C. Asylees
    D. Undocumented residents

14. The Equal Access Act of 1984, which was intended to protect religious speech in an educational environment, applies to _____ receiving federal funds.

    A. all K-12 public schools
    B. all colleges and universities
    C. public secondary schools
    D. public or private secondary schools

15. Once a job offer has been made, an employer may condition employment upon a satisfactory medical examination if it can be demonstrated that

    A. all applicants have to submit to the same examination
    B. the results of the examination will be kept confidential
    C. the examination does not specifically test for disability
    D. the results of the examination had no relevance to the hiring decision

16. Under the provisions of the Americans with Disabilities Act (ADA) of 1990, van-accessible parking spaces for disabled individuals must have an access aisle that is at least _____ feet wide.

    A. 4   B. 6   C. 8   D. 10

17. To which of the following types of organizations would federal AIDS discrimination legislation apply?
    I. A bona fide private membership club
    II. Corporations wholly owned by the United States
    III. Employment agencies
    IV. Corporations wholly owned by an Indian tribe
    The CORRECT answer is:

    A. II, III   B. III only   C. IV only   D. I, II

18. Federal minimum wage legislation requires that overtime work be compensated at a rate that is at least _____% of the rate of pay for normal working hours.

    A. 100   B. 125   C. 150   D. 200

19. In terms of human rights, *deferral states* are those that

    A. rely on the EEOC for investigation into claims of discrimination
    B. have shorter time limits on filing claims
    C. send claims directly to a federal district court
    D. make their own investigations prior to those of the EEOC

20. Which of the following federal laws awarded attorney's fees and costs to parents who were successful in litigation?
The

   A. Rehabilitation Act of 1973
   B. Education for All Handicapped Children Act of 1975
   C. Handicapped Children's Protection Act (HCPA) of 1986
   D. Individuals with Disabilities Education Act (IDEA) of 1997

21. In AIDS litigation, which of the following is most likely to be the context for a cause of action for negligence?

   A. A tainted blood transfusion
   B. A sexual relationship
   C. The physician/patient relationship
   D. Exclusion from certain educational activities

22. In 1980, the EEOC determined that

   A. gay, lesbian, or bisexual persons would be granted the same protections from discrimination as those of other groups
   B. sexual harassment is a form of gender discrimination that is prohibited under federal law
   C. privately-owned organizations are not subject to the same employment regulations as other groups
   D. persons with physical disabilities would be granted the same protections from discrimination as those of other groups

23. Which of the following would be protected from hiring discrimination by the Americans with Disabilities Act (ADA)-provided that he or she is qualified to perform the essential functions of the job?
A(n)
   I. alcoholic
   II. person with AIDS
   III. person addicted to illegal drugs who is currently using
   IV. person with Down's Syndrome

The CORRECT answer is:

   A. II only
   B. II, IV
   C. I, II, IV
   D. IV only

24. In general, the maximum civil penalty for employers who violate OSHA provisions is

   A. $10,000   B. $70,000   C. $250,000   D. $500,000

25. The Supreme Court's 1974 ruling in the case *Lemon v. Kurtzman* established a precedent for how public schools were expected to deal with the issue of

   A. attention deficit disorder (ADD)
   B. safety
   C. religious activity
   D. desegregation

KEY (CORRECT ANSWERS)

1. D
2. B
3. C
4. B
5. C

6. C
7. A
8. C
9. B
10. B

11. D
12. B
13. D
14. C
15. A

16. C
17. B
18. C
19. D
20. C

21. A
22. B
23. C
24. B
25. C

TEST 2

DIRECTIONS: Each question or incomplete statement is followed by several suggested answers or completions. Select the one that BEST answers the question or completes the statement. *PRINT THE LETTER OF THE CORRECT ANSWER IN THE SPACE AT THE RIGHT.*

1. Under the provisions of the Family Medical Leave Act (FMLA) of 1993, which of the following are considered to be members of an employee's immediate family?
    I. Spouse
    II. Children under 18
    III. Stepchildren under 18
    IV. Parents
   The CORRECT answer is:

   A. I, II
   B. I, II, III
   C. I, II, IV
   D. II, IV

2. Which of the following groups are generally covered by federal equal employment opportunity laws?

   A. Indian tribes
   B. Agricultural workers
   C. Aliens employed by United States employers in foreign countries
   D. Publicly elected officials and members of their personal staff

3. In order to prevail in an age discrimination lawsuit, an employee has the burden of proving a prima facie case, which includes a demonstration of each of the following EXCEPT

   A. the employee is a member of the protected class, i.e., over the stipulated age
   B. the employee was adversely affected by the employer's action
   C. age was a determining factor in the employer's action
   D. the employer's action was willful

4. In determining whether disparate impact in a workplace is illegal, the EEOC's standard is that the rate of selection for minority applicants must be _____ the rate for whites.

   A. at least half
   B. just over half
   C. at least four-fifths
   D. equal to

5. Most likely to be covered by the provisions of the Occupational Safety and Health Act (OSHA) is a

   A. self-employed person
   B. transportation worker
   C. textile worker
   D. miner

6. Of the following, _____ is a permissible means by which an employer may attempt to influence the decisions of employees.

   A. closing down a plant permanently after an election to unionize
   B. conferring economic benefits on employees prior to an election
   C. locking out employees in order to prevent them from working
   D. coercively interrogating employees about union activities

7. Which of the following are guaranteed protection from mandatory retirement under the provisions of the Age Discrimination in Employment Act?

    A. Air traffic controllers
    B. Tenured university faculty
    C. Senior middle managers at a private employer of more than 20 people
    D. Employees whose retirement pensions are worth $44,000 or more

8. Which of the following types of employers is most likely to be exempt from the provisions of the Fair Labor Standards Act?

    A. Local government agencies
    B. Employers who engage in interstate commerce
    C. Skilled laborers who employ apprentices
    D. Employers with annual sales of $500,000 or more

9. Which of the following types of rental units is most likely to be excepted from some of the federal statutes on housing discrimination?
A

    A. detached unit that is on the same parcel of real property as the residence of the landlord
    B. single room in an owner-occupied home that does not house other lodgers
    C. multi-room, single-family home in a residential area in which most homes are inhabited by the owners
    D. single unit in an apartment complex

10. The *Opportunity Wage Provision* of federal wage law applies to employees who are

    A. under 18 years of age during their first 90 days of employment
    B. under 20 years of age during their first 90 days of employment
    C. under 18 years of age at any time during their employment
    D. legal immigrants

11. Under the provisions of federal law, which of the following are legitimate practices for a creditor to undertake in dealing with an elderly client?
    I. Closing a credit account based on the client's advanced age
    II. Using age as one of its factors in a credit scoring system
    III. Considering whether a client's level of income will continue for a particular duration
    IV. Denying credit due to an applicant's advanced age due to the default risk
The CORRECT answer is:

    A. I, IV
    B. II, III
    C. I, II, III
    D. I, II, IV

12. Each of the following is a factor involved in establishing the *severe and pervasive* standard used in sexual harassment investigations EXCEPT

    A. whether the behavior was directed at one or more individuals
    B. the position of the offender
    C. whether the behavior was welcome or not
    D. the type of behavior (physical/verbal)

13. Under the provisions of the Family Medical Leave Act (FMLA) of 1993, a *key employee* is one who is

   A. directly or indirectly involved in at least 25 percent of all company revenues
   B. among the highest-paid ten percent of employees within 75 miles of the workplace
   C. the administrative head of any division which comprises 10 percent or more of the total number of employees
   D. among the highest-paid ten percent of employees in a management position

14. Which of the following types of employers is most likely to be subject to the provisions of the Employee Polygraph Protection Act?

   A. Private providers of security services
   B. Private manufacturers of Pharmaceuticals
   C. Private software manufacturers
   D. Federal government agencies

15. Which of the following constitutes *sponsorship* of religious activity in schools?
   I. Assignment of a teacher to a religious meeting for custodial purposes
   II. Expending public funds for the incidental costs of providing space for student-initiated meetings
   III. Payment to a teacher for monitoring a student religious club
   IV. Using school media to announce meetings of student religious groups

   The CORRECT answer is:

   A. II, III
   B. IV *only*
   C. I *only*
   D. None of the above

16. Federal labor laws permit an employer from barring an employee from soliciting other workers to engage in union activity when the

   A. employer can prove that the formation of a union will cause undue hardship
   B. employee is actually engaged in paid work
   C. employee is on company property
   D. employee is in areas that are open to the public

17. Rules on drug testing in schools

   A. are prohibited from being applied in public schools
   B. are entirely up to the school administration
   C. must follow certain federal guidelines
   D. are governed by guidelines that differ from state to state

18. Approximately what sector of the United States population is victimized by about 1/3 of all consumer fraud?

   A. Minors (under the age of 18)
   B. The elderly
   C. Young married couples
   D. Non-English speakers

19. Which of the following types of prayer is/are permitted in public schools?
    I. Voluntary participation in classroom prayer
    II. Moments of silent meditation for a classroom
    III. Student-led graduation prayers
    IV. Individual students praying quietly and unobtrusively
    The CORRECT answer is:

    A. I, II, IV   B. II, III
    C. IV *only*   D. I, III

    19._____

20. Under the Americans with Disabilities Act (ADA) of 1990, privately-owned buildings are entitled to an *elevator exemption* if they are under three stories or

    A. are located on a grade of at least 10%
    B. are not devoted entirely to private residence
    C. consist of floors that are each under 3,000 square feet
    D. have been constructed after 1995

    20._____

21. Title _____ of the Civil Rights Act of 1964 prohibits discrimination in federally-financed programs.

    A. II   B. IV   C. VI   D. IX

    21._____

22. Each of the following is a federal law which affects AIDS and one's right to an education EXCEPT the

    A. Civil Rights Act of 1964
    B. Rehabilitation Act of 1974
    C. Americans with Disabilities Act of 1990
    D. Individuals with Disabilities Act (IDEA) of 1997

    22._____

23. In the 1995 case *Vernonia v. Acton,* the Supreme Court ruled that a certain segment of the student population would be subject to drug and alcohol testing no matter what the circumstance. Which group was specified in this ruling?

    A. Student athletes
    B. Students with a known history of substance abuse
    C. Students whose parents requested testing
    D. Students in leadership or government positions

    23._____

24. Under certain conditions, some types of properties may be exempt from federal fair housing law. Which of the following is NOT one of these?

    A. All owner-occupied buildings
    B. Property occupied solely by persons who are 62 or older
    C. Property owned by religious organizations
    D. Property owned by private clubs

    24._____

25. Which of the following is TRUE of an economic strike?

    A. Employees remain eligible to vote.
    B. Employees must be reinstated even if the employer must discharge permanent replacement workers.
    C. The employer is under no obligation to reinstate a striker if his/her position has been filled during the strike.
    D. The employer can hire replacement workers only on a temporary basis.

KEY (CORRECT ANSWERS)

1.	C	11.	B
2.	B	12.	C
3.	D	13.	B
4.	C	14.	C
5.	C	15.	D
6.	C	16.	B
7.	C	17.	D
8.	C	18.	B
9.	B	19.	C
10.	B	20.	C

21.	C
22.	A
23.	A
24.	A
25.	C

EXAMINATION SECTION
TEST 1

DIRECTIONS: Each question or incomplete statement is followed by several suggested answers or completions. Select the one the BEST answers the question or completes the statement. *PRINT THE LETTER OF THE CORRECT ANSWER IN THE SPACE AT THE RIGHT.*

1. The pivotal factor in determining whether an event is an "emergency" is typically 1.____

    A. the degree to which the event was unexpected
    B. whether the event requires supplemental efforts to save lives and protect property, public health and safety
    C. whether the event causes a loss of life
    D. the severity and magnitude of the damage caused by the event

2. Which of the following is an activity that is included within the authority of the Federal Emergency Management Agency (FEMA)? 2.____

    A. Physically rescuing disaster victims
    B. Establishing building standards and zoning regulations that will help mitigate the adverse effects of a disaster
    C. Providing mobile communications systems that open emergency lines when commercial networks are down
    D. Taking the lead role in recovery efforts after a disaster

3. Which of the following is NOT a member of the command staff under the incident command system? 3.____

    A. Information officer
    B. Information officer
    C. Logistics officer
    D. Safety officer

4. The Federal Response Plan generally performs each of the following functions, EXCEPT 4.____

    A. grouping types of federal assistance under twelve emergency support functions
    B. designating a primary agency and support agency for each emergency support function
    C. providing loans and grants to state and local governments
    D. explaining how the federal government mobilizes and supports state and local response efforts

5. Under the Federal Response Plan, FEMA is the lead agency for the emergency support functions (ESFs) of 5.____
    I. Resources Support
    II. Communications
    III. Information and Planning
    IV. Urban Search and Rescue

    A. I only
    B. II and III

171

C. III and IV
D. I, II, III and IV

Questions 6 through 10 refer to the following scenario:

A freak winter storm has stalled out over Summit County, dropping a record 25 inches of snow in a single night. More snow is forecast over the next 2 days, and the temperature is supposed to remain well below freezing for at least the next week or so.

All over the county, stranded motorists and residents without power have overwhelmed the 911 dispatch center. Although road crews have been activated, many of the drivers can't get to their trucks. Local and state emergency operations centers have been activated, and a local state of emergency has been declared. The incident commander has set up the command post at the police precinct house in the heart of the downtown in the county seat. The incident will require a large number and range of resources.

6. The incident commander will activate general staff positions that will each be led by a(n)   6.____

    A. branch supervisor
    B. staging area manager
    C. division supervisor
    D. section chief

7. Because this incident covers a large geographic area and is likely to continue for a period   7.____
   of time, the incident commander should probably establish a(n)

    A. base
    B. casualty collection point
    C. staging area
    D. camp

8. After several hours, the operations section activates several staging areas, divisions,   8.____
   branches, and groups. Under the ICS's principle of unity of command, which of these
   managers are likely to report directly to the incident commander?

    A. Only the operations section chief
    B. The operations section chief and the staging area managers
    C. Branch supervisors and division leaders
    D. Any of the above managers

9. The incident commander has requested that the state department of transportation send   9.____
   road-clearing equipment to help with the incident. The department's representative
   would communicate with the incident command staff's

    A. information officer
    B. planning section chief
    C. liaison officer
    D. facilities unit manager

10. After several days, a worker at the ICP is told that his position will be demobilized at the conclusion of the current operational period. The worker should
    I. update all files and records
    II. complete all work in progress, unless otherwise directed
    III. return or otherwise transfer custody of all equipment that he has signed for
    IV. brief his relief or immediate supervisor on the status of all work, pending assignments, needs, and special situations

    A. I and II
    B. II only
    C. II, III and IV
    D. I, II, III and IV

11. As defined by disaster relief agencies, weapons of mass destruction (WMDs) include
    I. radiation or radioactivity
    II. diseases or organisms
    III. toxic or poisonous chemicals, or their precursors

    A. I only
    B. I and II
    C. II and III
    D. I, II and III

12. Without a presidential declaration of disaster, federal disaster assistance may include each of the following, EXCEPT

    A. firefighting assistance
    B. tax refunds
    C. unemployment insurance
    D. search and rescue

13. Typically, hazard analysis determines
    I. how hazards are likely to affect the community
    II. when the next disaster is most likely to occur
    III. how well the community will be able to respond to a disaster
    IV. the costs of risk

    A. I only
    B. I and II
    C. I, III and IV
    D. I, II, III and IV

14. Each of the following is a responsibility of an incident commander, EXCEPT

    A. managing assigned resources
    B. maintaining accountability
    C. coordinating the community-wide response
    D. protecting life and property

15. Federal mission assignments

    A. may be requested by counties and cities
    B. are usually issued to meet all eligible requests for federal assistance

C. can be issued before a disaster declaration
D. meet needs that exceed state and local government resources

16. The federal government's most important contribution to hazard mitigation efforts in any given community will likely be to

   A. ensure that all federal facilities in the community are built or retrofitted to reduce hazard vulnerability
   B. provide adequate funding for hazard mitigation
   C. take a leadership role in the planning stages of hazard mitigation activities
   D. controlling the costs of over-ambitious state and local mitigation programs

17. "Unity of command" in the incident command system refers to the fact that

   A. each member reports to only one supervisor
   B. each member reports to the incident commander
   C. all members share responsibility for decision-making in the operations function of incident response
   D. all members share responsibility for overall incident management

18. An emergency operations plan (EOP)
   I. assigns responsibility for mitigation concerns to local officials
   II. explains how people and property will be protected in emergencies
   III. identifies resources available for use during response and recovery operations
   IV. establishes lines of authority

   A. I and II
   B. II and III
   C. II, III and IV
   D. III and IV

19. What component of emergency management is defined as "sustained actions taken to reduce or eliminate the long-term risk to people and property from hazards and their effects?"

   A. Risk analysis
   B. Vulnerability assessment
   C. Preparedness
   D. Mitigation

20. Under federal regulations, all organizations that respond to _____ incidents are required to use the incident command system.
   I. flood
   II. fire
   III. hazardous materials
   IV. hurricane or tornado

   A. I only
   B. I, II and IV
   C. II and III
   D. III only

21. Which of the following is a federal program that funds state and local pre-disaster flood-plain planning and projects?

   A. Flood Mitigation Assistance
   B. 406
   C. Increased Cost of Compliance
   D. Hazard Mitigation Grant

22. The Community Rating System is an element of the National Flood Insurance Program that can

   I. decrease a community's flood insurance premiums
   II. provide an incentive for new flood mitigation, planning, and preparedness activities
   III. increase a community's flood insurance premiums
   IV. be made available to non-NFIP communities

   A. I only
   B. I and II
   C. I and III
   D. I, II, III and IV

23. At the scene of a major storm, an operations section chief understands that her span of control will be exceeded when the requested resources arrive. There is a need to assign resources geographically. One effective way to maintain her span of control would be to assign personnel to

   A. units
   B. divisions
   C. bases
   D. strike teams

24. The federal emergency public assistance program provides funds to

   A. businesses for economic recovery after a disaster
   B. individuals for temporary housing
   C. private nonprofit universities and colleges for mitigation research
   D. state and local governments for response and recovery activities

25. The federal cost share for _____ programs is 100%

   A. emergency work
   B. crisis counseling
   C. permanent, restorative work
   D. "other needs" assistance

KEY (CORRECT ANSWERS)

1.	B	11.	D
2.	C	12.	C
3.	C	13.	A
4.	C	14.	C
5.	C	15.	D
6.	D	16.	A
7.	A	17.	A
8.	A	18.	C
9.	C	19.	D
10.	D	20.	D

21. A
22. B
23. B
24. D
25. B

TEST 2

DIRECTIONS: Each question or incomplete statement is followed by several suggested answers or completions. Select the one the BEST answers the question or completes the statement. *PRINT THE LETTER OF THE CORRECT ANSWER IN THE SPACE AT THE RIGHT.*

1. An effective emergency management plan is characterized by
   - I. overlapping command functions between jurisdictions
   - II. modular organization
   - III. separate police and fire command posts
   - IV. common terminology

   A. I only
   B. I and III
   C. II and IV
   D. I, II, III and IV

   1.____

2. Emergency Management Mutual Aid (EMMA) is
   - I. a means of establishing federal control over a disaster situation
   - II. coordinated by FEMA
   - III. a system for moving emergency management personnel to other jurisdictions that need assistance
   - IV. a way of providing continuous 24-hour-a-day management during a disaster

   A. I only
   B. I and II
   C. III and IV
   D. I, II, III and IV

   2.____

3. A combination of personnel and equipment-such as a search and rescue team and an EMS team assigned to locate and treat several people trapped in the debris of a building collapse-is usually called a(n) _____ in the incident command system.

   A. division
   B. task force
   C. unit
   D. strike team

   3.____

4. In the Federal Response Plan, an Emergency Support Team (EST)

   A. responds to presidential disaster or emergency declarations
   B. coordinates multi-state and multi-regional operations
   C. deploys to high-visibility, catastrophic disasters
   D. coordinates early response operations with the state

   4.____

5. Disaster loans for homeowners, renters, business owners and nonprofit organizations are administered and funded by the

   A. Small Business Administration (SBA)
   B. Department of Housing and Urban Development (HUD)
   C. Federal Emergency Management Agency (FEMA)
   D. American Red Cross

   5.____

Questions 6 through 9 refer to the following scenario:

At around midnight, the 911 call center receives a call from the maintenance department of a local nursing home. Fire alarms have sounded in the west residential hall, which is a four-story win Smoke can be seen from the fourth floor. The hall houses 300 residents, and there are reports that some residents are trapped inside.

Fire Battalion 6 is immediately dispatched. After an initial assessment, the Battalion Chief requests a general alarm and assigns a safety officer, a liaison officer, and a full general staff.

6. The first priority of the planning section will be to

    A. develop response goals and objectives
    B. monitor safety conditions
    C. assess the resource needs of the situation
    D. contact other agencies assigned to the incident

7. In addition to the incident command post, the incident will require
    I. at least one staging area
    II. several bases
    III. a casualty collection point (CCP)
    IV. a camp

    A. I only
    B. I and III
    C. II, III and IV
    D. I, II, III and IV

8. A local counselor, a trauma expert, is asked to help calm arriving family members who fear their loved ones are trapped in the fire. Upon arriving at the scene, the counselor should check in with the _____ unit of the planning section.

    A. medical
    B. ground support
    C. facilities
    D. resources

9. Search and rescue teams are able to locate most, but not all, of the victims from the building. After some time, it becomes clear that these victims are dead. The incident commander has requested that several local churches, synagogues, and mosques help provide short-term shelter for the newly homeless victims of the fire. He has also requested the help of several local mental health professionals to assist the family members who are griev ing for the dead. After representatives from these outside agencies check in, they should work with the

    A. liaison officer
    B. planning section chief
    C. logistics section chief
    D. safety officer

10. Which of the following is an activity that is NOT included within the authority of the Federal Emergency Management Agency (FEMA)?

    A. Administering the National Flood Insurance Program
    B. Providing "buy out" funding to relocate homes and businesses away from high-risk areas
    C. Creating risk assessment maps to aid local planners
    D. Operating temporary feeding stations or shelters after a disaster

11. Under the incident command system, which of the following has the authority to bypass the chain of command when necessary?

    A. Logistics officer
    B. Liaison officer
    C. Operations section chief
    D. Safety officer

12. Which of the following agencies provides AmeriCorps assistance following a disaster?

    A. Peace Corps
    B. Corporation for National Service (CNS)
    C. Department of Labor
    D. Department of Health and Human Services

13. A community that wants to participate in the National Flood Insurance Program must
    I. elevate roadbeds and homes that lie within a floodplain
    II. eliminate all known flood hazards
    III. adopt and enforce a floodplain management ordinance
    IV. conduct a flood hazard assessment

    A. I only
    B. II only
    C. III only
    D. III and IV

14. In federal mission assignment processing, which of the following typically occurs FIRST?

    A. the mission assignment is routed in the National Emergency Management Information System (NEMIS) for electronic signature
    B. the mission assignment coordinator or action tracker enters information from the action request form into the National Emergency Management Information System (NEMIS)
    C. funds are obligated in the financial system for mission assignment
    D. an operations section chief directs issuance of a mission assignment

15. Upon arrival at the scene of a disaster, the response team's FIRST action would most likely be to

    A. form initial opinions about the incident's requirements
    B. appoint a logistics officer
    C. develop an action plan
    D. establish a media liaison

16. The predicted impact that a hazard would have on people, services, facilities, and structures in a community is known specifically as

    A. vulnerability
    B. hazard identification
    C. risk
    D. incidence

17. A state that is considered a "Managing State" under FEMA's mitigtion programs
    I. contributes up to 80 percent of HMGP project costs
    II. has concluded a Memorandum of Understanding (MOU) with FEMA to perform specific Hazard Mitigation Grant Program project review functions
    III. reviews infrastructure projects for mitigation opportunities
    IV. can approve Hazard Mitigation Grant Program projects subject to environmental review.

    A. I and III
    B. II and IV
    C. II, III and IV
    D. I, II, III and IV

18. Which of the following is NOT a member of the general staff of an incident command system?

    A. Logistics officer
    B. Operations section chief
    C. Safety officer
    D. Incident commander

19. The lists of hazards developed during a hazard analysis will be compiled using
    I. community records
    II. historical data
    III. existing hazard analyses
    IV. computer simulations

    A. I and II
    B. I, II, and III
    C. III only
    D. I, II, III and IV

20. Which of the following is NEVER an allowable cost that can be submitted by states to federal disaster reimbursement programs?

    A. advertisements seeking temporary personnel for the disaster recovery efforts
    B. services of state building inspectors
    C. expenses incurred by the Officer of the Governor
    D. messenger/courier services

21. The STAPLE criteria are a means of determining the feasibility of _____ actions.

    A. mitigation
    B. preparation
    C. response
    D. recovery

22. An incident command system has been fully expanded to accommodate large-scale operations. In this case, the staging area manager would report to the

    A. operations section chief
    B. incident commander
    C. facilities unit leader
    D. logistics officer

23. At the state level, which of the following actions would occur at the "response" phase of disaster response?

    A. Issuing a disaster proclamation
    B. Requesting federal assistance
    C. Conducting mitigation efforts
    D. Activating and staffing an emergency operations center

24. The responsibility for identifying hazards and launching mitigation strategies typically belongs to

    A. the federal government
    B. state governments
    C. local governments
    D. businesses and individuals

25. FEMA's role in disaster assistance includes
    I. responding to requests from local governments
    II. managing the president's Disaster Relief Fund
    III. evaluating a state's request for a presidential declaration
    IV. advising the president on whether or not to make a declaration

    A. I and II
    B. III only
    C. II, III and IV
    D. I, II, III and IV

KEY (CORRECT ANSWERS)

1.	C	11.	D
2.	C	12.	B
3.	B	13.	C
4.	B	14.	D
5.	A	15.	A
6.	C	16.	C
7.	B	17.	B
8.	D	18.	D
9.	A	19.	B
10.	D	20.	C

21. A
22. A
23. B
24. C
25. C

INVESTIGATIVE TECHNIQUES

We will begin with a discussion of the search warrant for financial records: what it is, how it differs from a "general" search warrant, and how one is issued to an investigator. We will then explore the undercover operation, surveillance, the use of informants, recovering information from trash, gathering information from a suspect's mail, and retrieving evidence from a computer. We will look at how document examiners apply forensic science techniques to aid in investigations. The chapter concludes with an examination of a tool called "link analysis."

- State the importance of obtaining a valid search warrant.
- Describe the terms "probable cause" and "curtilage".
- State the purpose of an affidavit.
- List and describe the types of information required in an affidavit for a search warrant for financial information.
- List the objectives of undercover operations.
- List the objectives of surveillance.
- Describe the different types of surveillance.
- Describe how informants contribute to an investigation.
- State why recovering evidence from a suspect's trash, reading the covers of a suspect's mail, and retrieving evidence from a computer are valuable investigative techniques.
- List and describe the types of analyses a document examiner can perform.
- Use link analysis to show relationships in an investigation.

Persons involved in criminal activities do not flaunt their indiscretions in the faces of law enforcement officers. They try to hide what they are doing. And some of the webs criminals weave are very complex. Because of this, investigators rely on certain investigative techniques to help them gather information concerning criminal activities. These techniques are discussed in this chapter.

THE SEARCH WARRANT

Special Agent Wilson Taggart is working on a narcotics investigation where Tim Anthony is the prime suspect. Taggart receives an anonymous letter indicating that David Anthony, Tim's father, recently paid cash for a new $23,000 car. Wondering if Tim provided his father with the money, Taggart decides to visit David Anthony. Taggart goes to Mr. Anthony's house, identifies himself, and says he'd like to ask a few questions about Tim. Mr. Anthony lets him in. Taggart asks if it is alright for him to take a look around and, even though Mr. Anthony says no, Taggart acts as if he doesn't hear. Taggart opens a briefcase that is sitting on a desk and finds that it contains $100,000. He asks Mr. Anthony where he got the money but Mr. Anthony just shrugs his shoulders. Then Taggart spies a checking account statement that indicates Mr. Anthony had a balance of $1,494 less than a month ago. Taggart wants to know if Mr. Anthony has other accounts, but, again, Mr. Anthony just shrugs his shoulders. "How did you get $23,000 to pay for a new car?" Taggart asks. "None of your business," Mr. Anthony replies. "Now, get out of here." When he leaves, Taggart takes the briefcase full of money and the checking account statement with him.

The scenario presented above is fictitious, but suppose it really happened. Will Special Agent Taggart be able to use what he collected as evidence against Tim Anthony?

The answer is no. Taggart obtained the evidence without a valid search warrant. Mr. Anthony was under the assumption that Special Agent Taggart wanted to ask him a few questions about his son. When he invited Special Agent Taggart in, he had no reason to believe that the agent was going to search the house. The Fourth Amendment to the U.S. Constitution protects citizens against actions such as Special Agent Taggart's. The amendment provides that the people have the right to be "...secure in their persons, houses, papers, and effects, against unreasonable searches and seizures...." If evidence is obtained by an unreasonable search and seizure, or in violation of the privileges guaranteed by the Fourth Amendment, the evidence will be excluded from trial. Investigators need to be aware of the importance of obtaining a valid search warrant. Otherwise, critical evidence will be ruled inadmissible.

What is a Search Warrant?

A search warrant is a written order issued by a judge or magistrate. It describes the place to be searched as well as the things to be seized. Search warrants are usually issued for the search of a premise, person, or vehicle. Generally, search warrants are issued based on evidence gathered by the investigator during the conduct of the investigation. This evidence must establish that a crime has been or will be committed.

A specialized form of search warrant is a search warrant for financial records. This specialized warrant directs a law enforcement officer to search for financial documents or records. If Company XYZ is a suspect in a kickback investigation, the investigators probably will not be interested in searching and seizing office equipment and personnel files. However, they will be interested in obtaining the company's journals, ledgers, and other financial records. That's what a search warrant for financial records will allow them to do.

A search warrant is usually prepared by the prosecuting attorney before it is submitted to a judge or magistrate. Search warrants are usually required to be executed during daytime hours on a given day and are executable within a 72 hour period. At the completion of the search, a detailed inventory of the items seized is prepared. A copy of the search warrant and the inventory are to be left at the place searched or with the person searched. The investigator will then return the warrant and the inventory to the judge or magistrate who authorized the warrant.

Probable Cause

A judge or magistrate will issue a search warrant only after a finding of probable cause. Probable cause is all the facts and circumstances within the knowledge of the investigator about a criminal activity that can be considered reasonable and trustworthy.

When developing probable cause, an investigator must keep the following two principles in mind:

- Probable cause must be current.
- Probable cause must be reasonable and trustworthy to a degree sufficient to ensure that a reasonable person will believe that a crime has been or will be committed and that the evidence sought exists in the place to be searched.

Probable cause may vary from investigation to investigation but only in matters of degree. It must be present and it must be sufficient to enable an impartial judicial officer to issue the warrant.

The Affidavit

Judges or magistrates issue search warrants and do so only after a finding of probable cause. To convince a judge or magistrate that probable cause exists, an investigator prepares a sworn statement called an affidavit. In affidavits, investigators summarize their expertise and the information gathered during their investigations. The investigator who prepares an affidavit is called the affiant.

An affidavit for a search warrant should contain certain types of information. Affidavits for "general" search warrants and search warrants for financial records should contain the following types of information:

- Affiant's experience
- Detailed account of the criminal activity
- Description of place(s) to be searched
- Financial evidence
- Items to be seized

An affidavit for a search warrant for financial records requires an additional type of information: conclusions based on the affiant's expertise.

The following paragraphs describe the types of information to be included in a search warrant for financial records. An example of a statement reflecting the type of information is also provided.

Affiant's Experience
The affidavit should contain a sufficient amount of detail concerning the affiant's experience, training, and investigative background.

I am a Special Agent with the IRS, Criminal Investigation Division, and have been so employed since March 2017. I have conducted or assisted in over forty investigations of alleged criminal violations of IRS laws; of the distribution of drugs and controlled substances; and of money laundering. For the past 2½ years, I have held the position of Intelligence Analyst. I have been in charge of the Division's High Level Drug Leaders Project, Project Narcotics Currency, and Project White Collar Currency. All of these projects analyze information relative to the flow of drug proceeds throughout the State of Wisconsin.

Account of Criminal Activity
The affiant must detail the illegal activity that has been uncovered during the investigation.

In January 2017, four FBI informants who have previously provided reliable information reported that Tom Trio was selling cocaine in the Milwaukee area. Two of the informants stated that Trio was selling cocaine out of his residence. One informant reported that a friend of his had seen several trash bags of currency in Trio's house.

Description of Place(s) To Be Searched
The affiant must show that the defendant exercises dominion and control over the location(s) to be searched. To do this, the affiant can cite information contained in documentation such as telephone and utility records. The affiant can also point to surveillance findings as well as information secured through interviews from third parties.

The Milwaukee City Phone Directory lists Tom Trio's address as: 102 North West Street, Milwaukee, Wisconsin.

Financial Evidence
The affidavit should document major asset purchases and expenditures made by the defendant. It should describe any acts of deceit or fraudulent schemes uncovered, such as the use of aliases or the existence of any money laundering activities. Tax information, if available, should be presented as financial evidence. Generally, a court order is needed before tax returns can be released to non-IRS law enforcement personnel because of confidentiality laws. However, tax returns can be obtained from non-IRS sources, such as an ex-spouse, bookkeeper, accountant or return preparer, or loan documents.

Federal income tax records reveal that Tom Trio has reported a total income of $54,000 during the past two years.

Items To Be Searched/Seized
An itemized list of specific property (documents and evidence) to be searched for and seized must be attached to the affidavit.

Search the residence located at 102 North West Street, Milwaukee, Wisconsin and the 2010 Mercedes with VIN number GIAB2323 for:
   U.S. currency
   Cocaine
   Books, records, receipts, notes, ledgers, and other papers relating to the transportation, ordering, sale, and distribution of cocaine

Conclusions Based on the Affiant's Expertise
As previously indicated, what distinguishes the affidavit for a search warrant for financial records from the affidavit for a "general" search warrant is the reliance on the affiant's expertise to establish that records and other evidence will be at specific locations.

Based upon my training and experience, and my participation in other investigations involving the distribution of cocaine, I know that:
a. Drug traffickers must maintain, on hand, large amounts of U.S. currency to maintain and finance their ongoing narcotics business.
b. Drug traffickers maintain books, records, receipt, notes, ledgers, and other papers relating to the transportation, ordering, sale, and distribution of controlled substances.

AFFIDAVIT

STATE OF WISCONSIN)
) ss
MILWAUKEE COUNTY)

John Smith, being first duly sworn on oath, here deposes and says:

1. I am a Special Agent with the IRS, Criminal Investigation Division, and have been so employed since March 2017. I have conducted or assisted in over forty investigations of alleged criminal violations of IRS laws; of the distribution of drugs and controlled substances; and of money laundering. For the past 2½ years, I have held the position of Intelligence Analyst. I have been in charge of the Division's High Level Drug Leaders Project, Project Narcotics Currency, and Project White Collar Currency. All of these projects analyze information relative to the flow of drug proceeds throughout the State of Wisconsin.

2. I have attended and instructed in-service training seminars which concentrated on currency reporting statutes (Title 31, U.S.C.), money laundering statutes (Title 18, U.S.C. 1956, 1957) and drug statutes (Title 21, U.S.C. 848, 852, 881). I have conducted net worth and expenditure investigations and I have planned, drafted and executed both financial and traditional search warrants. I have been qualified in the U.S. District Court as an expert in financial and money laundering investigations.

3. As part of my duties, I am involved in the investigation of Tom Trio for cocaine trafficking in violation of Title 21 of the United States Code. Special agents from the Federal Bureau of Investigation and the Drug Enforcement Administration and officers from the City of Milwaukee Police Department have participated in this investigation. The information in this affidavit comes from my own personal investigation and observation, or from the information provided to me by personnel of these other agencies.

4. In January 2017, four FBI informants who have previously provided reliable information stated that Tom Trio was selling cocaine in the Milwaukee area. Two of the informants stated that Trio was selling cocaine out of his residence. One informant reported that a friend of his had seen several trash bags of currency in Trio's house.

5. The Milwaukee City Phone Directory lists Tom Trio's address as 102 North West Street, Milwaukee, Wisconsin.

6. Real Estate records at the County Courthouse in Milwaukee, Wisconsin show that on August 12, 2016, Tom purchased the residence at 102 North West Street from John Jakes for $64,000. No mortgage documents have been located for the property.

7. In an interview with John Jakes, he stated that Trio attempted to pay cash at the time of settlement. Jakes refused to accept payment in cash and Trio subsequently provided him with eight $8,000 cashier's checks.

8. Tom Trio is employed by Penders and Associates, Inc. This is his only place of employment

9. Local income tax records reveal that Tom Trio has reported a total income of $54,000 during the past two years.

10. On February 6, 2017, I collected and went through the trash left for garbage collection at 102 North West Street. The garbage included bills addressed to Tom Trio of that address, M&I Bank envelopes, 12 money wrappers marked for $2,000 each, and the title to a 2015 Mercedes with VIN number GIAB2323. The garbage also contained freezer paper cut into small squares. Special Agent Thomas Gore of the Drug Enforcement Administration told me that such paper is commonly used to wrap 1 ounce quantities of cocaine. The garbage also included three large plastic garbage bags that contained fiberglass cartons. Special Agent Gore told me that cartons of that size and type commonly contain kilograms of cocaine. The inside of the packages had a powdery residue which Special Agent Gore tested for the presence of cocaine. The test was positive.

11. Documentation from the dealership where Tom Trio bought the 2010 Mercedes shows that he paid $27,000 in cash for the car.

12. Between February 16 and February 24, 2017, one of the previously mentioned informants purchased cocaine from Tom Trio three times. Each buy was a controlled buy. All three buys took place at Trio's house. Each time, the substance purchased was tested for the presence of cocaine. Each time, the substance tested positive.

13. Based upon my training and experience, and my participation in other investigations involving the distribution of cocaine, I know that:

    a. Drug traffickers must maintain, on hand, large amounts of U.S. currency to maintain and finance their ongoing narcotics business;
    b. Drug traffickers maintain books, records, receipts, notes, ledgers, and other papers relating to the transportation, ordering, sale, and distribution of controlled substances;
    c. The aforementioned books, records, receipts, notes, ledgers, etc. are commonly maintained where drug traffickers have ready access to them, i.e., homes, offices, automobiles;
    d. It is common for drug traffickers to hide contraband, proceeds from drug sales, and records of drug transactions in secure locations for ready access;
    e. Cocaine traffickers usually keep paraphernalia for packaging, cutting, weighing, and distributing cocaine;
    f. The courts have recognized that unexplained wealth is probative evidence of crimes motivated by greed, particularly trafficking in controlled substances.

14. Based on the information contained herein, and my experience and training, I have probable cause to believe that Tom Trio is involved in cocaine trafficking in violation of Title 21 U.S.C. 881(B). The locations to be searched and property to be seized are included on the attachment to this affidavit.

John Smith
John Smith
Special Agent

Attachment

Search the residence located at 102 North West Street, Milwaukee, Wisconsin and the 2010 Mercedes with VIN number GIAB2323 for:

- U.S. currency
- Cocaine
- Drug paraphernalia for packaging, cutting, weighing and distributing cocaine, including, but not limited to, scales, freezer paper, and spoons.
- Books, records, receipts, notes, ledgers, and other papers relating to the transportation, ordering, sale, and distribution of cocaine
- Books, records, receipts, bank statements and records, money drafts, letters of credit, passbooks, bank checks, and other items evidencing the obtaining, secreting, transfer, and concealment of assets and the obtaining, secreting, transfer, concealment, and expenditure of money
- Income tax returns

8

UNITED STATES DISTRICT COURT
EASTERN DISTRICT OF WISCONSIN
AT LAW AND IN ADMIRALTY

UNITED STATES OF AMERICA,
Plaintiff,   Warrant No. 1

vs.
                                    SEARCH WARRANT
                                    (21 U.S.C. 881(B))

Thomas Trio

TO: ANY DEPUTY UNITED STATES MARSHAL OR OTHER FEDERAL OFFICER

An affidavit has been made before me by Special Agent John Smith of the United States Internal Revenue Service that he has reason to believe that Tom Trio of 102 North West Street, Milwaukee, Wisconsin is involved in cocaine trafficking in violation of Title 21 U.S.C. 881(B). Special Agent Smith's affidavit further states that he has reason to believe that evidence needed to support such a claim is located at the residence of 102 North West Street. I am satisfied that there are sufficient facts and circumstances to support the probable cause standard to believe that the items listed on the attachment to this warrant are currently located at 102 North West Street in Milwaukee, Wisconsin, and that grounds exist for the issuance of this seizure warrant as stated in the supporting Affidavit.

YOU ARE HEREBY COMMANDED to proceed to 102 North West Street to seize the items listed or described on the attachment to this warrant within a period of three days, serving this warrant and seizing this property during daytime hours 8:00 A.M. to 5:00 P.M., leaving a copy of this warrant, preparing a written inventory of all the property seized, and promptly returning this warrant and bringing the inventory before this court as required by law within ten days after seizure.

Dated at Milwaukee, Wisconsin, this 2 day of March, 2017.

                                                              Alice Miller
                                                              United States Magistrate

UNDERCOVER OPERATIONS

Operation ABSCAM was an investigation into corruption among U.S. government officials. Over the course of a year and a half, FBI undercover agents approached public officials thought to be involved in political corruption and told them that oil-rich Arab sheiks would offer money in exchange for political favors. The agents met with the public figures and paid out considerable sums in cash. Several public officials were indicted and convicted.

In August 1989, 46 traders from the Chicago Mercantile Exchange and the Chicago Board of Trade were indicted on charges ranging from defrauding customers to tax evasion to racketeering. The charges were the result of a two-year undercover operation that put wired FBI undercover agents in the trading pits at the two exchange.

In March 1991, law enforcement agents raided three University of Virginia fraternity houses and arrested 12 students for selling drugs to undercover agents. The raids came after more than six months of investigation by federal and state officials. The investigation involved undercover purchases of designer drugs, LSD, cocaine, and marijuana.

What is an Undercover Operation?

The undercover operation is something we hear about all the time. In an undercover operation, law enforcement officers or private individuals assume an identity other than their own for the purpose of gathering information relating to criminal violations.

Undercover operations require the highest degree of skill and planning to be successful. Used in a timely manner and with great care, the undercover operation can bring results to investigations that cannot be achieved in any other way. Used in the wrong way or handled poorly, these operations can lead to death, injury, serious financial liability, and agency embarrassment[1].

An undercover operation is frequently the only investigative technique that can be used effectively against well-organized criminal groups or sophisticated criminal activities. Through the use of disguise and deceit, information is gathered directly from those involved in the criminal offense. Take, for example, the undercover activities of Joe Pistone. Pistone was an undercover agent who infiltrated the Bonnano and Columbo crime families, posing for five years (1976-1981) as jewel thief Donnie Brasco. Pistone was instrumental in gaining more than 100 federal convictions against organized crime members.

Undercover activities can last a long or short period of time. As was just indicated, Joe Pistone was undercover for five years. The length of the undercover operation is contingent on the amount of information necessary to develop a picture of the alleged criminal activity. Situations involving organized crime figures and sophisticated financial crime networks dictate lengthy undercover operations.

At the other extreme are short-term undercover operations called stings. The previously described drug raid at the University of Virginia is an example of a sting operation.

Objectives of Undercover Operations

Undercover operations are accepted by the courts as a legitimate function of public and private law enforcement personnel, provided that the undercover operation is conducted in those situations where sufficient probable cause exists to believe that a crime has been or is being committed. Entrapment issues make it essential to establish that the suspect has a predisposition or prior intent to commit the crime. The only factor the government provides is the opportunity for the suspect to commit the offense.

The courts will now allow covert operations to be conducted as law enforcement "fishing expeditions." Undercover operations should be based on a written plan that details time frames and specific objectives. Specific objectives of an undercover operation may include:

- Observing and attending planning sessions for future violations
- Identifying unknown violators and developing information related to violations currently in progress
- Purchasing contraband (i.e., drugs, firearms, counterfeit currency)
- Identifying the fruits of a crime (illegal proceeds and profits)
- Developing information related to past crimes or criminal activities
- Locating contraband or weapons
- Locating violation sites
- Identifying co-conspirators and/or key witnesses
- Obtaining probable cause for search and arrest warrants
- Checking the reliability of informants
- Corroborating a witness' statements and testimony
- Gathering information and documents relative to the criminal investigation
- Obtaining information and leads to purchases and expenditures

SURVEILLANCE

Jonathan J. Pollard was a civilian analyst for the U.S. Naval Intelligence Center in Suitland, Maryland. In November 1985, Pollard's supervisor, Jerry Agee, began suspecting that Pollard was taking classified documents from his workplace and providing them to a foreign government. Agee shared his suspicions with a senior naval intelligence officer. The Naval Investigative Service and the FBI agreed to investigate. As the investigation progressed, the agents determined that Pollard was providing classified information to a foreign government. They just did not know which one.

Eventually, the investigators discovered that Pollard was providing the classified information to Israel. How did they determine this? They placed a round-the-clock surveillance on Pollard.

On November 21, 1985, Pollard and his wife decided to make a run for it even though they knew that there were going to be followed. Pollard felt sure he could shake the surveillance as he and his wife drove in circles around Washington, D.C. Several unmarked FBI cars were involved in the surveillance; one car would pick up the tail then drop it when another car became involved. Would the Pollards lead them to the foreign government involved in the espionage ring? Yes. The Pollards revealed the government they were providing classified information to when they pulled up to the Israeli Embassy.

What is Surveillance?

Surveillance is the secretive and continuous observation of persons, places and things to obtain information concerning the identity and activity of individuals suspected of violating criminal laws. Like undercover operations, surveillance provides a means to obtain information and evidence which probably would not be available by any other means. It is a technique that requires experience, teamwork, and knowledge of the "thing" to be surveyed.

Private citizens who form neighborhood watch groups use surveillance to gather information. So do private companies that employ security cameras. Countries use intelligence agencies to set up surveillance operations that are a matter of national security. Even criminals perform surveillance on their suspects before committing crimes.

Objectives of Surveillance

The objectives of a surveillance are to:

- Obtain evidence of a crime
- Obtain probable cause for search and arrest warrants
- Identify co-conspirators and associates of the suspects
- Apprehend violators during the commission of a crime
- Develop investigative leads
- Provide protection and corroboration for undercover officers
- Locate persons and things
- Gather intelligence

Types of Surveillance

Various types of surveillance activities are utilized by law enforcement. They can be classified as follows:

- Stationary
- Moving
- Electronic

Stationary
Stationary surveillance is where neither the suspect nor the agent maintaining the surveillance are mobile. Sitting in an unmarked car and watching someone's home or office is an example of stationary surveillance. A common term for stationary surveillance is stakeout. The surveillance on Jonathan Pollard began as a stakeout. But when Pollard and his wife decided to make a run for it, the surveillance requirements changed. A moving surveillance was needed.

Moving
A moving surveillance is one where the suspect does not remain in one position. Following a suspect in an automobile is an example of a moving surveillance. Following a suspect on foot or in a boat, or watching a car from an airplane also would be considered moving surveillances.

The risk of detection is higher in a moving surveillance than it is in a stakeout. Also, a moving surveillance consumes significantly more manpower. In the instance of following an automobile, a minimum of three cars with radio contact would be necessary. In most investigative situations, surveillance techniques mandate that it is better to lose the suspect than compromise the surveillance.

Electronic
The FBI agents who went undercover as traders in the pits at the Chicago Mercantile Exchange and the Chicago Board of Trade secretly tape recorded hundreds of incriminating conversations.

To make sure they would not lose touch with the Pollards during a moving surveillance, the FBI planted an electronic tracking device inside the bumper of the Pollard's car.

In each of the incidents above, electronic devices were used to assist law enforcement officers in obtaining evidence against their suspects. Used in a secretive manner, electronic surveillance can be of tremendous assistance to an investigation, but it must be used with care. Some devices available for use may require court orders.

In the trading pit incident, at least one of the people involved in the taped conversations knew the conversations were being recorded. This is called consensual monitoring. At the federal level, such monitorings are constitutional and statutorily permissible; however, this investigative technique is subject to careful regulation in order to avoid any abuse or any unwarranted invasion of privacy. At the state level, some states have made consensual monitoring illegal. Therefore, it is important for an investigator to know the legal precedents in the state where an investigation occurs.

Today's sophisticated electronic monitoring devices can be concealed in virtually anything. Briefcases, light fixtures, and jogging suits can be used to conceal microphones and tape recording devices. Pen registers (telephone number recording devices) can be activated by the change in voltage and used to record the numbers dialed on outgoing calls. Other electronic devices can make a record of the incoming telephone calls to a suspect's number.

INFORMANTS

Larry Bullock was an Illinois State Representative who dreamed of becoming Chicago's first Black mayor. His district encompassed McCormick Place Exposition Hall, a place that would play an active role in the 1992 World's Fair if Chicago was selected as the host city.

By law, a certain percentage of all public construction projects had to be awarded to minority business enterprises (MBE). Eugene Blackmon was an MBE general contractor and he was experiencing difficulty in getting his money from another general contractor to pay his sub-contractors. Blackmon approached Bullock to enlist his aid in securing his money. Bullock said he could help—for a price! Bullock also promised Blackmon that he would play a prominent role in the awarding of the World's Fair contracts.

Blackmon did not have the money to pay Bullock. But he was desperate to get his money, so one Friday afternoon he went to the Office of the U.S. Attorney and told them about his encounter with Bullock. The government and Blackmon reached an agreement where Blackmon would become an informant and would meet with Bullock to discuss fixing contracts and other matters in political corruption. In return, the government would give Blackmon money to "pay" Bullock so that his contract money would be released.

Over the next few weeks, Blackmon had a series of meetings with Bullock and paid him thousands of dollars of FBI money. Blackmon wore a concealed recording device to the first meeting but something went wrong with the equipment and, instead of recorded conversations, all the FBI got was a mess of spaghetti tape because the tape had come off the spool. At all subsequent meetings, Blackmon wore a recording device and had a transmitting device concealed in his briefcase.

Toward the end of the investigation, Bullock and his attorney were invited to the U.S. Attorney's Office and were treated to selected portions of the recorded conversations. The government offered Bullock the opportunity to cooperate with them in investigating political corruption. Bullock refuses, choosing rather to go to trial. After a long trial, during which Blackmon spent a week on the stand testifying, Bullock was found guilty of a multitude of offenses. He was sentenced to six years in prison.

What is an Informant?

In the case described above, it is important to note that the role of the informant was key in carrying out the investigation. An informant is a person who has specific knowledge of a criminal event and provides that information to a law enforcement officer.

The development of an informant to provide confidential information is a legitimate function of investigators. If properly developed, informants can greatly enhance an investigation.

Many criminal cases have originated from informant information. Others have been successfully completed only because an informant supplied information that would have otherwise been unknown. Take, for example, the case against Al Capone. Capone was one of the United States' most notorious gangsters. You'd think that when he eventually went to prison, he would have gone for murder or racketeering. No, Al Capone was brought down by a mild-mannered tax investigator from the IRS. This investigator was able to build a case against Capone when one of Capone's associates told IRS agents where they could seize books reflecting Capone's income.

Perhaps the most common reason informants supply information is because they themselves are involved in the criminal offense and by furnishing information on the suspect they can diffuse suspicion from their own activities. Particularly when looking at jail time, individuals are willing to become informants in order to get a reduced sentence based on their cooperation.

Many informants are motivated by revenge. They sense that they've been wronged or taken advantage of by the suspect and want to get even. For example, in the case of drug dealing, an informant may furnish information on the suspect because the suspect is a "business" competitor. Other informants feel a social responsibility to provide law enforcement their knowledge of any criminal wrongdoing. It is critical that the investigator be able to determine why the informant is cooperating and to use that information to properly assess how the informant and information provided should be handled.

Informants can be used in surveillances, consensual monitorings, and as participants in undercover operations. Control is a key element in dealing with an informant. Informants should take directions from the investigator, not the other way around. Without control, not only is the investigation in jeopardy, but the investigator could be at risk. If informants are willing to violate a basic tenet of our culture and inform on someone close to them, consider how quickly they would be willing to blackmail agents if they can discover some wrongdoing.

Informants can be powerful tools in a financial investigation. However, all informant information should be corroborated through independent verification to ensure its accuracy.

EVIDENCE RECOVERED FROM TRASH

An informant tells an investigator that Billy Greenwood is dealing drugs. The investigator watches Greenwood's home and observes a number of cars making brief nighttime stops at the house. Based on the informant's information and the surveillance, the investigator asks the garbage collector for the plastic garbage bags in front of Greenwood's house. While sifting through the garbage, the police uncover drug-related paraphernalia, straws containing cocaine residue, and phone bills listing calls to people with drug records. Based on this evidence, the investigators obtain a warrant to search the house and find cocaine and hashish. They arrest Greenwood. Can the evidence the investigators collected from the trash be used against Greenwood at trial?

Yes. In May 1988, the Supreme Court ruled that police may freely rummage through ordinary household trash left at a curbside without obtaining a search warrant. This decision evolved from the incident described above.

Investigators often find that picking up a suspect's garbage is a useful tool for identifying leads. People often dispose of important documents and information pertaining to their criminal activities when they throw out their trash. Once the trash leaves the suspect's possession, they no longer have a reasonable expectation of privacy in the contents of their trash. However, the investigator must be careful not to violate the suspect's curtilage. Curtilage usually, but not always, refers to the area inside the boundary of a person's residence or business location, which has been marked off by any number of man-made or naturally occurring devices. These boundary lines include fences, sidewalks, tree lines, and rows of shrubbery. Inside this area, a person has a reasonable expectation of privacy base on the Fourth Amendment to the Constitution.

READING MAIL COVERS

Since letters, packages, and other documents travel through the U.S. and other mail delivery services, a person cannot attach a reasonable expectation of privacy to the outside of the mail itself. Therefore, an investigator, in conjunction with the U.S. Postal Service, can make a record of the outside of any mail. Return addresses and postmark information can provide an excellent source of financial leads (i.e., names of banks, credit card companies, etc.).

FORENSIC SCIENCE

Timothy Wilson Spencer was suspected of murdering a number of women in Richmond and Arlington, Virginia. Police had reason to suspect Spencer but had no confession, no witnesses, and a limited amount of physical evidence. Then it was found that Spencer's DNA perfectly matched that from semen found at three of the murder scenes. The likelihood that someone else could have produced all three matching patterns was 1 in 135 million. Subsequently, Spencer was found guilty on four counts of murder and sentenced to death.

Genetic fingerprinting played a crucial role in the case against Spencer. Genetic fingerprinting is a technique used in forensic science. Forensic science is the application of scientific techniques to legal matters, in particular to investigations of criminal activities. The forensic sciences have been utilized in the investigation of violent crimes for centuries. Traditional techniques such as fingerprint identification, ballistics classifications, and drug, blood, and urine analyses have served the purposes of law enforcement successfully in the past.

Not all criminal cases evolve around forensic evidence like fingerprint identification and ballistics classification. Sometimes evidence comes from the forensic analysis of documents involved in the crime. Take, for example, the Lindbergh kidnapping case. On March 1, 1932, 20-month-old Charles A. Lindburgh, Jr. was kidnapped. A ransom note left at the scene of the crime read:

Have fifty thousand dollars ready, 25,000 in twenty-dollar bills, 15,000 in ten-dollar bills, and 10,000 in five-dollar bills. In 4-5 days we will inform you where to deliver the money. We warn you for making anything public of for notify the police. The child is in gut care. Indication for all letter are signature and three holes.

On May 12, 1932, the child's body was found in some woods a few miles from the Lindbergh mansion. It wasn't until September, 1935, that a person was charged with the kidnapping and murder of the Lindburgh baby. On January 2, 1935, Bruno Richard Hauptmann went to trial. Since the ransom note was a key piece of evidence, the prosecution needed to show that Hauptmann wrote the note. They obtained other samples of his handwriting and compared them to the ransom note. Handwriting experts took the stand and stated that Hauptmann's handwriting and that of the ransom note were one and the same. This crucial testimony helped convict Hauptmann.

What is a Questioned Document?

Since the end product of financial investigation is documentary evidence, scientific examination of documents by a qualified expert can be an important aspect of the investigation. Besides verifying a person's handwriting, a document examiner can analyze checks, kidnapping and hold-up notes, hate letters, wills, contracts, birth/death/marriage certificates, passports or any other document to determine if they have been forged, erased, or changed in any way.

Document examiners are called into an investigation when a questioned document is involved. A questioned document is a document that has been questioned in whole or in part with respect to its authenticity, origin, or contents. For example, a suspect denies that she signed a check used to make a bribe payment. Or Cousin Jane accuses Cousin Larry of altering Uncle Charlie's will so that Larry receives the bulk of Charlie's estate.

Types of Forensic Analyses

Document examiners can perform many types of analyses on a document. The following types of forensic analyses are discussed in this section:

- Handwriting analysis
- Typewriter analysis
- Alteration analysis
- Ink analysis
- Paper analysis
- Document restoration

Handwriting Analysis
Over the years, an individual's brain, arms, and fingers create a pattern of handwriting. Everyone's handwriting possesses "normal" or "natural" variations. But the basic pattern does not change. When analyzing handwriting, the document examiner has the suspect submit an exemplar, a sample to be used in comparison to the questioned document. The document examiner determines the range of variation in a person's handwriting from the exemplar and compares that handwriting to the questioned document. The document examiner can determine if the writing on the questioned document falls within the individual's "normal" or "natural" range.

Typewriter Analysis
Every typewriter is unique. Each one types differently from every other one because typewriters develop individual characteristics during the manufacturing process and through use. Examiners attempt to determine a document's type style and escapement (pica, elite, or proportional) to establish the make and model of the typewriter that created it. Also, the examiner attempts to find horizontal and vertical misalignment of characters, which if significant, is considered to be an identifying characteristic. Examiners also search for any typeface defects or damaged letters.

Alteration Analysis
Document examiners can determine if a document has been altered. They look for additions (insets between lines, addition of a word, sentence, or paragraph to a document) and deletions (erasures or obliterations). Utilizing infrared and ultraviolet viewing techniques and photography, alterations unseen by the naked eye become apparent. By looking through a microscope, a document examiner can determine if information was erased by determining if paper fibers were disturbed due to abrasive action.

Sophisticated chemical deletions such as white-out obliterations or ink over-whites can be examined through infrared reflectants.

Interlineation, the addition of a word, sentence or an entire paragraph to a document can be detected because it is nearly impossible to perfectly realign paper in a typewriter once a document has been removed. The examiner can detect the misalignment of the added test plates.

Ink Analysis
The ink on a questioned document can be examined through the use of scientific techniques. One ink can be differentiated from another by microscopy, infrared reflectants, transmission, florescence, and thin layer spectro-chromatography. Inks are identified and dated by their chemical properties. Even pencil writing can be dated within 50 years based on carbon methods.

Paper Analysis
Paper can be identified by characteristics such as dimensions, texture, thickness, color, and opacity. Higher grades of paper have watermarks that identify both the brand of paper and its manufacturer. Some papers are coded by the manufacturer to show the year of make.

Document Restoration
It is possible to restore a document that has been torn, mutilated, or even burned. Through scientific processing, some documents that have been partially destroyed can be pieced together and used for investigative purposes.

In this age of desktop publishing, a new type of forgery has come about—desktop forgery. With a scanner, computer, and laser printer, desktop forgers can re-create almost anything: checks, invoices, etc. While some of the forensic analysis techniques described above can be applied to desktop forgery, new techniques will evolve.

EVIDENCE RECOVERED FROM COMPUTERS

Recent law enforcement reports suggest that—just as legitimate business managers have found computers indispensable in conducting business—organized criminals, drug dealers, and even child pornographers increasingly depend on computer transactions. The computer is a powerful tool in today's business society, providing access to many services and programs. Computers also can provide access to many services and programs. Computers also can provide evidence of criminal activity. A computer could contain a drug dealer's databases, the daily operations of a prostitution ring, or a pornographer's mailing list. Physical evidence including handwritten note, printouts, manuals, sales invoices, photographs, and fingerprints may also be found in the area of the computer.

LINK ANALYSIS

Link analysis is a technique for evaluating, integrating, and presenting complex information by taking bits of information collected from various sources and putting them together to show patterns and meanings. It provides a graphic picture of associations and relationships among various persons and organizations. Link analysis is ideally suited for showing the associations among identifiers, such as:

- Telephone numbers
- Vehicle license plates
- Aircraft/boat/vehicle registration numbers
- Property ownership
- Financial transactions

For the investigator, link analysis converts written information into a graphic summary called an association matrix. The association matrix is converted into a link diagram which graphically depicts relationships among people, organizations, and activities. Look at how an association simplifies the following relationships:

Smith is the Vice President of the ABC Corporation and President of DEF Corporation, a subsidiary of ABC. DEF is a general partner in two limited partnerships. Jones and Green are limited partners in the first partnership, Brown and Black are limited partners in the second partnership. Black is also a general partner in a third partnership. Smith may have an interest in the first partnership.

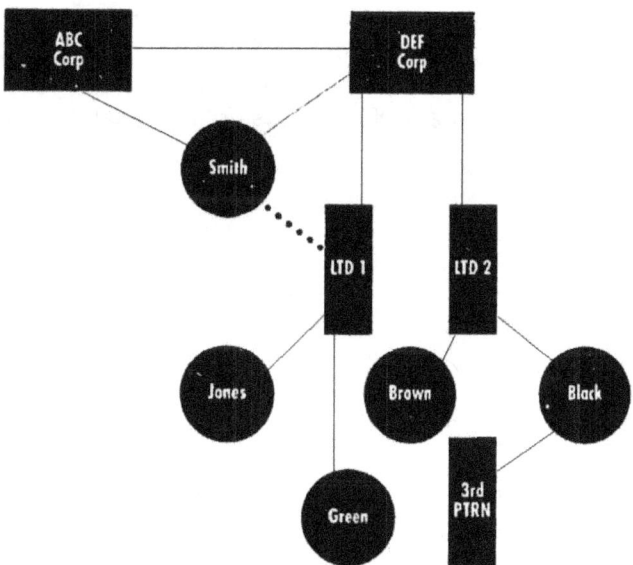

Link networking can also be used to identify the direction and frequency of telephone traffic between suspect parties. The numbers inside the small circles indicate the number of calls made to particular telephone numbers.

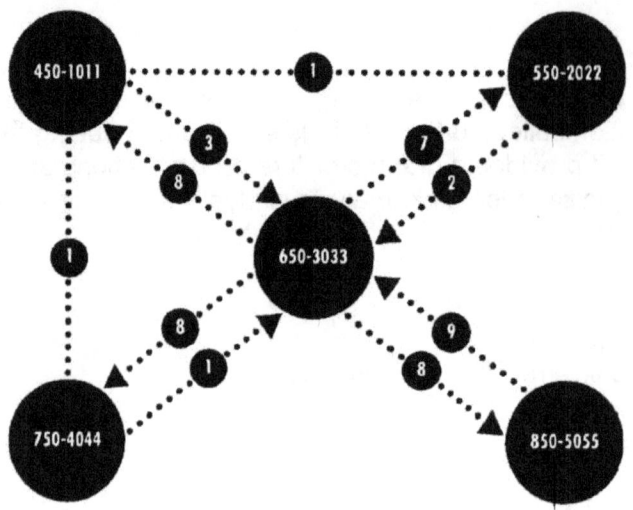

Link networking offers the investigator the ability to simplify and synthesize the relationships and suspected relationships of people in organizations involved in a criminal activity. This technique can be used to present material during the investigative process or at any legal proceedings that may occur subsequent to the investigation.

SUMMARY

An investigator's success or failure is often determined by the investigative techniques used. "Proving a financial crime" requires evidence of guilty beyond a reasonable doubt. This often can be achieved only through the use of specialized techniques. With the continuing growth and sophistication of financial crimes, knowing what investigative means are available and how to apply them is the trademark of a successful financial investigator.

QUESTIONS AND EXERCISES

Answer the following questions, then check your responses with those provided at the end of the book.

1. Why is it important that an investigator obtain a search warrant prior to searching a suspect's residence or place of business?

2. What is probable cause and how does an investigator show that probable cause exists?

3. List six types of information that should be included in an affidavit for a search warrant for financial information. After you have listed the six, place an * beside the type of information that is not required in an affidavit for a "general" search warrant.

   a.
   b.
   c.
   d.
   e.
   f.

4. You are developing an affidavit for a search warrant for financial information. You are trying to obtain a warrant to search John Winkler's residence at 34 Tremont Avenue. Winkler is an accounting clerk suspected of embezzling money from the company he works for. In your affidavit, you include the following statement:

   While going through the trash left for garbage collection at 34 Tremont Avenue, I found an electric and phone bill addressed to John Winkler of that address. I also found a bill from Haggler's Electronic Store indicating that Winkler recently bought $2,435 worth of stereo and video recording equipment.

   How does the statement support your quest for a search warrant?

5. During the execution of a search warrant, a typewritten contract between the suspect, Toni Tuesday, and Frank Friday is seized. Mr. Friday claims that the contract is a fake, that it is not the contract his office created. What could a document examiner contribute to the investigation?

6. The University of Muckraker's basketball team is under investigation for its suspected involvement with professional gamblers in a point-shaving scandal. You have been tasked with going undercover as one of the team's tutors. What do you suppose are some of the objectives of this undercover operation?

7. During your undercover activities at the University of Muckraker, you discover the following:

   - Sam Roundball and Terry Rebound are the starting forwards for the basketball team. They are also roommates and live in a fraternity house off campus.
   - Roundball's uncle, Joe Bench, served time in prison. Bench shared a cell with Jack Dice. Dice was convicted of running an illegal gambling operation.
   - Dice is a season ticket holder for University of Muckraker basketball games. Dice's son, Kurt, attends the university. Kurt Dice lives in the same fraternity house as Sam Roundball and Terry Rebound.
   - Jack and Kurt Dice often attend University of Muckraker basketball games together.

   Develop an association matrix that depicts the relationships described above.

8. How might an informant contribute to your investigation of the University of Muckraker's basketball team?

KEY (CORRECT ANSWERS)

1. If an investigator seizes evidence from a suspect's home or office without first obtaining a search warrant, the evidence collected could be ruled inadmissible.

2. Probable cause means that, based on the facts presented and the experience of the investigator, a reasonable person would think that the evidence sought exists in the place to be searched. Probable cause is shown via an affidavit.

3.
   a. Affiant's experience
   b. Detailed account of criminal activity
   c. Description of place(s) to be searched
   d. Financial evidence
   e. Items to be seized
   f. Conclusions based on the affiant's expertise

4. The statement supports two types of information that must be in an affidavit. The statement—*While going through the trash left for garbage collection at 34 Tremont Avenue, I found an electric and phone bill addressed to John Winkler of that address*—shows that the suspect exercises dominion and control over 34 Tremont Avenue, the place you want to search. The second statement—*I also found a bill from Haggler's Electronic Store indicating that Winkler recently bought $2,435 worth of stereo and video recording equipment*—is financial evidence of a major expenditure and asset purchase.

5. A document examiner could perform handwriting analysis to determine the authenticity of the signatures on the contract, could determine whose typewriter was used to create the contract, and could analyze the paper to see if it's the same type of paper used in the creation of contracts in Mr. Friday's office.

6. Undercover operation objectives could include:
   - Identifying persons on the basketball team and outside the team who may be involved in the point-shaving activities
   - Obtaining probable cause for search and arrest warrants
   - Gathering information and documents relative to the investigation
   - Obtaining information and leads to purchases and expenditures made by members of the basketball team

7.

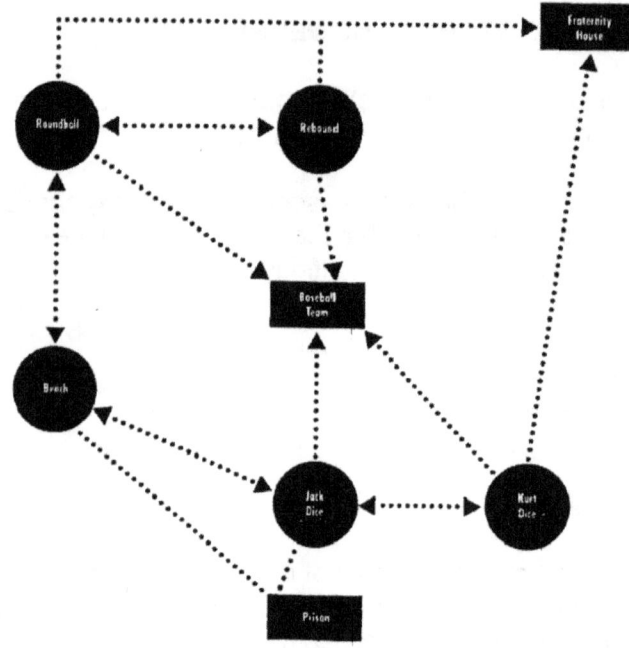

8. An informant could tell you many things including which basketball players are involved in point shaving, who on the outside directs the players to shave points, what past games were involved, what future games might be involved, and how the players are paid off.

INVESTIGATIVE REFERENCES

Appendix

This appendix contains a listing of selected sources of business information and government records available to the financial investigator.

Business Records

Abstract and Title Company Records
•Maps and tract books.

•Escrow index of purchasers and sellers of real estate (primary source of information)

•Escrow files (number obtained from index)

•Escrow file containing escrow instructions, agreements, and settlements

•Abstracts and title policies

•Special purpose newspapers published for use by attorneys, real estate brokers, insurance companies, and financial institutions. These newspapers contain complete reports on transfers of properties, locations of properties transferred, amounts of mortgages, and releases of mortgages.

Agriculture Records
•County veterinarians

•Commission merchants

•Insurance companies (insure shipments)

•Transportation companies

•Storage companies

•County and state fair boards

•County farm agents

•State cattle control boards (some states maintain records of all cattle brought in and taken out of state)

Automobile Manufacturer and Agency Record
•Franchise agreements

•Financial statements of dealers

•New car sales and deliveries (used car purchases, trade-ins, and sales)
•Service department (mileage, order, and delivery signature to indicate presence in area)

Bonding Company Records
•Investigative and other records on persons and firms bonded

•Financial statements and date

•Address of person on bond

Specialized Commercial Credit Organizations
•United Beverage Bureau

•National Fuel Credit Association
•Jewelers Board of Trade

- Lumbermen's Credit Association
- Produce Reporter Company
- Packer Produce Mercantile Agency
- Paper and Allied Trade Mercantile Agency
- Lyon Furniture Mercantile Agency
- American Monument Association

Credit Reporting Agencies

The Fair Credit Reporting Act of 1971 restricts the availability of information from credit reporting agencies to governmental investigative agencies. Credit reports may only be furnished:
— In response to the order of a court having the jurisdiction to issue such an order;
— Upon written request of the consumer; or
— To a person who has a legitimate business need for the information in regard to a business transaction involving the consumer, including but not limited to credit, insurance, and employment purposes.

There is no specific exception provided in the act that will allow law enforcement agencies to obtain credit reports for investigative purposes. The act provides criminal penalties for obtaining information under false pretenses and for unauthorized disclosures by officers or employees of consumer reporting agencies.

The identifying information which is available under the act is limited to a consumer's name, address, former addresses, place(s) of employment, and former place(s) of employment.

If identifying information is needed for investigative purposes the following credit reporting agencies can be checked:
- Local credit rating and collection agencies
- Local office of National Association of Retail Credit Men
  — Insurance applicants

  — American Service Bureau

  — Hooper Holmes Agency

  — Retail Credit Company
- Mortgage Loans
  — Loan exchange (clearing house loan information)

  — Retailer's Commercial Agency (performs credit investigations for credit cards, banking, and mortgages)

- Transportation
  — TRINC (furnishes statistics on the trucking industry).
  — Motor Carrier Directory (lists motor carriers with revenues totaling $50,000 or more).

- Manufacturers
  — The "Census File of Manufacturers" contains a census of manufacturing plants in the United States.

- Marketing Services
  — Dun and Bradstreet, Inc.

  — Market Service Bureau

  — Middle Market Director (business guide of firms with a net worth between $500,00 and $1,000,000)

  — Million Dollar Directory (business guide firms with a net worth of $1,000,000 or more)

  — Metal Working Directory (marketing director of metal working plants in the United States)

  — Vendor Account Services (used by retail stores in processing accounts payable, buying, and merchandise control)
- International

  — International Credit Reports (a division of Dun and Bradstreet which furnishes credit reports on overseas credit)

  — International Market Guides (Middle and South America only)

  — Continental Europe (lists European businesses in 39 countries)

  — Guide to Key British Enterprises (lists prominent firms throughout the United Kingdom)

  — Synopsis of Dun-Mexico

  — Synopsis of Dun-Brazil

  — Reference book- Argentina

  — Bradstreet Register

  International Mercantile Claims Division

Department Store Records
- Charge accounts

- Credit files

Detective Agency Records
- Investigative files
  — Civil

  — Criminal

  — Commercial

  — Industrial

- Character checks

- Fraud and blackmail investigations

- Divorce evidence

- Missing persons search

- Security patrols and guards

- Undercover agents

- Shadow work

- Lie detector tests

- Personnel screening and fingerprinting

- Service checking

- Restaurants

- Public transportation

- Stores

Distributors' Records
• Wholesale toiletry (cash rebates are paid by toiletry manufacturers). Details of available contracts which pay rebates to wholesale toiletry distributors are contained in publications issued by the Toiletry Merchandisers Association, Inc., 230 Park Avenue, New York, N.Y. 10017, and the Druggist Service Council, Inc., 1290 Avenue of the Americas, New York., N.Y. 10019
• Gambling equipment

• Wire service

• Factory, farm, home, office equipment, etc.

Drug Store Records
• Prescription records (name, address, date, and physician issuing prescription)
Fraternal, Veterans, Labor, Social, and Political Organization Records
• Membership and attendance records

• Dues, contributions, and payments

• Locations and history of members

Hospital Records
• Entry and release dates

• Payments made

Hotel Records
• Identity of guest

• Payments made by guest

• Credit record

• Forwarding address

• Reservations for travel (transportation companies and other hotels)

• Telephone calls made to and from room

• Freight shipments and luggage (in and out)

Insurance Company Records (Life, accident, fire, burglary, automobile, and annuity policies)
• Applications (background and financial information, insurance carried with other companies)
• Fur and jewelry floaters (appraised value and description)

• Customers' ledger cards

• Policy and mortgage loan accounts

• Dividend payment records

• Cash value and other net worth data

• Correspondence files

• Payment records on termination, losses, or refunds on cancellations

• Payments to doctors, lawyers, appraisers, and photographers hired directly by the insurance company to act for the company or as an independent expert

Laundry and Dry Cleaning Records
• Marks and tags (marks are sometimes invisible and are

brought out by use of ultraviolet rays)

•Files of laundry marks
—Local or State police departments

—National Institute of Dry Cleaning, Inc., Washington, D.C.

Lenders Exchange or Consumer Loan Exchange

An organization known as the Consumer Loan Exchange or Lenders Exchange exists in all of the large cities in the United States, as well as in some of the smaller cities. It is a nonprofit organization supported by and for its members. Most the lending institutions are members of the exchange. It can supply information concerning open and closed loan accounts with member companies, and is a good source of general background information. These organizations are not listed in directories or telephone books. Their location in a city may be obtained through local lending agencies.

National Charge Plan Records

National agencies, such as American Express, Diners Club, and Carte Blanche, which provide credit cards for use in charging travel, entertainment, goods and services, can determine whether an individual or business has an account from their central index files. If details of the account are needed, information requests should indicate whether only copies of the monthly statements or copies of both the statements and charge slips are desired, name, social security number, the time period to be covered, the subject's address, and the name and address of the subject's employer or business. Requests should be directed to:

American Express Company, 770 Broadway, New York, N.Y. 10003, and Diners Club/Carte Blanche, Adjustment Department, 180 Inverness Drive West, Englewood, CO 80111.

Newspaper Records (from a newspaper's morgue)
•Relatives, associates, and friends

•Previous places of employment (employee or company publications)

•Police and FBI files

•Schools (yearbooks, school papers, etc.)

•License bureaus (drivers, chauffeurs, taxis, etc.)

•Military departments

•Fraternal organizations

•Church groups

•Race tracks

•Nightclub or sidewalk photographers and photography studios

Public Utility Company Records

- Present and previous address of subscriber

- Payments made for service and "major" purchases

Publications

- *Who's Who in America* and various States

- Tax services

- City directories

- *Billboard* (amusements, coin-machines, burlesque, drive-ins, fairs, state, radio, TV, magic, music machines, circuses, rinks, vending machines, movies, letter lists, and obituaries)

- *Variety* (literature, radio, TV, music, state, movies, obituaries, etc.)

- *American Racing Manual* (published by Triangle Publications, Inc., 10 Lake Drive, P.O. Box 1015 Highstown, New Jersey 08520). Records showing amounts paid to owners of winning horses by each race track in the United States, Canada, and Mexico

- Professional, trade, and agriculture directories and magazines

- *Moody's Investors Service Inc.*

- *Standard and Poor's Corporation*

Real Estate Agency or Savings and Loan Association Records

- Property transactions

- Financial statements

- Payments made and received (settlement sheets)

- Credit files

- Loan applications. These do not contain quite the same information as loan applications given to a bank. A savings and loan association depends primarily upon real estate security rather than upon other assets and liabilities of a borrower.

Telephone Company Records

- Local directories, library of "out of city" directories

- Message unit detail sheets (in some areas) which list numbers called by a particular telephone

- Investigative reports on telephones used for illegal purposes

- Payments for service

- Toll calls. Because of the existence of more than one long distance carrier, toll records of a local phone company may be an incomplete listing of such calls. There may be a second telephone bill from another company, such as GT&E or MCI.

Transportation Company Records

- Passenger lists, reservations
- Destinations
- Fares paid
- Freight carrier-shippers, destinations, and storage points
- Departure and arrival times

Government Records
State Police (Central Records Section)

- Criminal cases
- Criminal intelligence
- Inflammable liquid installations
- Firearms registrations
- Investigations conducted for other departments
- Traffic arrests and motor vehicle accident investigations
- Noncriminal and criminal fingerprint records
- "Rogues gallery"
- Investigation of aviation rules and non-carrier civilian aircraft accidents
- Police training school files

City Police

- Criminal identification
  —Records of arrests, accidents, and general information
  —Alphabetical indexes of every complainant or suspect
  —"Aided" cards (citizen assistance)
  —Gun permits or applications and registrations
  —Lost or stolen articles Pawn shop files
  —Towed or repossessed autos
  —Ambulance files
  —Business information files
  —"Scofflaw files" (consistent violator of minor offense- primarily traffic)
- Other divisions
  —Criminal division files
  —Forgery squad (check squad)
  —Juvenile division
  —Morals or vice squad files
  —Narcotics bureau
  —Organized crime division
  —Police force personal history files
  —Public relations office (press file)
  —Traffic division files

Small Town Police

- Criminal index cards
- Criminal arrest cards

- Accident reports
- Complaint forms

- Offense reports

County Police (Sheriff)
- Criminal records

— Crimes involving bodily violence

— Crimes involving theft

— Crimes involving worthless checks

— Personal history sheets on people connected with the crimes

— Juvenile division records

— County business owners Traffic records

— Name, address, license plate number, driver's license number, arrest number, date and place of birth, sex, color, age, occupation, height, weight, complexion, color of hair, eyes, marks, and facts of arrest

National Sheriffs Association Directory
- List of State institutions and their superintendents

- State and Federal enforcement agencies and territorial jurisdictions
-
- Associate members of National Sheriffs Association

- County sheriffs

- Address of National Auto Theft Bureau

Other State and Local Law Enforcement and Quasi-Law Enforcement Organizations
- Specialized police organizations
- Public, semi-public, and private organizations
- The industrial security officer

- International Association of Chiefs of Police

- The monthly police administration review list of police publications

State and Local Court Records

Typically, there are three levels of courts within the State system. There is a Trial Court, where most litigation begins, an Appellate Court, which is the first level of appeal, and Court of Final Appeal. Sometimes you will find a court below the Trial Court which works much like the magistrate does in the Federal system.

Most litigation, such as divorce or breach of contract, takes place in the State and local system. Documents submitted to the court in connection with a divorce are particularly helpful in financial investigations. It is not unusual for detailed asset and liability information to be present in a divorce file.

Probate records describing estates and distribution of estates are also found in the State and local court system. These may be particularly helpful in negating nontaxable sources of cash.

Anytime a person is involved in a civil action, whether it be for breach of contract or some type of negligence action, a wealth of background information on the individual is usually provided to the opposing party through the court. A record of this information will be kept in the case files of the court and is available to an investigator.

Federal Government Records

Bureau of Alcohol, Tobacco, and Firearms (ATF)
•Distillers, brewers, and persons or firms who manufacture or handle alcohol, as a sideline or main product

•Inventory or retail liquor dealers and names of suppliers as well as amounts of liquor purchased by brand

•Names and records of known bootleggers

•Names of subjects of investigations by ATF

•Processors, manufacturers, and wholesalers of tobacco products

•List of all Federal firearms license holders, including manufacturers, importers, and dealers

•List of all Federal explosives license holders, including manufacturers, importers and dealers

•For weapons manufactured or imported after 1986, capability of tracing any firearm from manufacturer or importer to retailer

Bureau of the Public Debt
•U.S. savings bonds purchased and redeemed

•Requests for information must be addressed to:
Bureau of the Public Debt
Division of Transactions and Rulings
200 Third Street
Parkersburg, West Virginia 26101

Federal Aviation Agency (FAA)
This agency maintains records which reflect the chain of ownership of all civil aircraft in the United States. These records include documents relative to their manufacture and sale (sales contracts, bills of sale, mortgages, liens, transfers, inspections, and modifications). They also maintain licensing and medical information on pilots.

Federal Aviation Administration Civil Aviation Security Division AAC- 90, P.O. Box 25082 Oklahoma City, Oklahoma 73125

Department of Agriculture
•Licensed meat packers and food canners

•Inspections made under Pure Food and Drug Act

- Transactions with individuals and businesses (subsidies and adjustments)

Department of Defense
The Department of Defense maintains data concerning pay, dependents, allotment accounts, deposits, withholding statements (Forms W-2), and any other financial information relative to military personnel. This information is available at one the following offices, depending upon the branch of the Armed Forces to which the individual was or is presently attached:

United States Army Finance Center
Indianapolis, Indiana 46249
Request must include the complete name and Army serial number

Air Force Finance Center
RPTP

Denver, Colorado 80279
Director, Bureau of Supplies and Accounts Department of the Navy 13th and Euclid Streets Cleveland, Ohio 44115

Department of State
- Import and export licenses

- Foreign information

- Passport records (date and place of birth required). Recent data may be obtained from the local district court.

Drug Enforcement Administration (DEA)

- Licensed handlers of narcotics

- Criminal records of users, pushers, and suppliers of narcotics

Federal Bureau of Investigation (FBI)

- Criminal records and fingerprints

- Anonymous Letter Index

- National Stolen Property Index (stolen Government property, including military property)

- Nonrestricted information pertaining to criminal offenses and subversive activities

- National Fraudulent Check Index

U.S. Customs Service
- Record of importers and exporters

- Record of custom house brokers

- Record of custom house truckers (cartage licenses)

- List of suspects

- Records of persons who transport or cause to be transported currency of more than $10,000, or certain monetary instruments at one time into or out of the United States

U.S. Secret Service

- Records pertaining to counterfeit, forgery, and United States' security violation cases

- Records pertaining to anonymous letters and background files on persons who write "crank" letters

- Secret Service's central files in Washington, D.C., contain an estimated 100,000 handwriting specimens of known forgers. An electronic information retrieval system facilitates comparison of questioned handwriting with the specimens on file for identification purposes.

U.S. Postal Service

- Mail watch or cover

- Current or forwarding addresses of subjects and third parties

- Photostats of postal money orders. Requests for such records must be addressed to:
Money Order Division
Postal Data Center
P.O. Box 14965
St. Louis, Missouri 63182

- Addresses of post office box holders. These requests should be made only when efforts to obtain the information from other sources are unsuccessful. Information can be obtained from the Inspector-in-Charge or Postal Inspector. Check with the local post office to learn the identity of the inspector who can furnish the information.

Immigration and Naturalization Service (INS)

- Records of all immigrants and aliens

- Deportation proceedings

- Passenger manifests and declarations (ship, date, and point of entry required)

- Naturalization records (names of witnesses to naturalization proceedings and people who know the suspect)

- Lists of passengers and crews on vessels from foreign ports

- Financial statements of aliens and persons sponsoring their entry

Interstate Commerce Commission (ICC)

The ICC has information concerning individuals who are or have been officers of transportation firms engaged in interstate commerce. This information includes the officer's employment and financial affiliations.

In addition to the record information available from the ICC, most safety inspectors of the ICC are good sources of "reference" information because they have personal knowledge of supervisory employees of the various carriers in their region.

IRS National Computer Center

The National Computer Center is located in Martinsburg, West Virginia and it maintains the Master File, a tax record of all known taxpayers. The Master File is designed to accumulate all data pertaining to the tax liabilities of all taxpayers, regardless of location. The Master File is separated into several categories. Two of the categories are the Business Master File and the Individual Master File.

Securities and Exchange Commission (SEC)

- Records of corporate registrants of securities offered for public sale, which usually show:
  — A description of registrant's properties and business

  — A description of the significant provisions of the security to be offered for sale and its relationship to the registrant's other capital securities

  — Information as to the management of the registrant

  — Certified financial statements of the registrants

- Securities and Exchange Commission News Digest (a daily publication giving a brief summary of financial proposals files and the actions taken by the SEC)

- The SEC Bulletin is issued quarterly and contains information of official actions with respect to the preceding month. It also contains a supplement which lists the names of individuals reported as being wanted on charges of violations of the law in connection with securities transactions. It is available upon request at any of the SEC regional or branch offices in the following cities:

Atlanta, GA
Miami, FL
Boston, MA
New York, NY
Chicago, IL
Philadelphia, PA
Cleveland, OH
Salt Lake City, UT
Denver, CO
San Francisco, CA
Detroit, MI
Seattle, WA
Fort Worth, TX
St. Louis, MO
Los Angeles, CA
Washington, D.C.

- The SEC's Securities Violations Section maintains comprehensive files on individuals and firms who have been reported to the Commission as having violated Federal or State securities laws. The information pertains to official actions taken against such persons, including denials, refusals, suspensions, and revocations of registrations; injunctions, fraud orders, stop order, cease and desist orders; and arrests, indictments, convictions, sentences, and other official actions.

Social Security Administration

The Social Security Administration, headquartered in Baltimore, is responsible for the issuance of social security numbers. Records on social security paid by an individual or business are not available for review by the public.

If a social security number is known, it might lead to helpful information regarding the location in which the card was issued. Since many people apply for a social security number at a young age, this in turn can lead to locating the place of birth of an individual. There are nine digits in the social security number. With the exception of the 700 series, the first three digits reflect the state of issue. The last six digits are individual identifiers. The table on the next page contains a listing of the states of issue of the first three digits.

Initial Numbers	State of Issuance	Initial Numbers	State of Issuance
001 - 003	New Hampshire	449 - 467 627 - 645	Texas
004 - 007	Maine	468 - 477	Minnesota
008 - 009	Vermont	478 - 485	Iowa
010 - 034	Massachusetts	486 - 500	Missouri
035 - 039	Rhode Island	501 - 502	North Dakota
040 - 049	Connecticut	503 - 504	South Dakota
050 - 134	New York	505 - 508	Nebraska
135 - 158	New Jersey	509 - 515	Kansas
159 - 211	Pennsylvania	516 - 517	Montana
212 - 220	Maryland	518 - 519	Idaho
221 - 222	Delaware	520	Wyoming
223 - 231	Virginia	521 - 524	Colorado
232 - 236	West Virginia	525, 585, 648 - 649 allocated, not in use	New Mexico
237 - 246, 232 with middle digits 30	North Carolina	526 - 527 600 - 601	Arizona
247 - 251	South Carolina	528 - 529 646 - 647 allocated, not in use	Utah
252 - 260	Georgia	530	Nevada
261 - 267 589 - 595	Florida	531 - 539	Washington
268 - 302	Ohio	540 - 544	Oregon
303 - 317	Indiana	545 - 573, 602 - 626	California
318 - 361	Illinois	574	Alaska
362 - 386	Michigan	575 - 576	Hawaii
387 - 399	Wisconsin	577 - 579	Washington, DC
400 - 407	Kentucky	580 groups 01 - 18	Virgin Islands
408 - 415	Tennessee	580 (groups above 20) - 584, 596 - 599	Puerto Rico
416 - 424	Alabama	586	Guam, American Samoa, Northern Mariana Islands, Philippine Islands
425 - 428, 587 588 allocated, not in use	Mississippi	700 - 728	Railroad employees with special retirement act
429 - 432	Arkansas		
433 - 439	Louisiana		
440 - 448	Oklahoma		

Veterans Administration (VA)

•Records of loans, tuition payments, insurance payments, and nonrestrictive medical data related to disability pensions are available at regional offices. This information, including photostats, may be obtained by writing the appropriate regional office. All requests should include a statement covering the need and intended use of the information. The veteran should be identified clearly and, if available, the following information should be furnished:

—VA claim number

—Date of birth

—Branch of service

—Dates of enlistment and discharge

Federal Reserve Bank (FRB)

•Records of issue of United States Treasury Bonds

United States Coast Guard

•Records of persons serving on United States ships in any capacity

•Records of vessels equipped with permanently installed motors

•Records of vessels over 16 feet long equipped with detachable motors

Treasurer of the United States

Checks paid by the U.S. Treasury are processed through the Office of the Treasurer of the United States. Photostats of the canceled checks may be obtained by initiating a request through the U.S. government agency which authorized the check.

National Crime Information Center (NCIC)

The National Crime Information Center is a repository of data relating to crime and criminals gathered by local, State, and Federal law enforcement agencies. The NCIC's computer equipment is located at FBI Headquarters in Washington, D.C. The present equipment is capable of accommodating nearly 2 million records on criminal activities. In a matter of seconds, stored information can be retrieved through equipment in the telecommunications network. Connecting terminals are located throughout the country in police departments, sheriffs offices, State police facilities, and Federal law enforcement agencies. Dispatchers can respond quickly to requests. NCIC, as well as operating statewide systems, furnishes computerized data in a matter of seconds to all agencies participating in the centralized State systems. The goal of NCIC is to serve as a national index to fifty statewide computer systems and heavily populated metropolitan area systems.

NCIC Headquarters might be compared to a large automated "file cabinet" with each file having its own label or classification. Such a cabinet of data contains information concerning:

Stolen, missing, or recovered guns

Stolen articles

Wanted persons

Stolen/wanted vehicles

Stolen license plates

Stolen/wanted boats

Stolen/embezzled/missing securities

National Law Enforcement Telecommunications System (NLETS)

NLETS is a computerized communication network linking State and local enforcement agencies in all 50 States. It can provide information such as criminal history, driver's licenses, and vehicle registration.

El Paso Intelligence Center (EPIC)

EPIC is a multi-agency operation that collects, processes, and disseminates information on narcotics traffickers, gun smugglers, and alien smugglers in support of ongoing field investigations.

If a suspect is or has been engaged in any of the previously mentioned activities, it is possible that EPIC will have intelligence information on him or her. This information might include the name of the individual, his or her known activities, significant events, associations among individuals or activities, aircraft or vessels used by the subject, observations of both foreign and domestic movements of the subject, and his or her associates and their aircraft or vessels. EPIC also provides the name, agency, and telephone number of each investigator having expressed an interest in or having data regarding a subject. EPIC records often contain substantial *financial* information relative to the subject.

International Criminal Police Organization (Interpol)

Interpol is an international police agency with bureaus set up in member countries. In the United States, the National Central Bureau is under the direction and control of the Departments of Justice and Treasury.

The National Central Bureau can assist in such things as criminal history checks, license plate and driver's license checks, and the location of suspects, fugitives, and witnesses.

The Federal Courts

This system is basically a three step process. The first step is the U.S. District Court;, the second, the U.S. Court of Appeals; and the third, the U.S. Supreme Court. Since most court records are similar, we will only deal with the U.S. District Court in this appendix.

• U.S. District Courts

There are U.S. District Courts in every State (the larger States have several) and in the District of Columbia, Guam, Puerto Rico, the Canal Zone, and the Virgin Islands.

The U.S. District Court has exclusive jurisdiction in bankruptcy, maritime and admiralty, patents, copyright penalties, fines under Federal law, and proceedings against consul and vice consuls of foreign states. In addition, it has jurisdiction when the United States or a national bank is a party, and in cases where the law specifically states that the U.S. District Court has original jurisdiction. The U.S. District Courts have concurrent jurisdictions with State courts on "Federal questions" when the dispute arises under the Constitution, laws, or treaties of the United States; disputes between citizens of different States; one U.S. citizen and one citizen of a foreign state; or a citizen and a foreign state.

The U.S. District Court has broad criminal jurisdiction over all offenses against the laws of the United States. When both Federal and State laws are violated by one committing a crime, the offender is subject to prosecution in both the Federal and State courts for the separate crimes.

The files of the clerk's office of a U.S. District Court are not as complex as those of a State court of original jurisdiction. For the investigator, **the most important records in the custody of a clerk of a U.S. District Court are the case records.** These records consist of the files (case papers), the minutes, and the dockets.

—The files consist of pleadings, processes, and written orders and judgments of the court, and such other papers as pertain directly to the case.

—The minutes record, in summary form, of what happened during the proceedings. In some courts, the minutes are an integral part of the file.

—The docket sheet on each case is a chronological summary, not only of what takes place in court, but also of the papers in the file. The docket sheet can be very valuable to an investigator who is looking for only one item in a huge file. In most U.S. District Courts there are separate sets of dockets for bankruptcy, and civil and criminal cases. Some clerks have found it to their advantage to keep a set of miscellaneous dockets, and most clerks keep the docket sheets for closed cases in a separate area.

The clerk of a district court will have a record of banking institutions that have been designated as depositories for money of estates in bankruptcy.

The United States District Courts have jurisdiction to naturalize aliens and maintain copies of the certificates of naturalization as well as a name index of the individuals naturalized. If an alien elects to change his or her name at naturalization, both the old an new name appears in the index. In addition, a copy of the subject's Application to File Petition for Naturalization appears in the court records. This form (N-400) contains considerable information about the alien being naturalized.

•Other Federal Courts

To handle particular types of cases, Congress has established special courts. They are described in the *Guide to Court Systems* as follows:

—Court of Claims—The U.S. Government permits certain claims to be brought against itself in the U.S. Court of Claims.

—U.S. Customs Court— When certain merchandise is imported into the United States, customs duties have to be paid to the U.S. Government. Customs collectors at various ports in the United States classify merchandise and appraise it. When an importer complains on the rate, or that the merchandise was improperly excluded, the U.S. Customs Court is the court to which the case must be brought. Appeals from the U.S. Customs Courts are taken to the Court of Customs and Patent Appeals. This court also reviews certain decisions of the Patent Office and the U.S. Tariff Commission.

19

This appendix contains information regarding the American Bankers Association prefix numbers of cities and states and a listing of Federal Reserve Districts.

Federal Reserve Districts
1 -   Boston
2 -   New York
3 -   Philadelphia
4 -   Cleveland
5 -   Richmond
6 -   Atlanta
7 -   Chicago
8 -   St. Louis
9 -   Minneapolis
10 - Kansas City
11 - Dallas
12 - San Francisco

American Bankers Association Prefix Numbers

THE NUMERICAL SYSTEM
of The American Bankers Association
Index to Prefix Numbers of Cities and States
Numbers 1 to 49 inclusive are Prefixes for Cities
Numbers 50 to 99 inclusive are Prefixes for States
Numbers 50 to 58 are Eastern States
Number 59 is Hawaii
Numbers 60 to 69 are Southeastern States
Numbers 70 to 79 are Central States
Numbers 80 to 88 are Southwestern States
Number 89 is Alaska

Prefix Numbers of Cities in Numerical Order

1 New York, N.Y.	14 New Orleans, La.	26 Memphis, Tenn.	38 Savannah, Ga.
2 Chicago, Il.	15 Washington, D.C.	27 Omaha, Neb.	39 Oklahoma City, Ok.
3 Philadelphia, Pa.	16 Los Angeles, Ca.	28 Spokane, Wash.	40 Wichita, Kan.
4 St Louis, Mo.	17 Minneapolis, Minn.	29 Albany, N.Y.	41 Sioux City, Iowa
5 Boston, Mass.	18 Kansas City, Mo.	30 San Antonio, Tx.	42 Pueblo, Co.
6 Cleveland, Ohio	19 Seattle, Wash.	31 Salt Lake City, Ut	43 Lincoln, Neb.
7 Baltimore, Md.	20 Indianapolis, Ind.	32 Dallas, Tx.	44 Topeka, Kan.
8 Pittsburgh, Pa.	21 Louisville, Ky.	33 Des Moines, Iowa	45 Dubuque, Iowa
9 Detroit, Mich.	22 St. Paul, Minn.	34 Tacoma, Wash.	46 Galveston, Tx.
10 Buffalo, N.Y.	23 Denver, Colo.	35 Houston, Tx.	47 Cedar Rapids, Iowa
11 San Francisco, Ca.	24 Portland, Ore.	36 St. Joseph, Mo.	48 Waco, Tx.
12 Milwaukee, Wis.	25 Columbus, Ohio	37 Fort Worth, Tx.	49 Muskogee, Ok.
13 Cincinnati, Ohio			

Prefix Numbers of States in Numerical Order

50 New York	64 Georgia	77 North Dakota	89 Alaska
51 Connecticut	65 Maryland	78 South Dakota	90 California
52 Maine	66 North Carolina	79 Wisconsin	91 Arizona
53 Massachusetts	67 South Carolina	80 Missouri	92 Idaho
54 New Hampshire	68 Virginia	81 Arkansas	93 Montana
55 New Jersey	69 West Virginia	82 Colorado	94 Nevada
56 Ohio	70 Illinois	83 Kansas	95 New Mexico
57 Rhode Island	71 Indiana	84 Louisiana	96 Oregon
58 Vermont	72 Iowa	85 Mississippi	97 Utah
59 Hawaii	73 Kentucky	86 Oklahoma	98 Washington
60 Pennsylvania	74 Michigan	87 Tennessee	99 Wyoming
61 Alabama	75 Minnesota	88 Texas	101 Territories
62 Delaware	76 Nebraska		
63 Florida			

PLANNING, CONDUCTING AND RECORDING AN INTERVIEW

"Talk is cheap because supply exceeds demand."

The above statement may be true in many situations, but when it comes to an investigator trying to get answers out of a witness, the opposite will probably happen. One of the most important skills investigators can develop is the ability to get people to open up and talk to them. In this chapter, you will learn about the "art" of interviewing. Yes, it is an art because those who do it well are more successful than those who shrug interviewing off as just "asking questions and writing down answers."

An interview is more than just going to someone's house, knocking on the door, and then asking questions. It takes planning. If you come across in a threatening manner or can't adequately explain why you need to interview a witness, you'll never get any voluntary cooperation. If you ask complex questions or don't allow witnesses to tell their story in their own words, you're not going to get what it is you are after. And, finally, if you cannot adequately convey to others what you found out during the interview, it may as well not have taken place. The "art" of interviewing consists of three phases—planning, conducting, and recording—all of which are discussed in this chapter.

- State the purpose of a financial interview.
- List the objectives of a financial interview.
- Describe the elements that must be considered when planning an interview
- Describe techniques used when conducting an interview.
- Identify and describe methods used to record an interview.

"Just the facts." Remember Sergeant Joe Friday's famous phrase from the television Show *Dragnet*? For years, every week like clockwork, Joe had the uncanny ability to detect, investigate, and resolve criminal matters in 30 minutes or less.

Television makes it look easy. Unfortunately, it isn't. Detecting and investigating a financial crime can take weeks, months, and even years. So, while reality significantly differs from what happens on television, one thing remains the same—financial investigators, just like Joe Friday, search for facts by interviewing people.

Few skills are as important to the financial investigator as the ability to talk to people and successfully gather information from them. Yet, law enforcement officers are not empowered to force people to talk to them. These powers are granted only to courts, grand juries, and certain judicial and legislative bodies. Consequently, investigators face the double duty of convincing the interviewee (hereafter called the **witness**) to agree to be interviewed and then getting the witness to talk after getting inside the door.

WHAT IS AN INTERVIEW?

Phone interviews. Employment interviews. Counseling interviews. Investigatory interviews. As you can see, there are many types of interviews. And though they all serve different purposes, they are founded on the same definition: an interview is a specialized form of oral, face-to-face communication between people that is entered into for a specific task-related purpose associated with a particular subject matter.

For the financial investigator, two aspects of this definition should be noted. The first one is that an interview is a face-to-face communication. Not only will investigators listed to what witnesses say, they will be able to see what the witnesses do. The visual and non-verbal aspects of an interview are very important and should not be overlooked. Secondly, the interview has a specific task-related purpose. This task-related purpose is what makes an interview different from mere conversation. A conversation can take off in many directions; an interview must be focused on relevant content.

INTRODUCTION TO THE FINANCIAL INTERVIEW

Before we get into a general discussion of the interview process, we should look at some specifics of the financial interview. The purpose of a financial interview, its objectives, and the type of question to be asked during a financial interview are discussed below.

Purpose and Objectives

For the financial investigator, the interview is a tool used to determine what knowledge a witness has concerning an investigation. Knowledge in this context includes information about the allegation or crime in question, and any relevant records in a witness's possession. The information and documents provided to the investigator form the basis of the witness's testimony.

A financial interview is different from a financial interrogation. Financial interviews are conducted to obtain information and documentation from witnesses. Financial interrogations are conducted with suspects and hostile witnesses to elicit confessions or admissions of culpability. An investigator may plan on conducting an interview and have it turn into an interrogation. Conversely, interrogation can commenced only to discover that the witness appears to be innocent, and with that, an interrogation turns into an interview.

The financial interview is not something that investigators undertake haphazardly. Prior to each interview, they must decide what they hope to accomplish by interviewing a particular witness. In other words, they must determine the interview's objective(s).

The objectives of a financial interview are:

- To obtain information that establishes or refutes the allegation or crime under investigation.
- To obtain leads for further development of the case
- To obtain all information and documents in the witness's possession relative to the financial investigation
- To obtain background and personal information about the witness and motivation for involvement in the crime

Type of Question Asked

A financial interview is a special type of investigatory interview. During most investigations, people are interviewed to obtain their recollections of events. For example:

- "Can you describe the person who came into the bank?"
- "Do you remember if anyone was with him?"
- "What color was the car she purchased?"

Financial interviews go beyond recollection questions. Like the financial investigation itself, they are concerned with specific details of financial transactions and the movement of money. For example:

- "Why did you have this check cashed?"
- "You notarized two signatures on this document. One is the suspect's. Who is the other individual?"
- "How did she pay for the car?"

THE THREE PHASES OF AN INTERVIEW

For any investigator, an interview is more than just asking a witness some questions. Who should be interviewed? What questions should be asked? In what order should the questions be asked? Where should the interview take place? How can the witness be put at ease so that he or she cooperates? What happens to the information collected? These are just some of the questions an investigator must ask before, during, and after the interview.

A good interview requires a lot of forethought, skillful execution, and an ability to convey what happened during the interview to others. The interview process is comprised of the following three phases:

- Planning
- Conducting
- Recording

Planning an Interview

Prior to planning any interview, the investigator is usually faced with one or more of the following conditions:

- A crime has been alleged or committed, but the facts relating to the situation have not yet been established.
- A complainant or victim has been identified. This could be an individual, business, or governmental entity.
- Records or documents reflecting financial transactions relating to the suspected criminal activity have surfaced.
- Rumors, innuendo, or factual information pointing to a specific suspect have emerged.

The investigator uses the interview to develop information about these existing conditions. The information collected will be used to support or dispel the allegations.

Selecting Witnesses

When an investigation begins, investigators must determine who they want to interview and in what order. Traditional criminal cases are generally investigated by first contacting the outer circle of honest, disinterested witnesses and then working inward to the co-conspirators and ultimately to the target. Law enforcement normally starts the interview process with the complaining witness and after exhausting his or her knowledge of the facts and reasons for suspicion, proceeds in a similar manner around the outer circle of witnesses.

In a financial investigation, this traditional sequence is often altered. Following the movement of money dictates talking to witnesses that have knowledge of financial transactions. Accordingly, the hierarchy of interviews is determined by the degree of knowledge or participation in financial activities created by the alleged criminal event or crime at issue. For example, in a political corruption investigation, documents showing the movement of money from the payer of the bribe to the taker of the bribe would be of paramount importance to the investigator. People with documents (bankers, money couriers, business associates) would be priority contacts. In an embezzlement or tax evasion investigation, the key interviews would be with custodians of accounting records and internal audit files, and tax return preparers. Even in a drug case, financial transactions decide the order of contacts for the investigator. The priority witnesses will have records reflecting the suspect's use of proceeds from the drug trade. While each investigation offers a different set of interview options and priorities, the bottom line in a financial investigation is that every person who has documents pertaining to financial transactions, or knowledge about them, should be interviewed.

Types of Witnesses

One of the things an investigator must consider prior to contacting an individual for an interview is what type of witness will that person be. Will he or she be cooperative, hostile, or have no feelings one way or the other? Prospective witnesses can be categorized into three general types.

Neutral
This is an uninterested third party such as a custodian of public or financial records. This person has no interest in the outcome of the investigation and provides documents and/or unbiased information.

Friendly
A friendly witness is one who cooperates. Witnesses are friendly for a variety of reasons. Certain people naturally tell anybody everything. Others realize that they stand to benefit from providing information about the suspect to authorities. Also, many people seem to enjoy "playing detective" and get caught up in the excitement of being a part of an important investigation.

Reluctant or Hostile
This is an uncooperative party who is typically a friend or associate of the suspect. This witness may also be hostile due to his or her own culpability in the criminal activity under investigation.

Neutral and friendly witnesses usually agree to interviews upon request. No more than proper identification and introduction by the investigator opens the door. Interviewing hostile witnesses often presents greater challenges. Most likely, these witnesses will not voluntarily submit to an interview. They refuse to provide information and documents.
Since law enforcement cannot, on its own, compel any witness to say or do anything, investigators need assistance from the legal system. With approval from a government attorney (i.e., city or district attorney, or U.S. Attorney), the investigator can be issued a document (i.e., summons, subpoena) which commands a witness to appear and submit to an interview. The investigator serves this document on the witness and, if the witness disregards the document, contempt charges and incarceration possibly could result. But even an investigative tool that can command appearance before the investigator does not override a witness's constitutional

guarantees. So, while a hostile witness can be ordered to open the door and submit to an interview, he or she cannot be compelled to say anything incriminating.

Contacting the Suspect

The suspect is a valuable source of information. It follows then that deciding when to interview the suspect is an important decision. Should he or she be contacted at the start of the investigation or confronted upon its completion? Should the investigator contact the suspect at all? The decision is determined by the investigator and is different for each investigation. Interviewing the suspect during the early stages of the investigation makes good sense if it is feared that records in his or her possession may be destroyed or an alibi may be concocted. Often, catching the suspect off guard results in a more responsive interview filled with more answers and more documents. Also, early interviews have resulted in quick confessions and/or early indications of innocence.

On the other hand, delaying contact with the suspect may be advantageous if information and documents gathered from other witnesses can be used to refute the suspect's alibis and lies. Additionally, confessions sometimes occur when the suspect is confronted face to face with the evidence of guilt.

In certain situations, the suspect may not be interviewed at all. He or she may be beyond the reach of law enforcement (i.e., out of the country) or may be represented by an attorney who refuses to allow his or her client to be interviewed on constitutional grounds.

Method of Questioning

While planning an interview, the investigator must determine the method of questioning to use. Questioning can be organized in a number of ways:

- **Chronological Method.** The witness is questioned about the events in the order that they occurred from beginning to end. This is the usual organization of questioning.

- **Questioning According to Documents.** In this type of interview format, a particular document (financial statement, canceled check, tax return) is the focus. The witness may be the legal custodian of the record and have no other involvement in the investigation.

- **Questioning According to Transactions or Events.** The witness may have sold the subject of a house or delivered a package for him or her. The questions in this situation would center on the event and radiate from there.

During the planning phase, the investigator should prepare a written outline that lists main topics to be covered in the interview. An outline allows the investigator to concentrate on important ideas and areas to be covered. However, writing down every specific question to be asked and in a specified order should be avoided as this has the tendency to make the investigator inflexible and tied to the next question. The investigator unwittingly becomes guided by what is written on the sheet of paper instead of what is being said by the witness. Also, the witness may catch a glimpse of the upcoming questions and prepare responses in advance. The following page contains a simplified example of an interview outline. The outline used for an actual interview would be more extensive.

Sample Interview Outline

Ray Austin Interview

Introduction: Identify Self
                 State Purpose

Background: DOB
                 SSN
                 Address
                 Married
                 Wife (Maiden Name)
                 Children
                 Source of Income
                 Parents
                 Education
                 Military
                 Prior Arrest, Convictions

Assets
Liabilities
Cash-on-Hand

Associates: Adkins HTB Inc.
                Allen Cleveland
                Massey TB Trust
                Rosemary Westbury
                Tony Idaho
                Toni Boise
                Marc Fresno

Conducting an Interview

Once an investigator is finished with the planning phase, he or she is ready to conduct the interview. The interview itself is composed of three distinct parts:

- Introduction
- Body
- Close

Introduction

The introduction is critical as it sets the tone for the whole interview. It serves the following two purposes:

- Allows the investigator to identify himself or herself to the witness
- Allows the investigator to state the purpose of the contact

The following shows right and wrong ways for an investigator to introduce himself or herself.

Wrong
"Mr. Smith, my name is John Jones and this is Mary Adams. We're with the government. We're investigating Jim Dealer and we need to talk to you."

Right
"Mr. Smith, my name is John Jones. I am a Special Agent with the Internal Revenue Service's Criminal Investigation Division. This is Special Agent Mary Adams from the Drug Enforcement Administration. We are currently conducting an investigation involving alleged violations of money laundering laws by Jim Dealer. May we speak to you for a few moments?"

The objective of the introduction is to put witnesses at ease and to get them to agree to answer questions. However, once the investigator identifies himself or herself, the next question normally is asked by the witness.

Witness: "Why are you contacting me?"
Investigator: "We would like to ask some questions about your financial dealings with Jim Dealer and his associates."

Since the investigator's goal is to put the witness in a frame-of-mind to answer questions, he or she must supply a reason which leads the witness to perceive that he or she will benefit from cooperating with the investigator. If the witness believes that the investigator represents a threat, voluntary cooperation is generally lost. The next page shows some right and wrong ways to gain the cooperation of a hesitant witness.

During the introduction, the investigator should ask general, almost generic, questions such as name, address, telephone number, and date of birth. Since many witnesses are apprehensive, the investigator needs to be patient and avoid rushing into important questions. Through reassuring the witness that his or her cooperation will not cause any undue hardships, inconveniences, or embarrassment, a rapport can be established that will assist both the witness and the investigator during the interview process. When the introduction has been completed and the witness is ready to talk, the investigator moves on to the second part of the actual interview—the body.

Right and Wrong Ways to Gain the Cooperation of a Witness

Wrong
Witness: "Why should I talk to you? I don't want to get involved."
Investigator: "You should have thought of that sooner; it's too late now. We can talk here or we can talk downtown. It's your choice."

Right
Witness: "Why should I talk to you? I don't want to get involved."
Investigator: "You certainly are not required to talk to me. I am just seeking some information on a serious matter which may or may not result in legal action. By speaking informally with me now, it may save you the trouble of having to testify later, depending on the information you have. Is that okay?"

Or

Witness: "I don't want to answer any questions at this time without first talking to my lawyer."

Investigator: "You certainly don't have to talk to me, with or without your lawyer. Let's do it this way. Let me ask you a few questions; and if you don't want to answer them, just say so. I'm not trying to get you into trouble. I'm just trying to do my job and get some answers. Is that okay?"

The Body

The body of the interview is the fact finding part of the interview process. Questions are asked and answers are provided. The structure of the interview is determined by the method of questioning (chronological, by document, or by transaction or event) which should have been pre-determined and outlined by the investigator.

In this stage of the interview, witnesses should be allowed to tell their story in their own words. Recognizing that a witness's story will usually be disjointed and rambling, the investigator must be prepared to put order to the material—find the details, focus for clarity, and ensure the accuracy. For the investigator, conducting an interview is much more than just asking questions and writing down answers. This process requires concentration and active participation by the investigator if his or her objectives are going to be achieved.

The time-honored questioning devices of *who, what, where, why, why,* and *how* allow investigators to push witnesses for details. Investigators should continue the questions until they are convinced that a witness's knowledge of a topic is exhausted. Details, details, details! Whether recollections or records, it is the detail provided by the witness that lays the foundation for a successful financial investigation. The following exchange between an investigator and a witness illustrates how to pursue the detail in a line of questioning.

Investigator: "How was the kickback payment made?"
Witness: "At a meeting."
Investigator: "Where did this meeting take place?"
Witness: "In Mr. X's office."
Investigator: "How many people were there?"
Witness: "There were three of us."
Investigator: "Who were they?"
Witness: "Mr. X, Bill Baker, and me."
Investigator: "How was the kickback divided?"
Witness: "Mr. X split it into three piles."
Investigator: "How much did each of you get?"
Witness: "I don't know. Mr. X didn't count the money. He just estimated the size of each pile."
Investigator: "Did you all get the same size piles?"
Witness: "Yes. I counted it at my office. I had just a little over $100,000."
Investigator: "Would you say that Mr. X received about $100,000 also?"
Witness: "That would seem about right."

A witness's opinion of events often clouds the facts. Although there is nothing wrong with requesting an opinion from a witness, the investigator, through proper questioning, needs to separate the facts (what was said) from the opinions (what was talked about). The goal is a verbatim recollection from the witness. For example:

Wrong
"What did you and Jim Dealer talk about?"

Right
"What did Jim Dealer say to you? What did you say to him?"

As was stated earlier, an investigator must actively participate in the interview process. It's not as simple as ask a question, write down a response. The investigator must constantly analyze responses, and continually check for inconsistencies, and incompleteness. For example:

Investigator: "How long did your meeting with Mr. Grey last?"
Witness: "It lasted all day."
Investigator: "What did Mr. Grey say?"
Witness: "Not much."

An all-day meeting with not much said should raise a red flag in the investigator's mind. This line of questioning needs to be pursued.

During an interview, investigators have a multitude of tasks to handle simultaneously. From listening to a response and recording it, to formulating the next question, they have a lot to do. There are some general "do's and don'ts" that investigators should consider when performing an interview.

Interview Do's and Don'ts

- *Do* interviews as a team. One investigator listens and controls the questioning while the second records the responses.

- *Do* interview witnesses individually. Attempting to interview two witnesses in the same room at the same time results in one of two things—one witness influences the other's responses or one witness becomes mute, thereby allowing the second witness to answer all the questions. Always separate witnesses and conduct their interviews simultaneously.

- *Do* control the interview. For example, don't let an attorney who is present disrupt the interview. Before beginning the interview, advise each participant of their role in the process. This should help eliminate any control problems.

- *Do* provide the witness with an "out". If a witness has previously denied knowledge, or has supplied false information, there is often reluctance to admit it. The investigator should provide this witness an "out". It normally will be taken. For example:
"Mr. Smith, I know when we talked before you denied knowing Mr. Dealer. You probably forgot about meeting him. Can we start over?"

- *Don't* ask compound/complex or negatively phrased questions (i.e., "you didn't see the money, did you?"). Questions should be simple, to the point, and positively phrased.

- *Don't* make threats and avoid threatening remarks. Threats rarely work, so overbearing tactics should be avoided. The "good cop/bad cop" interview technique looks good on television, but is usually inappropriate in financial investigations.

In our legal system, documents cannot speak for themselves, either figuratively or literally. A witness must identify, explain, and introduce every financial document to give it meaning in any legal proceeding or court action. So what does interviewing have to do with the introduction of documents into a legal proceeding? Plenty! Successful interviewing creates cooperative witnesses who breathe life into financial records involving the movement of money.

Technical areas such as accounting procedures or business specialties should be covered in detail during the body of an interview. The investigator should ask questions concerning the document's entries, meanings, and purposes. The investigator should also determine the identity of the document's custodian and solicit the authenticity of the document. Investigators should not be afraid to ask questions and should keep that old saying, "There is no such thing as a stupid question" in mind. Any question can lead to a surprising answer.

The investigator's job during the interview process is not complete until he or she has exhausted the witness's knowledge on the important topics relative to the ongoing investigation. Successful interviews obtain information and financial leads, as opposed to solving the case. If enough interviews are conducted and enough information is uncovered, the case will solve itself.

The Close

After the witness has provided information, the investigator should review the key points gathered during the body of the interview. This process of summing up the important facts serves the following two purposes:

- It allows the investigator to clarify the facts.
- It provides an opportunity for the investigator and witness to agree with the investigator's summation.

Once the summation has been agreed on, the investigator should ask the following three questions:

- **"Is there anything that I have forgotten to ask?"**
  Probably the number one reason investigators fail to get the answers they seek is that they simply fail to ask the question. Using this "catch-all" question allows the witness the opportunity to play detective.

- **"Is there anyone else you think I should speak with?"**
  This question is designed to find more leads. If the witness is hesitant, it's okay to say that his or her name will not be revealed to the person(s) suggested.

- **"Is there anything else that you would like to say?"**
  This should be the investigator's last question. It gives the witness one final chance to say anything that he or she wishes.

Exit gracefully, even after encounters with hostile witnesses. Soothe the apprehensive witness by mentioning that all the information that he or she provided will be held in confidence and/or for official purposes only. If the witness was cooperative, thank him or her for the cooperation; if nothing was said, express regrets and leave the door open for future contacts.

Recording an Interview

Investigators conduct interviews to obtain information and documents in an attempt to resolve financial crimes. It is also necessary to prepare a permanent record of each interview for future reference and use. Often in a financial investigation, persons interviewed become trial witnesses. The record of the financial interview as prepared by the investigator can be used to refresh the witness's memory and assist the witness in the identification process relative to a financial document.

The complexity and investigative importance of an interview determines the best method to record it. In situations where no information is secured, a limited report or record of interview is acceptable. However, in situations where "case critical questions" are answered, or denials are made by an important witness, a more formal record becomes necessary. The only constraint in the recordation process is the requirement for accuracy and completeness by the investigator preparing the written summary.

When an investigator plays the role of an interviewer, he or she must be accurate, fair, and just. The prosecuting attorney relies on the investigator's written notes taken during an interview. The investigator's portrayal of the interview process should accurately and completely reflect the witness's testimony.

Informal Notes

The "informal notes" taken by investigators during the course of the interview, in conjunction with their recollections, provide the basis for the written record. Informal notes should contain sufficient detail to permit investigators to refresh their memories as to what transpired during the interview. Any method of recording the details is sufficient if it shows the date, time, place, persons present, and what occurred. The following is an example of the informal notes taken by Special Agent John Jones during an interview with Richard Smith. Special Agents Jones and Adams interviewed Smith concerning a financial transaction (the purchase of a car) he had with the suspect, Jim Dealer.

Re: Jim Dealer
Talked with Richard Smith
123 A Street

John Jones, IRS
Mary Adams, DEA
July 25, 2018
10 A.M. - 10:47 A.M.

Dealer called Smith about truck Smith advertised. Dealer came to see truck about ½ hour after call. Test drove truck around block, then paid $25,000 in cash, in $100 bills, for truck.

2015 truck, serial #1173945

Memorandum

A second way to record interviews is to "formalize" the investigator's informal notes into a "memorandum of interview." A memorandum should be prepared when details of an interview are too numerous to be fully and properly related through informal notes. It should state what occurred during the interview and show the date, time, place, and persons present. If the person interviewed was advised of his or her constitutional rights during the interview, this fact should also be noted in the memorandum. The final typed memorandum should be prepared as soon as possible, and promptly signed and dated by the investigators present during the interview. The actual date of preparation should be shown at the bottom of the memorandum. If it becomes necessary to correct or supplement a memorandum after it has been finalized, the supplemental memorandum should clearly state the date and reason for such action, and the previous memorandum should be attached.

Handwritten notes made during an interview and used as the basis for a more detailed memorandum may be subject to inspection by a court and should be retained in the case file. Investigators should confine memorandums to the facts developed in the interviews and should avoid opinions, conclusions, and extraneous matters.

When deciding whether or not to use a memorandum as a means of recording interview notes, an investigator should consider the following advantages and disadvantages.

Advantages and Disadvantages of the Memorandum

Advantages	Disadvantages
Informal	Does not contain the exact words of the interviewee
Contains all pertinent testimony obtained in the interview	Since information was not mechanically recorded, there is a a chance for some information to be forgotten
Memorandums can be prepared by topic and, therefore, are easy to follow	
Does not require an oath or affirmation	

An example of a memorandum appears on the following page.

Example of Memorandum of Interview

In re: James Dealer
         115 South Street
         Miami, Florida

Present: Richard Smith, Witness
         Special Agent, Mary Adams
         Special Agent, John Jones

Place: Office of Richard Smith
         117 Elm Street
         North Miami, Florida

Date: July 25, 2018

Time: 10:00 A.M. to 10:47 A.M.

1. S/A Adams and I made a field call to a travel agency located at 117 Elm Street, the known employer of Richard Smith. Records obtained from State vehicle registration files reveal that Smith transferred the title of a truck (serial number 1173945) to Dealer in May 2017.
2. After proper introduction and identification (by displaying our credentials and badges), I asked Mr. Smith if he would answer a few questions about the sale of his truck. Mr. Smith agreed and, when asked, stated the following:

   a. He advertised his truck for sale in a newspaper at $25,000.
   b. Dealer responded to the ad and bought the truck by paying $25,000 in currency, composed of one hundred dollar bills.
   c. The sale was completed on May 29, 2017, when the currency was exchanged for the truck and registration paperwork.

3. Mr. Smith further stated that he would agree to reducing the information to a written affidavit and swear to its accuracy.
4. I suggested that we meet again tomorrow at his home to prepare the affidavit. Mr. Smith agreed.
5. This interview concluded at 10:47 A.M. when we left Mrs. Smith's office.

I (prepared/dictated) this memorandum on July 26, 2018, after refreshing my memory from notes made during and immediately after the interview with Richard Smith.

John Jones
Special Agent

I certify that this memorandum has recorded in it a summary of all pertinent matters discussed with Richard and immediately after the interview with Richard Smith.

Mary Adams
Witness

Question and Answer Statement

A question and answer statement is a complete transcript of the questions, answers, and statements made by each participant during an interview. It may be prepared from a stenographer's notes or from a mechanical recording device. The source used to prepare the transcript should be preserved and associated with the case file as it may be needed in court to establish what was said.

A question and answer statement should contain:

- When and where the testimony was obtained

- The name and address of the person giving the testimony

- The matter the testimony relates to, including the purpose of the interview

- The name and title of the investigator asking questions and the name and title of the person giving answers

- The names and titles of all persons present during the testimony and the reason for each person being present, if not obvious

- The consent of the person being interviewed to use a tape recorder if a mechanical recording is being made

- Information given to the person being interviewed concerning his or her rights to counsel and against self-incrimination, if appropriate

- Administration of an oath if given

- Questions and answers establishing that the statement was made freely and voluntarily, without duress, and that no promises or commitments were made by the investigators

- Signatures of the investigators who conducted the interview and the person being interviewed

- Signature and the certification of the person transcribing the statement, showing the soured of the original information used

- Information that the person being interviewed was given the opportunity to examine the statement, correct any errors, and sign it

Question and Answer Statement Format

Testimony of (name, address) given at (location including address) at (time) on (date) about (subject of investigation and their address).

Present at this interview are (names and titles of all persons present).

Questions were asked by (name and title of person asking the questions) and answers given by (person being interviewed).

This interview is being recorded, as agreed upon, by means of (method of recording).

1. Q. You were requested to appear at (location) to answer questions concerning (subject matter). (If appropriate, advise the person being interviewed of his or her rights to counsel, etc.).

2. Q. Please stand and raise your right hand. Do you (person being interviewed) solemnly swear that the answers you are about to give to the questions asked will be the truth, so help you God?

3. Q. Did you sell a truck that you owned to Mr. Jim Dealer?
   A. (answer)

4. Q. How much did he pay you for the truck?
   A. (answer)

NOTE: The interview is brought to a close with the following questions?

120. Q. Have I, or has any other investigator or officer, threatened or intimidated you in any manner?
   A. (answer)

121. Q. Have I, or any other investigator or officer, offered you any rewards, promises, or immunity, in return for this statement?
   A. (answer)

122. Q. Have you given this statement freely and voluntarily?
   A. (answer)

123. Q. Is there anything further you care to add for the record?
   A. (answer)

After this statement has been transcribed, you will be given an opportunity to read it, correct any errors, and sign it.

NOTE: When transcribing the statement include the following:

I have carefully read the foregoing statement consisting of page 1 to (last page number), inclusive, which is a correct transcript of my answers to questions asked me on (date of statement) at (location where statement was given), relative to (subject of investigation and their address). I hereby certify that the foregoing answers are true and correct, that I have made the corrections shown, have placed my initials opposite each correction, and that I have initialed each page of the statement.

    (signature of person giving statement)

Subscribed and sworn to before me at (time), on (date) at (present location).

    (signature and title of investigator)
    (signature and title of witnessing investigator)

I (name of person transcribing statement), do hereby certify that I took the foregoing statement of (person giving statement) from (method of recording) and personally transcribed it and have initialed each page.

    (signature and title of transcriber)

Normally, people will review and sign a question and answer statement after it has been put in its final form. Sometimes, for various reasons, the person may change his or her position and refuse to sign the statement. When an investigator is faced with such a refusal, he or she should request that the statement be read and verified for correctness. In such situations, the following can be inserted at the end of the statement.

This statement was read by (name) on (date) who stated that it was true and correct, but refused to be placed under oath or to sign it.

Just as there are advantages and disadvantages to using a memorandum as a recording device, so there are for the use of a question and answer statement.

Advantages and Disadvantages of the Question and Answer Statement

Advantages	Disadvantages
Reflects both questions and answers	Usually contains unnecessary material
Questions are generally asked in a logical sequence	Is often very long and involved
Is difficult to dispute with claims of misunderstanding	It is unedited; therefore, it picks up incorrect grammar, etc.
Is preferred when the issues are complicated	Tape recorder will pick up outside noises which can disrupt recording
Is useful when the person testifying under oath is illiterate or below average intelligence	Unable to make voice distinction
	Mechanical failure (if tape recorder used)
Can be used to challenge or discredit a witness	Can be viewed as intimidating by deponent; therefore, witnesses are often not willing to participate

Affidavit

An affidavit is a written declaration of facts made voluntarily and confirmed by oath or affirmation. The text of an affidavit may be prepared extemporaneously or composed by agreement between the affiant, the person making the statement, and the investigator. An affidavit can be either typed or handwritten, and prepared either by the affiant or investigator. There are certain advantages to allowing the affiant to compose and write an affidavit. These advantages are:

- The affidavit will be in the affiant's own words.
- The affidavit will be more credible because it is in the affiant's own handwriting. It would be difficult for the affiant to later deny the affidavit was his or hers.

One advantage to having the investigator prepare the affidavit is that the investigator will ensure that only relevant information will be covered and that the information will appear in an orderly fashion. In cases where the affiant is unable to either read or write, a witness other than the affiant or the investigator must read the affidavit to the affiant before he or she signs it. The affidavit must also be signed by both the investigator and witness.

No particular form of affidavit is required by common law. It is customary that affidavits have a caption or title, the judicial district in which given, the signature of the affiant, and the jurat. A jurat is the certification on an affidavit declaring when, where, and before whom it was sworn.

The affidavit is one of the most commonly used forms of recording testimony. It can be used during trial to impeach a witness, refresh memory, or it can be introduced as evidence. An affidavit should not contain hearsay or information about which the witness has no direct knowledge. If the person being interviewed was advised of his or her constitutional rights, this should be included in the affidavit.

A sample affidavit is found on the next page.

Sample Affidavit

United States of America
Southern Judicial District of Florida

I, <u>Richard L. Smith   </u> state that:
I reside at <u>123 A Street, Miami, Florida   </u>.
I am currently employed as a travel agent at Miami Travel, located at 117 Elm Street, Miami, Florida. On May 28, 2018, I placed a newspaper advertisement in the Miami Herald classified ads offering my 2017 truck for sale. I listed the asking price as $25,000. On May 29, I received a phone call from a man who said that he read the ad and would like to see my truck. He stated that he would like to look at it that afternoon. I gave him my address, and he came over about 30 minutes later. I gave him the keys, and we took a ride around the block. He said that he would buy the truck for $25,000. He opened the trunk of the car he was driving and pulled out a briefcase. We went into my house where he took $25,000 in one hundred dollar bills from the briefcase to pay for the truck. I was surprised at being paid in currency, but the man stated that he wanted the truck today and knew that it would take time for a check to clear the bank, so he brought cash. I gave him the ownership papers for the truck. I said thanks for buying the truck and gave him my business card requesting that he give me a call if he needed any travel planning. He gave me his business card and said he was in the import-export business. Jim went to his car and made a telephone call and a couple of minutes later two guys arrived and one drove Jim's car while Jim drove the truck away. I have not seen or heard from Jim since that day. On today's date, I gave Special Agent Jones a copy of the truck registration, serial number 1173945, that I sold to Jim Dealer on May 29, 2018, and the business card I received from Jim Dealer on that same date. I have received a receipt for both of these items from Special Agent Jones.

I have read the foregoing statement consisting of <u>1   </u> page(s) and have signed it. I fully understand this statement and it is true, accurate, and complete to the best of my knowledge and belief.

I made this statement freely and voluntarily without any threats or rewards, or promises of reward having been made to me in return for it.

Richard L. Smith
(Signature of affiant)
Subscribed and sworn to me before this <u>29</u>[th]
day of <u>July   </u>, <u>2018</u>.
at <u>Miami, Florida   </u>

John Jones
(Signature)

Special Agent
(Title)

Mary Adams
(Signature of witness, if any)

The affidavit, like the memorandum and the question and answer statement, has advantages and disadvantages to its use. Prior to using an affidavit, the items listed below should be considered.

Advantages and Disadvantages of an Affidavit

Advantages	Disadvantages
Preserves probable testimony	Does not reflect questions asked
Frequently used in requiring testimony from:	May contain non-related information if prepared by affiant
Hostile witnesses	May not contain all pertinent information when prepared by affiant
Witnesses who have changed allegiance	May not be well written or clear if prepared by affiant
May be used as grounds to impeach witness	
Usually is easier to write than other types	
Valuable in developing an investigation	
May be written or typed and prepared on the spot	
May be concise and brief	

Sworn Statement

A sworn statement is, in a general sense, a declaration of matters of fact. It may be prepared in any form and should be signed and dated by the person preparing it. A sworn statement has the same judicial bearing as an affidavit. The investigator taking the statement administers an oath prior to the witness signing the statement. The following is an example of an oath that can be administered.

Do you (name of person giving statement) solemnly swear that everything contained in this statement is true and correct?

Mechanical Recordings

A mechanical recording device may be used to record statements when a stenographer is not readily available if all parties to the conversation consent. A recording device also may be used in conjunction with a stenographer, when necessary, again provided that all parties consent. When mechanical recording devices are used, the following guidelines are suggested:

- Identify, on tape, the individuals engaged in the conversation, any other persons present, and the time, date, and location.

- Immediately after the original has been made, make a copy of the tape for use in transcribing the conversation. If the recording was made during an undercover operation, seal and store the original after a transcribed copy has been made.

- Keep a written record of the tape's custodians and storage arrangements from the time it was recorded to the time it is submitted as evidence.

- When tape recordings are going to be used in taking a confession, advise the suspect of his or her rights and have the suspect state at the start of the tape recording that he or she is aware that a recording is being made.

- Off the record discussions between the investigator and the suspect should not be permitted during a recorded interview and should be kept to a minimum during a recorded interview with anyone else.

Form Letter

A form letter can be used to request information of a similar nature from several third parties. Following is an example of a form letter.

Sample Form Letter

Prosecuting Attorney's Office
Glynn County
300 South Main Street, 4th Floor
Brunswick, GA 31523
Telephone: (912) 555-5982
June 4, 2018

Ms. Michelle Tallmadge
1111 B Street
Glynco, GA 31520

Dear Ms. Tallmadge:

This office is conducting an investigation concerning Rosemary Westbury for the years 2016, 2017, and 2018. Ms. Westbury is a corporate officer of Massey TB, Inc. She is also the trustee for Massey TB Trust. We have reviewed the bank records of Massey TB, Inc. and Massey TB Trust. We found several checks made payable to you. Please answer the questions below which relate to the checks we found. We have included copies of the checks for your review.

Should you have any questions, please call investigator Dennis S. Paul at the telephone number listed above.

1. Did you receive check numbers 1521, 1571, 1681, 1952, 1991?
2. Did you endorse these checks?
3. Please explain why these checks were deposited into Massey TB Trust's bank account.
4. We would like to talk to you about these checks. Please call us, or provide your daytime telephone number so we can schedule an appointment.

Sincerely,

Dennis S. Paul

Grand Jury Transcript

A complete grand jury transcript will contain the questions, answers, and statements made by each participant before the grand jury. This transcript can be used as basis for a charge of perjury if the witness gives false information before the grand jury.

THE ART OF INTERVIEWING

Through practice, an investigator can improve his or her interview skills. But, equally important is practicing the art of critical self-analysis when dealing with others. This starts by stripping away the prejudices and other self-imposed barriers to impartiality that surface when communicating with people. It continues by learning to converse in different styles of language. Interviewing a college graduate and a fifth grade drop-out require different communication skills. How something is said is just as important as what is said. Everyone communicates through speech patterns and non-spoken behavior patterns. Witnesses sense the presence of the investigator's questions, not only with their ears, but by watching his or her gestures, making or avoiding eye contact, and feeling the stress in the room.

The interview process should flow naturally. The investigator should enter into the interview with general questions in mind. After the first question is asked, the investigator assumes a new role as the listener. Contingent upon what is heard, the investigator leads the interview toward the next question and then listens. This asking and listening process, controlled by the investigator, continues until the objectives of the interview have been achieved.

A successful interviewer has empathy for others. No one likes the thought of appearing foolish. Many witnesses are actually victims of fraudulent actions committed against them by the subject of the investigation and are embarrassed about being victimized. For example, businesses victimized by insiders are often reluctant to let the public know that they were vulnerable to fraud. A business may have more than money at stake. It becomes a matter of confidence and prestige in the public or industry's eye. An investigator who can become sensitive to a witness's situation quickly improves his or her interviewing techniques.

SUMMARY

The goal of an investigator is to conduct each interview in such a manner as to gather all available information and documents pertaining to the investigation and then make a permanent record of each witness's testimony for further reference.

The planning phase of the interview process is the foundation of an interview. Poor planning will have the same effect on an interview as a weak foundation has on a building. Proper planning enhances the probability of a successful interview. A successful interview can create a cooperative witness who can breathe life into financial records. It could also provide additional leads for the investigator to solve the case.

Once the investigator has decided on who, when, where, and how to interview the witness, the investigator should prepare a topical outline of the questions to be asked. Just as planning is the foundation of the interview process, the opening of an interview sets its tone. The body of the interview is the fact finding part of the process. The closing summarizes the key facts and provides an opportunity for the witness and the investigator to agree with the summation.

The medium used to record an interview should be reflective of the significance of the witness and the information and records provided by the witness.

Interviewing is a skill that can be developed and improved upon through practice. Few skills are as important to the financial investigator as the ability to talk to people and successfully gather information from them.

QUESTIONS AND EXERCISES

Answer the following questions and then check your responses with those provided following the questions and exercises.

1. How does an interview differ from an interrogation?

2. How do questions asked in a financial interview differ from those asked in other types of investigative interviews?

3. What are some things an investigator should consider when planning financial interviews during the course of an investigation?

4. Identify and describe the three methods of questioning that can be used in a financial interview.

5. Why is the introduction critical to a successful interview?

6. How can an investigator gain the cooperation of a hesitant witness?

7. Explain the following statement:
   The interview process is more than just asking questions and writing down responses.

8. What is wrong with the following question?
   He didn't have anyone with him when he came into the bank did he, but if he did, do you remember if the person was male or female and can you give a description of the person?

9. What is the last question an investigator should ask during an interview?

10. You are preparing to record an interview and you can't decide which method of recordation to use. You are torn between the memorandum and the question and answer statement. Describe the pros and cons of each.

11. What advantages are there to having a witness compose and write his or her own affidavit?

23

KEY (CORRECT ANSWERS)

1. A financial interview is conducted to obtain information and documentation from a witness. A financial interrogation is conducted for a different purpose. Its purpose is to elicit confessions or admissions of culpability from suspects or hostile witnesses.

2. Many investigative interviews focus on the recollection of witnesses. Questions such as, "Do you remember seeing any suspicious cars in the neighborhood?" or "What color jacket was he wearing?" are asked. Financial interviews go beyond recollection questions and deal with the specific details of financial transactions and the movement of money.

3. When planning interviews, an investigator should consider the following:

   - Who should I interview?
   - In what order should I interview the witnesses?
   - What type of witness is this person going to be?
   - Should I contact the suspect?
   - When should I contact the suspect?
   - What method of questioning should I use?

4. There are three general methods of questioning an investigator can use during a financial interview:

   - The chronological method
   - Questioning according to documents
   - Questioning according to transactions or events

   With the chronological method of questioning, a witness is questioned about the events in the order that they occurred, from beginning to end. With questioning according to documents, a particular document (financial statement, canceled check, tax return) is the focus of the interview. When questioning according to transaction or event, questions focus on a particular situation.

5. The introduction is critical as it sets the tone for the whole interview. Its primary objective is to put the witness at ease and get him or her to agree to answer questions.

6. To get hesitant witnesses to agree to cooperate, an investigator must avoid coming across as a threat. He or she should try to lead witnesses to believe that they will benefit from cooperating with the investigator.

7. An investigator must actively participate in the interview process. He or she must constantly analyze responses, and continually check for inconsistencies, inaccuracies, and incompleteness. Also, investigators must attend to what witnesses do during an interview. The visual and non-verbal aspects of an interview are very important.

8. The sentence is negatively phrased, and so long and complex that no one is going to understand it. Investigators should avoid asking complex and negatively phrased questions. All questions should be simple, to the point, and positively phrased.

9. The final question an investigator should ask is: "Is there anything else that you would like to say?" It gives the witness one final chance to say anything that he or she wishes.

10. The major advantage of the question and answer statement is that it contains all of the questions asked and answers provided during an interview. Of course, this could be viewed as a disadvantage also. The statement will be long, unedited, and could contain unnecessary material. On the other hand, the memorandum is more informal and it contains all pertinent testimony obtained during the interview. However, the testimony is recorded as the investigator recalls after refreshing his or her memory through informal notes. The memorandum does not contain the exact words of the witness. Both the memorandum and question and answer statement are good methods for recording an interview. The choice the investigator makes should be based on the complexity and investigative importance of the interview.

11. By allowing the affiant to create the affidavit, the investigator ensures that the affidavit will be in the affiant's own words and the credibility of the affidavit will increase because it is in the affiant's own handwriting. It would be difficult for the affiant to later deny the affidavit was his or hers.

www.ingramcontent.com/pod-product-compliance
Lightning Source LLC
Chambersburg PA
CBHW081804300426
44116CB00014B/2234